Reshaping Europe: Strategies for a Post-Cold War Europe

Edited by
Kim R. Holmes
and
Jay P. Kosminsky

Contributors

Leon Aron, an emigre from the U.S.S.R., is Salvatori Senior Policy Analyst in Soviet Studies at The Heritage Foundation. He holds Ph. D., M. Phil., and M.A. degrees in media and political sociology from Columbia University.

William D. Eggers is a Research Associate at The Heritage Foundation. He formerly served as a research fellow at the Reason Foundation, Santa Monica, California.

Kim R. Holmes is Director of Foreign Policy and Defense Studies at The Heritage Foundation. He has a Ph. D. and M.A. from Georgetown University.

Jay P. Kosminsky is Deputy Director of Defense Policy Studies at The Heritage Foundation. He is a graduate of Georgetown University's School of Foreign Service.

Douglas Seay is a Heritage Foundation Policy Analyst specializing in East European Affairs. A former Foreign Service Officer in Turkey, he also was a Fellow at the Harvard Center for Science and International Affairs.

Ronald D. Utt is Vice President of the National Chamber Foundation, Washington, D.C. A former John M. Olin Fellow at The Heritage Foundation, he holds a Ph. D. in economics from Indiana University.

ISBN 0-89195-225-X
Copyright © 1990 by The Heritage Foundation

Table of Contents

Introduction
Kim R. Holmes..1

Chapter 1
The New Political Landscape of Europe
Douglas Seay...21

Chapter 2
A New American Role in Europe's Balance of Power
Jay P. Kosminsky..55

Chapter 3
*Beyond 1992: Protecting America's Economic Interests
in Post-Cold War Europe*
Ronald D. Utt and William D. Eggers...105

Chapter 4
Orchestrating Retreat: Moscow and the Changing Europe in the 1990s
Leon Aron..145

Conclusion
Jay P. Kosminsky..181

Appendix
Men Who Have Reshaped Europe..191
NATO Chronology...195
What U.S. Presidents Said About NATO....................................201
Milestones in German-Soviet Relations.....................................203
Profiles of Soviet Leaders...209

Introduction

Kim R. Holmes

In a commitment without precedent in American — and perhaps world — history, the United States for over four decades has devoted vast amounts of its resources and troops to safeguard the freedom and security of Western Europe. Now that the Soviet empire is collapsing in Eastern Europe and the continent of Europe is becoming whole again, the need for a large U.S. military in Europe may be diminishing. If the Soviet military threat in Europe recedes, then so, too, will the U.S. military presence and consequently its diplomatic influence. This will revolutionize the U.S. role in Europe. The new task for America will be less as chief protector and captain of a military alliance comprising half of Europe, than as a distant diplomatic arbiter and largely offshore military power that has as its goal the preservation of peace and democracy and the protection of American interests by protecting against a resurgence of Soviet power and balancing the new alignment of forces in a reunited Europe.

The reshaping of Europe in the postwar era has been a smashing victory for America's policy of containment. In his famous "Mr. X" article in the July 1947 issue of *Foreign Affairs*, George Kennan wrote that "...the United States has it in its power to increase enormously the strains under which Soviet policy must operate, to force upon the Kremlin a far greater degree of moderation and circumspection than it has had to observe in recent years, and in this way to promote tendencies which must eventually find their outlet in either the break-up or the gradual mellowing of Soviet power." It may be late in coming, but the policy of containment, primarily as it was practiced in the 1980s by Ronald Reagan, paid off. Through Western perseverance, the loss of nerve of the Soviet leadership, and the courage of the East European peoples, containment ultimately laid the groundwork for a tremendous peaceful revolution not only of political values and institutions in Europe, but of its state and military system.

Reshaping Europe

Acknowledging the U.S. victory in Europe is important for the morale of the Western world and for understanding the causes of the changes in Europe. Americans deserve to feel jubilant and vindicated. Yet recognizing Moscow's defeat in the Cold War does little to provide guidance on where to go from here. U.S. policy will have to change fundamentally to cope with the new realities in Europe. If George Bush is serious about developing a strategy that "goes beyond containment," he will have to think very hard about what America's enduring interests are in Europe, what new strategies can protect and advance those interests, and what can be done in the meantime to ensure that all the gains of the East European revolutions of 1989 are not lost.

As his first and most important task, Bush should strive to promote peaceful change in Europe. Bush said on May 4 in Stillwater, Oklahoma, that "...our enemy today is uncertainty and instability." In some respects Bush is correct to worry about instability, particularly since it invites violence. But Bush and the nation must be careful not to equate stability with resistance to change or with the status quo. While Americans want the peaceful and democratic transformation of Eastern Europe, they also want all Soviet forces eventually to be withdrawn to the U.S.S.R. Fear of instability in Europe must not paralyze Washington and make it a champion of the status quo. The new European stability that should be sought by Bush emerges from Europe's revolutionary changes. This stability must be based on peaceful change, the legitimacy of democratic governments and market economies, and the withdrawal of foreign military forces from countries that do not want them.

Thinking boldly about America's future role in Europe will mean saying farewell to some cherished beliefs. If all Soviet forces return home, U.S. forces, too, will come home in large numbers. The U.S., of course, should not disengage entirely from Europe. The U.S. has learned from two world wars that it is better to keep thousands of troops in Europe in peacetime than to bring them back in the millions to fight a war started in America's absence. But neither should the U.S. continue to shoulder the principal burden of defending Western Europe. Washington should redefine the concept of "Atlanticism" so that the close trans-Atlantic ties which form the fabric of Western collective security will include a larger European role in the defense of Europe and a smaller American one. NATO should be

Introduction

"Europeanized," managed and financially supported more by Europeans than by Americans.

A reduced U.S. military role in Europe would be a welcome change. Americans have spent hundreds of billions of dollars defending Europe from the Soviet Union since 1945. The U.S. contributed a larger percentage of its national wealth for the defense of the West than any European nation. The U.S. certainly benefited from the successful containment of Soviet military power in Europe, but not nearly as much as did West Europeans. Whereas the U.S. gained by not having Europe dominated by a hostile totalitarian power, the West European members of the NATO gained immensely more: their freedom, the security of their borders, and the stability necessary for economic prosperity. At no time in human history have nations benefited so much from the generosity of another nation as West Europeans have from the United States.

Despite these inequities, which America has borne graciously, the U.S. should remain engaged militarily in Europe. The U.S. has security interests in ensuring that neither the Soviet Union nor any other hostile power can threaten to control Europe and its vast resources by military force. The U.S. has an abiding interest in securing peace in Europe, where hundreds of thousands of American lives have been lost in this century. By the same token, Washington has an equally important interest in ensuring that the financial burden of defending Europe be no more than is absolutely necessary. Americans take no pleasure in spending billions of dollars to defend countries overseas, and they certainly do not pay their money to buy international prestige or superpower status in global affairs. Americans, however, do wish to see democracy and market economies spread into Eastern Europe and the Soviet Union, while expanding free trade between Europe and the United States. Increasingly they may wish to see more of their tax dollars dedicated to educating East Europeans and even Soviets about free market economics, rather than to defending Europe with military force.

If the Soviet Union continues to retreat from Europe – though there is no guarantee that it will – then all of these U.S. interests can be protected at less cost to the American taxpayer, with more flexibility for a U.S. diplomacy less burdened by the collective decision making procedures of the NATO alliance, and more independence in negotiations with the Soviet Union. If the Soviet threat does not recede, then

Reshaping Europe

the U.S. should not only continue its commitment to NATO as it currently is configured, but lead the alliance in a military modernization program sufficient to continue the deterrence of Soviet military power in Europe. Only the complete and final demise of Soviet military power in Europe will make possible a fundamental change in U.S. security policy in Europe.

The changing political landscape in Europe also has important implications for the economic future of Europe and for economic relations with the U.S. Market economies are emerging in Eastern Europe and the European Economic Community (EC) is marching toward complete economic integration in 1992. Although the road to complete economic unity for Europe will be rocky, the U.S. will benefit if East European countries join the EC, and if they and their West European partners keep Europe's market open to the U.S. Since there is no guarantee that they will, America should be negotiating an expansion of free trade area agreements in this hemisphere — asking Mexico to join the U.S.-Canada free trade area agreement, for example — as a hedge against the rise of protectionism in a united Europe. But Washington should begin plans to negotiate a free trade area agreement with Europe as well. Many Europeans may welcome closer economic relations with the U.S. to balance out what they see as the economic power of a resurgent Germany.

While the U.S. may have a lesser role in Europe in the future, today, as leader of a victorious military alliance, Bush has an opportunity to shape the Europe of the 21st Century. He must devise a strategy to get the U.S. successfully through the series of negotiations on conventional arms, German unification, security, and human rights, trade, possibly even short-range nuclear forces. He must also not only preserve parts of the old security and political order worth saving, but boldly propose new political, security, and economic institutions and architectures to protect and promote U.S. interests in a new European order. To do this, Bush's European policy should be guided by several premises. They are:

Premise #1. America should not fear change. Fear of instability should not lead Washington to champion the status quo in Europe. Bush should promote the peaceful consolidation and spread of democracy and market economies in Europe and the U.S.S.R.

Introduction

Premise #2. U.S. interests should be safeguarded as Europe changes. The U.S. has an enduring interest that Europe not come under the military domination of a hostile power. It is also in the U.S. interest that democracy and free markets spread peacefully. Bush should ensure that these interests are safeguarded not only during the period of transition, but in the new European security order as well.

Premise #3. Washington should take an active role in reshaping Europe. While the U.S. military role in Europe is likely to decrease, Washington will still be highly important in shaping the new security order in Europe. Bush should not abdicate to others the task of safeguarding U.S. interests in Europe.

Premise #4. The U.S. military presence in Europe should be reduced as the Soviet threat recedes. Washington committed U.S. troops to NATO because of the magnitude of the Soviet military threat to Western Europe. If that threat disappears or subsides substantially, then the U.S. need not keep large numbers of military forces stationed in Europe.

Premise #5. Nothing is irreversible. Despite encouraging signs that Moscow is abandoning its East European empire, these changes remain reversible. Bush should remain on guard during this period of transition, ensuring that the U.S. is not left unprepared if the Soviet Union refuses to withdraw its forces from Europe or, as seems unlikely, seeks to reimpose its political rule over Eastern Europe.

Premise #6. European security should be grounded on a balance of power. NATO has kept the peace in Europe for the past forty years by balancing Soviet power. Even if Moscow withdraws all of its forces from Europe, European security will require military forces to deter the Soviet Union.

Premise #7. Tyranny is the main impediment to a lasting peace in Europe. The threats to peace in Europe for the past century have been attempts by tyrannical powers to dominate Europe: Germany's Kaiser Wilhelm II; Germany's Adolf Hitler; and the Soviet Union's Joseph Stalin, Nikita Khrushchev, and Leonid Brezhnev. Europe's best chance for a genuine and lasting peace lies ultimately in the spread of democracy and economic prosperity not only to Eastern Europe, but to the Soviet Union itself.

Premise #8. Europe will become less strategically critical to the U.S. If the Soviet threat to Europe declines, so too will Europe's strategic importance to the United States. Washington's critical interest

Reshaping Europe

in Europe has always been primarily derived from fears for U.S. security. Freed of its European burden, the U.S. will not only concentrate more on other regions of the world, such as Latin America and Asia, but will have to face such threats unrelated to Europe as Iraq, Islamic fundamentalism, international terrorism, the proliferation of missiles and nuclear weapons in Third World, and international drug trafficking.

Premise #9. The transition to market economies in Eastern Europe should proceed as rapidly as possible. The best way to ensure continued economic stagnation in Eastern Europe is to move slowly toward market economies. Half-measure free market reforms will not produce the economic benefits of a completely free market. East European democracies should make the transition to free market economies without delay.

Premise #10. Free trade with Europe benefits both America and Europe. One of the best insurances of economic prosperity for Europeans and Americans is free trade. The expected waning U.S. interest in Europe, plus the economic integration of Europe itself, should not be allowed to hamper greater free trade between the U.S. and the emerging unified continent of Europe.

These premises should be the intellectual foundation of a new and bold U.S. strategy for Europe. To see that they are translated into policy, Bush should prepare a long-range plan to reduce the U.S. military presence in Europe if the Soviets diminish theirs, create a new institutional and architectural framework to secure peace, freedom and stability in Europe, and maximize the opportunity to spread free trade, market economies, and thus economic growth, into Eastern Europe and the Soviet Union.

PREPARING FOR A REDUCED U.S. MILITARY ROLE IN EUROPE

If Soviet forces leave Europe, and are constrained through an effective and verifiable conventional arms control agreement, the U.S., too, should reduce its military role in Europe. If the Soviet threat is diminished substantially in this way, the U.S. should:

♦ ♦ **Eventually reduce U.S. ground forces to approximately 50,000 troops.** These forces would be mainly symbolic, demonstrating the U.S. commitment to the defense of Europe. Their main task should be to

Introduction

protect weapon depots, secure airfields, and provide the administrative staff to prepare for a massive return of U.S. forces in time of war.

♦ ♦ **Demobilize at least half of U.S.-based troops available for rapid reinforcement of NATO allies, while continuing to provide reserve manpower.** If all Soviet forces are out of Europe, the U.S. should have adequate warning of a Soviet mobilization against Europe. With this, America should be able to mobilize its own army in time to meet an attempt by the Soviet Union to attack Western Europe.

♦ ♦ **Maintain a Navy strong enough to keep the North Atlantic open for the free passage of U.S. reinforcements to Europe in time of war.** A strong fleet of U.S. attack submarines, escort ships, and aircraft carriers will be necessary to prevent the Soviet Navy from blocking U.S. reinforcements in time of war.

♦ ♦ **Continue to base airpower in Europe if requested by allies.** While the number of U.S. aircraft would be substantially lower, the U.S. would still wish to base fighter aircraft and fighter bombers in Europe to ensure not only the U.S. right to station such forces in Europe, but to react quickly to an unexpected Soviet attack.

♦ ♦ **Base U.S. aircraft armed with long-range nuclear missiles in Europe if requested by allies.** George Bush already has announced that the U.S. will negotiate over the future deployment of nuclear artillery and Short-Range Nuclear Forces (SNF) in Europe. Long-range nuclear missiles with ranges of hundreds of miles, however, could be placed on U.S. aircraft. Based on European soil, these U.S. weapons would help "couple" Europe, particularly Germany, strategically with the U.S. They would be capable of reaching the Soviet Union and thus would serve to deter a Soviet attack on Europe.

♦ ♦ **Prepare for a reduction in NATO's role in European defense.** While the U.S. has no interest in hastening NATO's demise, the current changes in Europe likely will lead to a lesser role for NATO. NATO was founded to respond to a Soviet threat. To ensure that Western defense remains strong, Washington should begin planning for a new security order in which Europeans take over the primary responsibility for their own defense.

Bush should encourage Europeans to take the lead in organizing new European defense structures either through the Western European Union, a defense organization founded in 1954 and composed of Britain, France, and other West European nations, or the European Economic Community, West Europe's common market.

Reshaping Europe

Bush also should strengthen U.S. bilateral defense ties to such key allies as Britain and Germany. As the influence of NATO wanes, the importance of bilateral security relations with West European nations will increase. The most important security relationships for the U.S. will be with Britain and Germany. Britain has a longstanding close relationship with the U.S., while Germany is important because it will, outside the U.S.S.R., be potentially the most powerful nation on the continent of Europe.

♦♦ **Develop new U.S. military strategies and force postures to accommodate reduced military role.** If U.S. forces in Europe are reduced to 50,000 troops, new military strategies and force postures will have to be developed to make them effective. Instead of the strategy of "forward defense," which envisages defending against a massive Soviet attack along the inter-German border, a new strategy of "mobilization defense" should be developed whereby the U.S. plans for a massive mobilization of U.S. forces to reinforce Europe in time of war. Forces stationed in Europe would be the skeleton crew of a much larger force rushed to Europe by air and sea. And new military tactics emphasizing the rapid mobility of ground forces would have to be developed to deal with a battlefield no longer dominated by fixed lines of defense and offense.

♦♦ **Maintain NATO's military strength until Soviet forces are withdrawn from Europe.** U.S. force withdrawals from Europe are predicated on a substantial reduction of the Soviet military threat. If the Soviet threat remains, so too should the U.S. forces and the current structure of NATO needed to deter it. If Moscow retains its current force posture in Europe, the U.S. should be prepared to lead the way in maintaining NATO's military strength. If the Soviet threat does not continue to decline, the U.S. will have to consider proceeding with such military programs as production of new short-range missiles, expansion of its airlift capabilities, and developing a new generation of tanks, fighter aircraft, artillery, and helicopters.

♦♦ **Maintain close ties between Germany and its allies.** On July 17, 1990, in the Soviet Union, West German Chancellor Helmut Kohl and Soviet leader Mikhail Gorbachev announced that a united Germany would be free to choose NATO membership. Still, Moscow is likely to continue to press for concessions which will weaken German ties with its Western allies. To ensure that Germany remains secure in coming years, the U.S. and other allies should continue to resist any

Introduction

Soviet efforts to deny Germany's rights to: contine stationing foreign troops on its soil; remain within NATO's unified military command; and station NATO nuclear weapons on its territory.

CONCLUDING THE CONVENTIONAL FORCES IN EUROPE (CFE) TALKS

These talks began on March 9, 1989, in Vienna and involve the members of NATO and the Warsaw Pact. The aim is to reduce substantially conventional forces in the region from the Atlantic Ocean to the Ural Mountains. In these talks Bush should press for a swift but favorable conclusion that redresses military imbalances favoring Moscow and lays the groundwork for further reductions in follow-on negotiations. Also he should:

♦ ♦ Insist that both alliances agree to a "sufficiency rule" barring the Soviet Union or any other country from possessing more than 30 percent of the total amount of military equipment deployed from the Atlantic to the Urals. The aim of this provision is to ensure that the Soviets cannot maintain a predominance of conventional military power on the continent.

♦ ♦ **Ensure that a CFE Treaty contains a clause upholding the sovereign rights of all signatories to bar foreign forces from their territory if they wish.** This is needed to avoid the impression that a CFE Treaty legitimizes the presence of Soviet forces on the territory of Warsaw Pact states.

♦ ♦ **Propose that a CFE Treaty require the complete destruction of Soviet tanks, artillery, armored troop carriers and aircraft reduced under the agreement.** Otherwise Moscow could bring these weapons back to the U.S.S.R. and store them there for future use in Europe.

♦ ♦ **Rescind the U.S. offer to limit to 30,000 the number of troops Washington stations outside of Central Europe.** The U.S. has proposed that Washington and Moscow be limited to no more than 195,000 troops in a "central zone," mainly Germany, while 30,000 additional troops could be stationed in the rest of Europe. This proposal was a mistake because it would overly restrict where and how many forces the U.S. could place in Europe. Germany conceivably could tell the Americans to take all their troops home, leaving the U.S. with only 30,000 troops in all of Europe. The U.S. should modify its proposal and insist that the "central zone" allowing 195,000 troops be

Reshaping Europe

expanded to include France, Britain, and other allies. This way the U.S. could put forces withdrawn from the "central zone" elsewhere in Europe.

TRANSFORMING THE CONFERENCE ON SECURITY AND COOPERATION IN EUROPE (CSCE)

Begun in Helsinki in 1973, the 35-nation CSCE focuses on resolving human rights and relatively minor security issues. Until recently it was not considered a very important negotiating forum. This has changed as Europeans have looked to the CSCE as an institution for creating a new security framework for Europe. Bush should try to transform the CSCE into a more practical forum for settling regional disputes and other lesser security concerns. Also he should:

♦ ♦ **Argue strenuously against proposals to replace NATO with a CSCE security framework.** Some French and West Germans, along with the Soviets, contend that the CSCE could someday replace NATO as the most important institution guaranteeing European security. Although NATO could become less central to ensuring the security of Europe if the Soviets withdraw their forces from Europe, it could not be effectively replaced by the CSCE. The reasons: it has no enforcement mechanisms, no military forces under its command, no common concept of a threat, and no clear community of political interest (since it includes both communist and non-communist countries such as the U.S.S.R. and the U.S.). The CSCE would be no more effective today in resolving intractable security disputes than the League of Nations was between the two world wars.

♦ ♦ **Propose a European Nuclear Non-Proliferation Treaty to prevent the spread of nuclear weapons in Europe.** As the U.S. and U.S.S.R. withdraw from Europe, some European countries such as Poland or even Germany may be tempted to acquire nuclear weapons. To remove this temptation, the 35 nations of the CSCE should sign a treaty committing themselves to nuclear non-proliferation, to supplement existing treaties and agreements.

♦ ♦ **Ask that the CSCE uphold the sovereign rights of all European states to decide whose forces can be stationed on their territory and to seek allies of their choosing.** No country, for example, should be forced to stay in either NATO or the Warsaw Pact against its will, or to have foreign forces occupy its territory.

Introduction

PROPOSING NEW INSTITUTIONS AND ARCHITECTURES

NATO, the European Community, and other European institutions have defended European freedom and promoted economic prosperity in Western Europe. The reunification of Europe will change these institutions and usher in the need for new ones. The U.S. should be prepared to influence the creation of Europe's new security, political, and economic institutions as it did with NATO and the EC at the beginning of the Cold War.

Building a "Three Pillar" Security Structure

Western Europe's security now rests on a single pillar: NATO. If the Soviet threat wanes, the U.S. should propose a new security structure consisting of three pillars. They are:

Pillar #1: NATO with a greater role for Europeans. NATO is likely to evolve into a less centralized military organization and become more of a forum to clarify security commitments and coordinate military planning. The U.S. role in NATO would be primarily as an offshore military power, with a smaller contingent of ground forces, that would be committed to return in force only if the Soviets or some other power threatened to dominate Europe militarily. Although less powerful than before, NATO would still be Europe's premier military organization dedicated to deterring the Soviet Union, primarily because it would still provide a U.S. nuclear guarantee to Europe. America would still be coupled strategically to Europe, albeit less closely. In short, NATO would still remain the key player in any "big war" involving the Soviet Union. Under these circumstances, the position of supreme military commander of NATO could alternate routinely between an American and a European.

NATO's military organization should not be expanded to include former Warsaw Pact members, excepting East Germany, which will likely join NATO as part of a unified Germany. In particular, the U.S. nuclear guarantee should not be extended to new countries. The U.S. has no business extending nuclear protection to Eastern Europe, which is an area that could be highly unstable in years to come, and for which it has been unwilling to fight for in the past. If former Warsaw Pact members join the Western European Union or any other West European defense organization, however, they could participate in

Reshaping Europe

NATO's political councils as observers, but staying out of NATO's military command structure.

Pillar #2: An expanded Western European Union (WEU) or European Community (EC) to organize Europeans into a common defense organization. These organizations could develop common defense policies and coordinate the development and procurement of weapon systems. The Western European Union could coordinate defense policies for military operations outside of Europe, such as the Persian Gulf, and for maintaining regional security in Eastern Europe. The European pillar could have primary responsibility for Europe's ground defense. The WEU could coordinate its military plans with the U.S. through NATO, acting as a West European caucus within that organization.

Former Warsaw Pact members should be free to join the WEU, the EC defense community, or any other European defense organization if they so choose. The WEU is better suited than the EC because it has been involved in coordinating the defense policies of West European members. Existing alongside NATO, these expanded organizations could supplement the capabilities of NATO to deter Soviet aggression not only against Western Europe, but if they join, the emerging democracies of Eastern Europe as well.

Pillar #3: A CSCE dedicated to resolving regional disputes and other European security problems. The CSCE is a diplomatic forum for discussing security and human rights issues in Europe. Unlike NATO, it is not a military organization dedicated to deterring an expansionist power, but a diplomatic forum.

With Europe becoming whole again, however, the CSCE could take on a new and more useful role of helping to mediate regional disputes that may emerge as Soviet power recedes in Eastern Europe. As a member of the CSCE, the U.S. could become involved in settling national and ethnic disputes between Hungary and Romania, for example. But Washington should not become militarily involved in European regional disputes unless Soviet or any other major military power intervention threatens the general peace and stability of Europe.

Creating a North Atlantic Conference

The U.S., Western Europe and the emerging democracies have one thing in common: a dedication to democratic institutions. A new

Introduction

political institution, called the North Atlantic Conference (NAC), consisting of any North American or European democracy that wishes to join, should be created to discuss the major political issues facing its member states. The NAC could become a forum for working out political disputes before they become too serious and also serve as the principal cooperative organization of the Western democracies. This institution also could be particularly important in promoting and managing technical, educational and political assistance for the emerging democracies of Eastern Europe. If the Soviet Union were to become a true democracy, it, too, could join.

Establishing a North Atlantic Economic Community

Free trade between America and Europe is mutually beneficial. Bush should propose opening negotiations to create free trade areas between the U.S. and the EC, with the countries of Eastern Europe, and with the smaller European Free Trade Association.[1] While the EC has little interest currently in such an arrangement, some of the Eastern European countries, especially Hungary and Poland, would welcome such an arrangement. The prospect of the U.S. selling goods in Eastern Europe without facing trade barriers would give the EC a strong incentive to seek a free trade area as well. Bush should announce that he intends free trade areas one day to result in a genuine common North Atlantic Economic Community based on free trade and free market principles, stretching from San Francisco to Warsaw, and from Mexico City to London. It should be made up of all market economies in North America and Europe, including Canada, Mexico, and the emerging democracies of Eastern Europe. Unlike the EC, however, Bush should insist that the Community not create a centralized bureaucracy like the EC's European Commission to run and regulate the member countries' economies. Rather, it should become an economic conference meeting periodically to discuss ways to promote

---

1 The European Free Trade Association includes Austria, Iceland, Norway, Sweden, and Switzerland, with Finland as an associate member.

Reshaping Europe

and enhance free markets and free trade between the North American continent and Europe.

COUNTERING SOVIET STRATEGY IN EUROPE

The Soviet Union may be giving up the military and political domination of Eastern Europe, has not decided to retreat entirely. Gorbachev apparently wishes to ensure that the military retreat be as orderly as possible, while ensuring that Eastern Europe still remains an area in which Moscow has important political influence. The U.S.S.R. wants to rid itself of the financial burden of Eastern Europe, diminish U.S. influence in Europe, persuade Western Europe to bail out the Soviet economy, and emerge as the preeminent superpower in Europe.

Bush needs to develop a strategy to counter Soviet policies when they violate U.S. interests. The U.S. has an enormous opportunity in Europe, which will be missed if it is passive or overly concerned about pleasing Gorbachev with diplomatic concessions. As part of a Soviet "counter strategy," Bush should:

♦ ♦ **Support the peaceful democratization and decolonization of the Soviet Union.** The expansion of genuine democracy into the Soviet Union will lead to Soviet "decolonization," as such captive nations as the Baltic states, Georgia, Ukraine and others seek freedom from Moscow's control. If this effort succeeds peacefully, the stage will be set for a just and lasting peace in a democratic Europe. In pursuit of this objective, Washington should take such measures as: establishing official contacts with republics seeking independence from the Soviet Union; warning Moscow that any use of force against national movements will jeopardize Moscow's economic and political ties to the U.S.; and using the CSCE to promote sovereignty and independence for Soviet republics which have declared their independence from Moscow.

♦ ♦ **Ask the Soviet Union to sign a new Atlantic Charter dedicating itself to freedom, self-determination, and democracy.**

Like the original Atlantic Charter signed off the coast of Newfoundland in August 1941 by Franklin Roosevelt and Winston Churchill, Bush and Gorbachev should sign a new Atlantic Charter dedicating the U.S. and the U.S.S.R. to respect the freedom, independence, and self-determination of the people of Europe. This document would

Introduction

enable Bush to hold Gorbachev more accountable for his actions. It could be seen not only as a Soviet official recognition of Eastern Europe's freedom and independence, but as the standard by which Gorbachev's behavior should be judged as the Soviet republics seek their independence.

◆ ◆ **Counter Soviet propaganda and public diplomacy aimed at alienating the U.S. from Europe.** Gorbachev often talks about the "Common European Home," saying that Russia is part of Europe, while implying that America is not. This is a theme that is attractive to many Europeans, especially Germans, who long for an end to Europe's conflicts. This concept should be vigorously opposed by Bush. It represents a variation on a longstanding Soviet theme: the attempt to decouple Europe from America. To counter the "Common European Home" idea, Bush should propose the creation of a "Common Democratic Home" from San Francisco to Warsaw. United in its dedication to Western civilization, democracy, and free enterprise, this home should include all democratic nations west of the Soviet border, and even the Soviet Union itself, if it should become free. What matters to Europe, far more than geography, are the values of Western civilization.

◆ ◆ **Rebuff Soviet attempts to slow democratic change in Eastern Europe in the name of "stability."** The Soviet Union has tried to slow the democratization of Eastern Europe and the Soviet Union by warning that stability in Europe is threatened by the fast pace of change. Bush should emphasize that the changes in Europe so far have been remarkably free of violence, and that real stability in Europe should be based not on fear but on freedom of political and national choice throughout Europe and inside the borders of the Soviet Union.

◆ ◆ **Prevent Gorbachev from using the CSCE to slow democratic change inside the Soviet Union.** The U.S. should lead the Western opposition to Soviet attempts to secure Western support for repression of democratic movements inside the Soviet Union in the name of stability. The CSCE review conferences should be used to press for Moscow's compliance with Article VIII of the "Declaration on Principles Guiding Relations between Participating States" of the 1975 Helsinki Final Act. This commits signatories, including the Soviet Union, to "respect the equal rights of peoples and their right to self-determination," declaring that "all peoples always have the right,

Reshaping Europe

in full freedom, to determine, when and as they wish, their internal and external political status...."

♦ ♦ **Preserve the Committee for Multilateral Export Controls (COCOM) until the Soviet threat is dramatically reduced.** COCOM is a Western organization that includes all NATO members, except Iceland, as well as Japan and Australia. It controls the export of militarily significant technology to the Soviet Union and its allies. The Bush Administration announced on May 2, 1990, that it intends to liberalize COCOM restrictions on Western exports.

Until the Soviet Union is a fully democratic state, some COCOM restrictions should be maintained. Washington needs to retain its historic leading role in COCOM to ensure that Europeans do not liberalize its restrictions too quickly. While easing restrictions on high technology exports to the new democracies of Eastern Europe, COCOM also should simultaneously create strict rules against the transfer of such technologies to the Soviet Union. Above all, Bush should control the export of technologies which could be used to make a smaller Soviet army more effective in combat. These include advanced telecommunications, computers, optics, imaging systems, and other items which could strengthen the command and control capabilities of Soviet forces.

♦ ♦ **Prepare contingency plans for a Soviet crackdown in Eastern Europe.** The gains of the 1989 revolutions in Europe are reversible. The Soviet Union still has the military power to crack down on democracy in Europe. Although it is not likely to do so, Bush should be prepared in case it does. Bush should emphasize in public statements that while he welcomes the changes in Europe, he will not rest easy until every last Soviet tank is out of Europe. If Gorbachev tries to reimpose Soviet rule over Eastern Europe with armed violence, Bush should respond in the harshest terms, cutting off all negotiations, and returning with grim determination to modernize and expand America's military forces. Conveying this message quietly and privately to Gorbachev could help Gorbachev convince hardliners in the Kremlin that they could never afford to alienate the U.S. and the West in this way.

Introduction

PROMOTING FREE MARKET REVOLUTIONS IN EASTERN EUROPE

Most of the emerging democracies of Eastern Europe want to transform their communist economic systems into a free markets. Poland is moving rapidly, while Romania and the Soviet Union are hardly moving at all. Free markets are an indispensable aspect of a free society and should be encouraged not only because they create prosperity, but because they tend to promote and support democratic institutions. To ensure that the free market revolutions continue in Eastern Europe and even the Soviet Union, Bush should:

♦ ♦ **Develop a foreign assistance program which encourages East Europeans to make free market reforms.** This could be done not by granting huge sums of money to East European governments, but by using U.S. foreign aid to provide finance technical assistance, for example, on establishing uniform commercial codes to protect private property rights and contracts on privatizing state-owned enterprises, and creating convertible currencies. Aid might also be used to provide managerial assistance, educational and cultural exchanges, and emergency projects such as buying fertilizers and pesticides for agriculture. The sooner East Europeans learn to create their own wealth, the sooner their economies will improve.

♦ ♦ **Use an Index of Economic Freedom to establish goals to be advanced by foreign assistance and to gauge the success of such assistance.** The U.S. Foreign Assistance Act of 1961 should be reformed by adding an Index of Economic Freedom. This Index would establish as goals for U.S. foreign aid the preservations of private property rights and open markets. It would emphasize giving individuals the maximum freedom to benefit from their own productive economic activities. How well foreign aid programs meet these goals would be the standard by which to measure their efficiency. If adopted, this amendment could be applied specifically to Eastern Europe to assure that U.S. assistance is put to the best possible use.

♦ ♦ **Support the removal of trade barriers between the various East European countries and, as they become free market economies, their economic integration into Western Europe.** Far more important for the economic well-being of Eastern European countries than Western financial aid is the full integration of their economies into the international market. Many East European countries want to join the

Reshaping Europe

EC as soon as they can. Further, Eastern European countries would benefit from integration with one another. Although they are not ready to do so yet, the U.S. should support their aspirations and encourage the West Europeans to render immediate assistance to them by removing barriers to East European exports. The U.S., too, should help stimulate economic growth in Eastern Europe by eliminating such barriers.

♦ ♦ **Consider writing off East European debts to the U.S. in exchange for privatization of state-owned firms in Eastern Europe.** East European nations owe the federal government $ 4.2 billion. This debt is an enormous burden on their economies. Bush should consider some form of debt forgiveness. This could take the form of a debt/equity swap. In return for debt relief, Eastern European governments would privatize state-owned enterprises, selling them to the employees themselves.

MOVING TOWARD A U.S.-EUROPE FREE TRADE AREA

As the two largest markets in the world, North America and Europe have a mutual interest in promoting cooperation in trade and economic relations. At present, however, each has concentrated on developing its own continental market. In North America, the U.S. and Canada have concluded a free trade agreement and negotiations will soon be underway for concluding a similar agreement between the U.S. and Mexico. The EC, of course, is attempting to eliminate its remaining internal trade barriers by the end of 1992.

The waning of the Cold War may loosen America's military ties with Europe, but its economic interest in freer trade with Europe can only increase. The U.S. should seek to establish freer trade with and between Europe and the countries themselves. To achieve this, Bush should:

♦ ♦ **Offer to begin negotiations for a free trade area with Eastern Europe, the EC, EFTA, and Turkey.** U.S. interests favor free trade in Europe. The economic integration of the EC, however, could produce trade barriers which would discriminate against American products. In the absence of alternatives, the pull of the EC's giant market may force other European states to cooperate in such measures.

To counter this danger, as well as to promote a lowering of trade barriers in general, the U.S. should offer to negotiate free trade areas

Introduction

with a number of European countries and organizations. The East European countries, especially Hungary and Poland, may find such an arrangement attractive and likely would welcome talks with the U.S. Guaranteed access to the huge U.S. market would offer opportunities for East European goods and would attract investors to newly established or privatized East European industries. And since developing countries require imports, a free trade area with Eastern Europe would give U.S. exports a more competitive position against other foreign suppliers.

Similarly, the U.S. should offer a free trade area to the EFTA countries, which have no interest in pursuing integration with the EC other than increasing economic cooperation. And the U.S. should offer such a package to Turkey, which the EC is unlikely to admit as a full member.

The EC currently has the least interest in some form of North Atlantic free trade area since it already has a large internal market and since its attention is focused on its upcoming 1992 integration. If, however, the Bush Administration begins free trade area talks with Eastern European countries, and with EFTA it is interested, the EC will have an incentive to seek trade liberalization with the U.S. as well.

♦ ♦ **Support European economic integration so long as it does not become protectionist.** Even as it supports the creation of a continental market in Europe, the U.S. must ensure that European economic integration is not used to erect market barriers to U.S. goods. The U.S. should oppose European protectionism in bilateral negotiations and in the General Agreement on Tariffs and Trade (GATT). But it should also inform the Europeans that a great North American free trade area encompassing the U.S., Canada, Mexico, and the Caribbean could someday be created.

♦ ♦ ♦

America has an abiding interest in promoting the changes underway in Europe and to make them as irreversible as possible. This can be done by negotiating the withdrawal of Soviet forces to within their own borders, firmly establishing the freedom and sovereignty of the states of the former Soviet East European empire, and sharply limiting the Soviet arsenal through arms control. If America can accomplish these

Reshaping Europe

goals, it will have won the Cold War, and will be able to bring home most of its own ground forces from Europe. If it accomplishes one further goal, the democratization and decolonization of the Soviet Union itself, the U.S. will have transformed fundamentally the European state system, establishing the foundation for a just and lasting peace based on common values and interests among democratic states.

While triumphant, NATO was not always a happy partnership. Europe's military dependence on America created tension and resentment on both sides of the Atlantic. With Soviet forces pushed back behind their own borders, however, this dependency can come to an end. The U.S. can then begin the task of building a new relationship with Europe, based on equality and partnership among democracies. The tasks of managing this new relationship should not be underestimated. They may well require a more subtle and complex American strategy in Europe than has been required for the past forty years.

Chapter 1

The New Political Landscape in Europe

Douglas Seay

Among the many remarkable developments transforming the political shape of post-war Europe, the most important are the collapse of the Soviet empire in Eastern Europe, the economic and political integration of Europe, and German unification. The disintegration of the Soviet Union itself may join this list. Each of these alone challenges American and European policy makers enormously. Their simultaneous unfolding promises quickly to transform the entire continent in ways that at present are perceived only dimly.

The most dramatic development in Europe, of course, is the collapse of Soviet political and military control over Eastern Europe. As the Soviet threat diminishes, the post-war European political order built up around it will change fundamentally. The 1989 revolutions in Eastern Europe largely destroyed the Soviet Union's puppet regimes, and new governments have moved quickly to dismantle the physical and other barriers separating them from the rest of Europe. One result of this is that the pair of long-dominant superpowers are likely to exercise considerably less influence than they have over the past half-century and to bring home most of their military forces. Another result is that the restraints on all European states long imposed by the Soviet military

Chapter 1

threat and Moscow's military occupation of Eastern Europe will be loosened considerably, giving them greater freedom of action.

As a consequence, new sources of discord and instability will emerge within Europe, and between the new Europe and the United States. Long-buried ethnic, national, and border conflicts will re-emerge as the Soviet grip on Eastern Europe is loosened and instability grows inside the Soviet Union itself. Historical patterns of diplomatic relations and alliances are likely to re-emerge as the Cold War's clear political lines of demarcation are blurred. An example could be the creation of a new political association among the countries once belonging to the pre-World War I Austro-Hungarian Empire. On August 1, 1990, the leaders of Austria, Czechoslovakia, Hungary, Italy, and Yugoslavia announced the creation of a "pentagonal grouping" among themselves aimed at improving economic and political cooperation.

With German unification, Europe again will come face-to-face with the question, unresolved after more than a century of efforts and wars, of how to integrate a large and powerful Germany into a peaceful European order. As part of the solution, Europe itself may become more united politically and economically, and in so doing potentially create a powerful political and economic rival to the U.S.

These are difficult problems, yet they pale beside the benefits from Europe's changes. For the first time in the post-World War II era an opportunity exists to reduce greatly the Soviet conventional military threat to Europe. Eastern Europe is demolishing enthusiastically the remaining institutions of communist rule, and the eventual creation of a continental market with significantly reduced economic barriers is a real possibility.

America will have an important role to play in the creation of this new Europe, albeit a diminishing one. U.S. diplomacy already has helped ensure that German unification poses a minimal threat to peace and stability. The U.S. too can help stabilize the new democracies of Eastern Europe and help spread free market principles there. It also can help ensure that the process of Soviet decolonization proceeds smoothly, by supporting a peaceful and negotiated solution to the demands by the many nationalities for self-determination.

In this new era, U.S. diplomacy must be aimed at accomplishing several goals: ensuring that the political and economic transformation of Eastern Europe continues and produces stable democracies and

The New Political Landscape in Europe

free market economies, integrating a reunified Germany into Europe, ensuring that Soviet decolonization occurs peacefully and orderly, maintaining a U.S. institutional connection in European affairs, and promoting U.S. economic interests in the new Europe.

To accomplish these goals, the U.S. should:

♦ ♦ **Support democratization in Eastern Europe and develop a foreign aid strategy that promotes free markets.** The U.S. can encourage democracy and movement toward free market economies in Eastern Europe by making American foreign assistance to these countries contingent on their holding democratic elections and adopting free market reforms such as removing restrictions on the private sector, privatizing the state-owned enterprises, and lowering barriers to trade.

♦ ♦ **Support a peaceful and negotiated Soviet decolonization.** European peace and stability require that the Soviet Union not break up violently. At the same time, the U.S. should support peaceful self-determination inside the Soviet Union. The U.S. can help ensure that Soviet decolonization avoids violence by supporting those democratic groups which advocate a peaceful break from Moscow.

♦ ♦ **Ensure that its ties to Europe remain strong.** As the need for the U.S. military commitment to Europe wanes, the U.S. must ensure that its political ties to Europe remain strong. NATO will continue to be the principal security organization linking the U.S. to Europe, but because it is primarily a military organization, NATO's ability to play a political role will be limited. Replacing NATO as America's main line to Europe could be a North Atlantic Conference, encompassing all European and North American democracies. This organization would focus upon strengthening trans-Atlantic ties through regular discussion of political and other issues.

♦ ♦ **Prevent European integration from discriminating economically against non-European goods, services, and investments.** U.S. interests can be served by greater European political and economic integration if this contributes to peace and stability on the continent. U.S. policy, however, should be guided by the goal of preventing European integration from discriminating economically against the U.S.

♦ ♦ **Use the Conference on Security and Cooperation in Europe (CSCE) to press for peaceful change in Europe.** Since it includes every European state, plus the U.S., Canada, and the Soviet Union, the

Chapter 1

CSCE is likely to emerge as an important forum for discussing and resolving issues facing the new Europe. The U.S. should use the CSCE to try to create a consensus for addressing Germany's unification and the dangers posed by Soviet decolonization.

EUROPE'S CHANGING POLITICAL ORDER

Despite the dangers long presented by Europe's post-war political and military divisions and even by the possibility of nuclear showdown in the heart of Europe, Europeans fear the breakdown of the post-war order and the new dangers that it may bring. This apprehension stems less from concern over any known future threats than from fear over a return of Europe's unstable and warlike past.

Throughout most of its history, Europe's political system has consisted of a relatively large number of states in constantly shifting alliances and frequent periods of conflict. In the latter 19th Century, for example, German Chancellor Otto von Bismarck created and managed a bewildering array of alliances and limited wars to disable potential opponents and promote first Prussia's and then Germany's freedom of action. This pattern of European diplomacy continued until the outbreak of World War II.

By contrast, the post-World War II European order has been characterized by the division of all major states on the continent into two huge opposing camps: the North Atlantic Treaty Organization and the Soviet-dominated Warsaw Pact. Diplomacy, as practiced in the pre-war period, came to an end, and Europe settled into a political deep freeze from which it just now is beginning to emerge.

The most important factor shaping the structure of post-war Europe was the overwhelming military and political presence of America and the U.S.S.R.

The Soviet impact was forceful and unsubtle. Its political control in Eastern Europe amounted to the establishment of an empire, with local communist regimes held in place ultimately by force of Soviet arms. The Soviet presence also served to galvanize West European efforts to cooperate to counter the Soviet threat. The defensive alliance of the West European Union (WEU) between Britain, France, and several smaller European powers was formed in 1948 to defend against Soviet expansionism as well as against a revival of German power. NATO, including the U.S. and most of Western Europe, was established a year

The New Political Landscape in Europe

later. The Soviet post-war military buildup reversed the process of U.S. military disengagement from Europe, begun after World War II, and led to a permanent and unprecedented U.S. peacetime commitment to Europe.

The impact of the U.S. on Europe has been as pervasive as Moscow's, but in a very different way. Not only did U.S. involvement in World War II ensure the survival of democracy in Britain, it also reestablished it in France, the Netherlands and other countries, following their liberation from German occupation. The U.S. also was the principal promoter of democracy in areas where it had been weak, such as in Germany and Italy. From this secure and increasingly prosperous West European base, democratic institutions eventually spread to Spain, Portugal, and Turkey, where authoritarian rule had been the norm.

As important as America's political role in post-war Europe has been its economic impact. Washington was the principal actor in establishing the post-war liberal international economic order with free trade at its core. The international economic organizations established at U.S. insistence include: the International Monetary Fund (IMF) and the World Bank (International Bank of Reconstruction and Development), both founded in 1944 and originally established to provide capital for Europe's economic revival; in 1947, the Organization for European Economic Cooperation, which in 1961 became the Organization for Economic Cooperation and Development (OECD), the principal economic grouping of the world's industrialized nations; and in 1948, the General Agreement on Tariffs and Trade (GATT), an international trade negotiating body devoted to removing barriers in trade.

More directly, the U.S. provided unprecedentedly generous loans and grants to rebuild Europe. The Marshall Plan pumped approximately $13 billion (in 1949 dollars; over $65 billion in 1990 dollars) into Europe from 1947 to 1952, which along with free market and currency reforms in West Germany sparked Europe's economic recovery. This was approximately same amount that Moscow stole from Eastern Europe in the late 1940s as the Soviets forcibly removed and transplanted factories, railroads, and other parts of Eastern Europe's industrial infrastructure to the U.S.S.R.

The U.S. also played an essential role in creating the framework for West European security. In addition to being the principal player in

Chapter 1

establishing NATO, the U.S. was responsible for broadening NATO to include almost all of Western Europe, insisting over the objections of France and other allies on the admission into the Alliance as equal members of Italy (1949), Portugal (1949), Greece (1951), and Turkey (1951), as well as West Germany (1955). The U.S. was not only the most important member of NATO, providing hundreds of thousands of troops and a nuclear guarantee, but also its indispensable political leader.

Finally, the U.S. had an extraordinary influence on the political unification of Western Europe. Through the operation of the economic and security organizations that the U.S. had established and maintained, political cooperation among the states of Western Europe, especially between West Germany and its traditional enemies, became routine. The legacy of cooperation that resulted was essential to establishing new European political institutions, including the European Economic Community (EC) in 1957, which despite its name and economic orientation has in its charter a commitment to eventual political integration.

SOURCES OF INSTABILITY IN THE NEW EUROPE

So thoroughly has Europe been transformed in the post-war decades that it bears little resemblance to the Europe of previous generations. The changes since 1989, however, may upset this relative tranquility. Most directly, the retreat of Soviet power frees East Europeans to pursue independent foreign policies. Declining Soviet power also removes the threat that has driven West Europeans to cooperate more closely with each other and the U.S. The prospect of German unification already is causing tension between Bonn and London, Bonn and Paris, and even Washington and London.

The replacement of the relatively rigid and stable post-war order by a more dynamic and fluid system is likely to increase political and possibly military instability in Europe. Not all instability need be worrisome, however, especially if it is confined to peripheral areas, such as the Balkans or even the Baltic states, in contrast to Central Europe. Nevertheless, several sources of instability could create problems in the wider community. These are: 1) ethnic problems, 2) border disputes, and 3) the fallout of a disintegrating Soviet Union.

The New Political Landscape in Europe

Ethnic Disputes

An unintended consequence of the political liberation of Eastern Europe is the revival of disputes between ethnic groups. The long process of redrawing political boundaries to coincide with ethnic populations largely ended in Western Europe with the consolidation of nation-states in the 19th and 20th centuries. In Eastern Europe, however, this process has yet to be concluded, largely because the area has remained under imperial domination, earlier by the Austro-Hungarian and Ottoman Empires and most recently by the Russians.

Ethnic disputes have been the cause or pretext of war in Europe on a number of occasions in the past two centuries. The most disastrous was in World War I, which grew out of a dispute between Austria-Hungary and Russia over attempts by the Serbs to unite the Slavic population of the Balkans under Serbian control. Moscow sided with the Serbs' challenge to Vienna's rule.

Many of those ethnic disputes that occupied the attention of European leaders in the early part of this century have now reappeared. Example: the efforts by Serbia's leadership to extend its control over all of traditionally Serbian areas, like the largely Albanian area of Kosovo, have triggered increasing conflict in Yugoslavia. The large Hungarian minority in Romania, a source of tension between the two countries even when both were allied as communist states, now threatens to become an invitation to conflict.

Likely to contribute to the growth of ethnic disputes is the rebirth of nationalism, especially in the newly liberated countries of Eastern Europe and in Germany. Germany's renewed nationalism stems from excitement over the prospects of reunification, pride in West Germany's remarkable economic and political accomplishments, and the sense that Nazi Germany now belongs to another era. A dramatic example of this is West German Chancellor Helmut Kohl's impassioned November 8, 1989, speech in Berlin to the crowds that had gathered for the opening of the Berlin Wall, followed by an emotional singing of the West German national anthem. While Poles, Frenchmen, and other Europeans understandably may be concerned over the prospect of a renewal of German nationalism, there have been few signs that it reflects either militarism or xenophobia beyond the slogans of fringe parties. West German officials repeatedly state the need for

Chapter 1

Germans to remember the destruction that Germany has wreaked on Europe in the past and to prevent its reoccurrence.

Nationalism is surging in Eastern Europe as well. Tense relations among differing ethnic groups are a serious problem in Yugoslavia, where the dominant Serbs are in conflict with Slovenes, Albanians, and other ethnic groups. The Serbian government and Communist Party led by Slobodan Milosevic have tried to use Serbian nationalism as an instrument for increasing their control over non-Serbian areas like Albanian-populated Kosovo and multi-ethnic Bosnia. This has raised fear and resentment among Yugoslavia's other major nationalities, primarily the Slovenes and Croatians.

This ethnic conflict well could lead to the break-up of Yugoslavia. The country is a federation of six republics: Bosnia-Herzegovina, Croatia, Macedonia, Montenegro, Serbia, and Slovenia. Since the federal government of Prime Minister Ante Markovic is very weak, the country could fragment along ethnic lines. The Slovenian Communist Party broke away from the Yugoslav Communist Party on February 4, 1990, which followed the Slovenian government's amendment of the republic's constitution on September 27, 1989, to give itself the right of secession. In Yugoslavia's first multi-party elections, on April 8, 1990, voters in Slovenia elected a parliament dominated by a non-communist coalition, following a campaign in which independence for Slovenia was openly debated.

A division into its constituent republics would not solve Yugoslavia's nationality problems, since the various ethnic groups are extensively intermixed in each of the republics and have a history of intolerance toward one another. A partition of Yugoslavia, even one that is contested, need not destabilize the rest of Europe as long as it does not prompt intervention by a major power like the Soviet Union; this is very unlikely given Moscow's lack of influence in Belgrade and its preoccupation with problems at home.

Some ethnic problems in Eastern Europe, however, could involve other outside powers. Germany, for example, could take a prospective interest in the well-being of the approximately 200,000 ethnic Germans in Hungary, the approximately 400,000 in Romania, and the several hundred thousand in Poland, primarily in the former German territories of Pomerania and Silesia. Since there is a potential border dispute between Poland and Germany over territories east of the Oder-Neisse rivers that Germany lost to Poland after World War II, the

The New Political Landscape in Europe

fate of ethnic Germans in Poland could become a serious problem. As long as emigration remains open and Germans in Hungary, Poland, and Romania do not become the victims of overt, or state-supported, persecution, tension involving German minorities is unlikely to be the source of international conflict that it was in the past.

Persecution of Jewish minorities could erupt into an international issue. The once-thriving Jewish communities of Eastern Europe were almost totally annihilated by the Germans in World War II; most of those Jews who survived fled to America or Israel after the war. Still, 80,000 Jews remain in Hungary and 20,000 in Romania. As in the case with German minorities in Eastern Europe, as long as immigration remains open and state-supported persecution does not reappear, the issue is not likely to prompt outside intervention.

The large Muslim Turkish population in Bulgaria, by some estimates up to 15 percent of the total population of 9 million, has been persecuted for years. The Bulgarian government has tried to force cultural assimilation, including requiring the Turks to adopt Bulgarian names and punishing the use of the Turkish language. When it became clear that this policy was failing, more drastic measures were taken. In the summer of 1989, 300,000 Turks were expelled to Turkey. The fall of Bulgaria's hardline Todor Zhivkov regime in November 1989 has led to a dramatic improvement in the treatment of the Turkish minority; still, ethnic relations remain tense. As a NATO member, Turkey's understandable interest in this minority, as well as in the Turkish minorities in Greece and Cyprus who long have suffered both subtle and overt persecution, gives the problem of Turkish minorities the potential for involving outside powers.

The Hungarian minorities are the most extensive and they overlap several Eastern Europe borders. In Romania's Transylvania live 2 million Hungarians. Significant Hungarian minorities also inhabit Yugoslavia's Vojvodina region and Czechoslovakia along the border with Hungary. This situation was created after World War I when the victorious allies separated large areas with a Hungarian population from the newly created Hungarian state to punish Hungary for its alliance with Germany.

Eastern Europe's ethnic problems pale beside those of the Soviet Union. The rise of independence forces among the Soviet nationalities raises the possibility of the rapid disintegration of Moscow's control and the emergence of new states. Most of these states, such as

Chapter 1

Lithuania and Ukraine, contain significant minorities. In Latvia, for example, non-Latvians make up almost half the population; in Estonia the figure is around 40 percent. Of Ukraine's 50 million citizens, Russians comprise over 10 million. All told, the disintegration of the Russian empire likely will create many ethic conflicts, especially if the process of decolonization is violent.

Border Disputes

More worrisome are ethnic problems which involve possible changes in international borders. The case of Romania, for example, is potentially dangerous because it directly involves the Soviet Union. The Soviet republic of Moldavia, bordering on Romania, is overwhelmingly composed of an ethnically Romanian population. Given the choice, the population most likely would vote to nullify the illegal Soviet seizure of Moldavia from Romania in 1940 and to rejoin Romania. The Moldavian Popular Front, a grouping of nationalist and democratic organizations, won control of Moldavia's government in the March 25, 1990, elections. It proclaimed Moldavia's sovereignty on June 23, giving its laws precedence over Soviet law, and openly backs independence and eventual reunion with Romania.

Developments in Moldavia could lead to a broader European conflict. The most serious would be between Romania and the Soviet Union. This could be triggered were Romanians to assist those Moldavians actively resisting Soviet rule. Soviet action against Romania could involve other European states, particularly France, which is becoming Romania's principal Western supporter.

No border question in Europe today is more sensitive and potentially explosive than the German-Polish, which has been revived by the prospect of imminent German unification. The problem lies in the ambiguities of the post-World War II redrawing of European borders.

Although no peace treaty exists between the victorious allies and Germany formally ending World War II, a *de facto* settlement establishing Germany's borders was reached among the allies at the July 1945 conference in Potsdam. In this agreement, Poland was given the eastern German lands of Silesia, Pomerania, and southern East Prussia in compensation for the Soviet annexation of Poland's own eastern territories, now comprising western Byelorussia and western Ukraine. Over 90 percent of the German population of the territories given to

The New Political Landscape in Europe

Poland by the allies were expelled or fled to Germany after the war. Estimates of the size of the German population remaining in Poland vary widely because of assimilation and intermarriage, but there may be as many as 500,000.

As long as Moscow imposed division on Germany, the matter of Germany's borders was only a theoretical problem which few West German politicians cared to address. Careful to protect their new image as good European citizens, West German leaders routinely have attempted to reassure the world of their peaceful intentions toward Poland. As part of its *Ostpolitik* policy of improving relations with the Eastern bloc, for instance, the West German government of Willy Brandt signed the Warsaw Treaty with Poland on December 7, 1970, which recognized the present East German-Polish border. Although West Germany has no border with Poland, the Poles thought it prudent to secure Bonn's recognition of the Polish border. West Germany's recognition of it was reinforced by the August 1, 1975, Helsinki Accord, signed by both Germanies, which commits all European states to seek border changes only by peaceful means.

The dangers of the ambiguity of Germany's borders became clear in early 1990. In a subtle but important departure from Bonn's routine pledges to respect Poland's post-war borders, West German Chancellor Helmut Kohl suddenly became vague, taking the legalistic position that only a united German government would have the constitutional authority to determine Germany's borders. This notion was met with an international outcry. Bowing to intense international pressure, Kohl stated on March 7, 1990, that the parliaments of both Germanies should adopt identical resolutions accepting the permanence of the Polish border — called the Oder-Neisse line, for the two rivers that define it — and that the resolution should be adopted by a united Germany. On April 8, 1990, the West German parliament declared that the present Polish border would not be challenged. And, in one of its first acts, the newly elected East German parliament did the same on April 12. Although the Oder-Neisse dispute is not as serious as it once was, it will remain an underlying source of tension between Germany and Poland.

Chapter 1

Disintegration of the Soviet Union

Two key questions facing the future of Europe are whether the Soviet Union will unravel, and if so, whether it will be violent or peaceful. Although the U.S.S.R. portrays itself as a voluntary federation of peoples, it is in fact the last of the European colonial empires, a direct descendent of the Russian Empire, and one now facing decolonization.

The collapse of Soviet authority in Eastern Europe and the overthrow of the imposed communist regimes is part of a larger process that is shaking the foundations of the Soviet Union itself. This is not surprising: the subject peoples within the Soviet Union share the same hopes of freedom, liberty, and prosperity as those of Eastern Europe. Several of the national republics in the Soviet Union already have asserted their sovereignty and many actively are planning for independence.

Following democratic elections in the Baltic states in which independence advocates captured large majorities, their new governments have moved toward establishing their sovereignty and independence. Lithuania declared its independence on March 11, 1990; Estonia's new parliament voted on March 30 to begin the "transition" to a restoration of that country's independence, and Latvia followed in early May.

In the March 4 elections for the Ukrainian parliament, the Democratic Bloc won 27 percent of the seats despite intense repression by the Ukrainian Communist Party. The Bloc is led by the Ukrainian nationalist organization *Rukh*, which is committed to independence for Ukraine. The growth of the nationalist forces has forced the hard-line Ukrainian Communist Party to adopt pro-nationalist policies, such as proclaiming Ukraine's sovereignty on July 16. The Georgian parliament has declared illegal that country's forcible incorporation into the Soviet Union in 1921, and pro-independence forces dominate the political landscape.

Moscow's only means of restraining these national liberation movements is the use of massive force; even then the success of repression is not guaranteed. Conversely, a decision by the Kremlin to allow subject nationalities to secede from the Soviet Union would mean the end of the Soviet Union and the historic Russian empire. Russia then would stand alone, its borders rolled back to the early 18th Century boundaries of the reign of Peter the Great. The Russian remnant of course, would still be huge; its 150 million citizens would make it

The New Political Landscape in Europe

Europe's most populous country. Without the burdens of empire, however, Russia may even find it easier to become democratic and to grow economically.

The key development in the dissolution of the Russian empire would be the independence of Ukraine.[1] Not only would Moscow's power be severely diminished by the loss of Ukraine's 50 million people and its extensive industrial capacity, natural resources, and agricultural output, but an independent Ukraine would create a vast buffer between Europe and Russia and itself would be a major power.

There are of course many dangers in the possible dissolution of the Soviet Union, as there have been with the dissolution of all empires. Any large-scale attempt by Moscow to suppress these nationality movements by force would shed blood and risk the conflict spilling over into Eastern Europe. Similarly, attempts by countries such as Poland or Romania to exploit Soviet weakness by reasserting historical claims to areas formerly under their control, like Polish claims on the Ukrainian city of Lvov and Romanian designs on Moldavia, could produce armed clashes with the Soviet military.

Moscow's ample stockpile of nuclear weapons makes it unlikely that war between Russia and a seceding republic would bring a Western military response. No Western military power would risk nuclear retaliation by Moscow to support an independence movement with military force. Should any conflict spill over into Eastern Europe, however, some sort of Western involvement could be imagined. The precedent for such action: French military assistance to newly independent Poland was crucial in helping Warsaw repel a Soviet invasion in 1920.

It is unlikely that even a massive use of force by Moscow could eliminate the independence forces within the U.S.S.R. They have become too entrenched organizationally, and their goals are broadly shared by the respective populations. Instead of producing submission, the use of force is likely to radicalize the population and eventually provoke conflict. The Soviet Union is awash with weapons, both legal

---

1   Common American usage usually prefixes "the" before Ukraine. Ukrainian nationalists object to this, explaining that it derives from the imperial Russian attempt to demote Ukraine from a nation to a region.

Chapter 1

armaments such as hunting rifles, and heavier equipment stolen from, or sold by, Soviet soldiers.

An even more explosive situation exists in the Soviet Union's Muslim areas, primarily Azerbaijan and Central Asia. Although Muslim fundamentalism has yet to make serious inroads there, a rising nationalism based on religious identity and increasing anti-Soviet and anti-Russian sentiment is creating an increasingly tense situation. Moscow already has helped radicalize the population in Azerbaijan when the armed forces were dispatched to restore order in the republic in January 1990. What had been a limited movement for sovereignty has become an independence movement with broad popular support.

The events in Azerbaijan had an important ethnic dimension, namely the conflict between the Armenians and Azeris. Similar communal hatreds exist throughout Central Asia between Muslim and non-Muslims as well as between differing Muslim groups. In March 1990 in Dushambe, the capital of Tadzhikistan, local groups attacked Armenians and Russians without provocation and killed several people. And in Uzbekistan, groups of the dominant Uzbeks have carried out a number of attacks on a minority people called the Meskhetians.

The mix of ethnic conflict, a desire for independence, and Soviet intervention to restore control could lead easily to wide-scale conflict. As Central Asia borders on Afghanistan, China, and Iran, the prospect of foreign intervention is real. The area's huge expanse and strategic location could invite outside involvement as Moscow's authority wanes. One possibility is Chinese-Iranian-Pakistani co-operation against an anti-Muslim Indian-Russian alliance, with local groups in Central Asia acting as surrogates.

There are other dangers of a Soviet descent into chaos. The seizure of power in Moscow by hard-line radicals could have catastrophic consequences for the world. And the prospect of loss of central control over even a portion of the nuclear weapons stockpiled in the U.S.S.R.'s non-Russian areas is troubling. Such weapons need not be used by local forces, but could be sold or given to regimes in such countries as Iran or Libya, which are both unstable and intensely anti-Western.

THE GERMAN QUESTION

The reunification of Germany and the termination of the residual occupation rights of the four major World War II victors — the U.S.

How a United Germany Compares

	Population (millions)	Gross National Product ($ billions)	Active Military Forces	Medals in 1988 Olympics
Austria	8	126	42,500	12
Belgium	10	153	92,400	2
Britain	57	826	311,560	24
Denmark	5	99	31,600	4
France	56	940	466,300	1
E. Germany	17	207*	173,100	127
W. Germany	61	1,206	494,300	49
Greece	10	53	208,500	1
Ireland	4	32	13,000	0
Netherlands	15	210	103,600	16
Norway	4	90	34,100	11
Portugal	10	41	75,300	1
Spain	39	344	285,000	4
Sweden	8	179	64,500	17
Switzerland	7	184	39,500	20
Turkey	53	64	650,900	2
USA	249	4,839	2,123,000	100
USSR	288	2,193*	4,258,000*	161
United Germany	78	1348*	667,400	176

* Estimates

Sources: *The Military Balance 1989-1990*, (London: International Institute for Strategic Studies, 1990). *The World Almanac 1989* (New York: Pharos Books, 1989). All figures for 1988.

Chapter 1

Britain, France, and the Soviet Union — will create a powerful state in the center of Europe. European apprehension regarding the impact of the new power has produced a great deal of hand-wringing and prediction of German political and economic domination. But the so-called "German problem" is not simply a question of Germany's future behavior and its capacity to threaten Europe. Rather, it is a broader question of the strength of Europe's institutions and the ability of its governments to secure the peace in a dynamic and increasingly unfamiliar environment. With its 63 million people, West Germany was the most populous country in Europe, save the Soviet Union. Its well-trained 500,000-man armed forces were the largest in Western Europe, except for Turkey. And its 1989 Gross Domestic Product of $1.2 trillion was comfortably ahead that of the second largest economy, France, at $950 billion. West Germany's 1989 trade surplus even exceeded that of Japan: $80 billion vs. $77 billion.

Despite its impressive economic performance, West Germany has had limited political influence. This is the result of a number of factors. The legacy of Nazism, particularly the Jewish holocaust, created a psychological climate in which German nationalism was restrained and in which West Germans made strenuous efforts to avoid being seen as imposing their views on other nations or on international bodies. Bonn typically deferred to its allies, particularly America, in light of the need for protection from the Soviet Union. This was evident in Germany's traditional deference to Washington on deciding which U.S. nuclear weapons should be placed on West German soil. West Germany also sought acceptance from Europeans by strongly supporting such postwar European institutions as the European Economic Community. Often this required West Germany's taking a secondary role and being particularly careful to mollify French sensibilities.

For these reasons, the prospect of a politically more assertive Germany, its unity restored and its freedom of action expanded by the reduction in the military threat from the East, worries its neighbors. Given Germany's victimization of Poland in World War II, Warsaw's anxiety about Germany's ultimate intentions are understandable. The border issue in particular has heightened Polish concerns, despite Kohl's attempts to assuage them by insisting he has no desire to challenge existing borders.

Poland's problem is historical and geographic. It is perched precariously between powerful neighbors and always has required a

The New Political Landscape in Europe

A United Germany and Its Neighbors

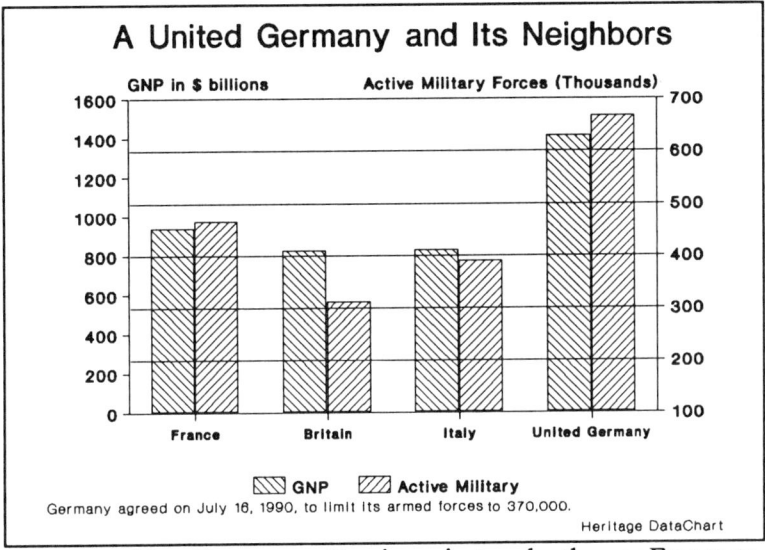

[Bar chart showing GNP in $ billions and Active Military Forces (Thousands) for France, Britain, Italy, and United Germany]

GNP · Active Military

Germany agreed on July 16, 1990, to limit its armed forces to 370,000.

Heritage DataChart

protector: either Germany or Russia against each other, or France or Britain against both Germany and Russia. While openly anti-German defensive alliances in Europe are unlikely to be revived, it is possible that such alignments may arise implicitly through, for example, close security and political coordination between Paris, on the one hand, and Warsaw and other East European capitals on the other. It also is possible that Polish fears over Germany could provide Moscow a permanent protective role in Poland, even after a general Soviet military withdrawal from Eastern Europe. This prospect was held out by Polish Prime Minister Tadeusz Mazowiecki, on February 22, 1990, when he said that Soviet forces might stay in Poland as long as the question of the border with Germany remains open.

France's strategy toward Germany was to avoid openly opposing German unification, while expressing a general concern about the rise of instability if events moved too quickly. French President François Mitterrand emphasized his desire to cooperate with a united Germany in building a new Europe, not only to encourage greater European independence from Washington and Moscow, but to benefit from closer economic cooperation.

But this cooperative attitude may not last in Paris. French leaders supported German unification only reluctantly, largely because France

Chapter 1

could not prevent it. Consequently, they have taken compensatory measures. For one thing, France was an important force in accelerating the political and economic integration of the EC. Its aim was to embed Bonn's economic and political decision-making within the framework of a united Europe in which Bonn could be outvoted. For another thing, Paris has bolstered its ties with Eastern European countries. Even before the recent upheaval in Eastern Europe, Mitterrand made a series of high-profile trips in the first half of 1989 to such traditional French allies as Czechoslovakia and Poland.[2] And France has taken a lead role in establishing ties to the new Romanian government. Most significantly, the day after the Berlin wall fell, on November 8, 1989, Mitterrand went to Kiev in the Soviet Union to confer with Gorbachev over German reunification.

This East European diplomacy, although intended to complement France's strategy of anchoring Germany in Europe, could at some point anger the Germans and create anti-French backlash. Germany, too, after all, has options: historic German-Russian ties rival Franco-Russian ties. Cooperation between Russia and Prussia (later Germany) was a fixture of 19th Century diplomacy. The connection was revived after World War I, when the two engaged in extensive economic, political, and secret military cooperation. And Stalin and Hitler entered into a far-reaching alliance against the West in 1939.

German unification promises to place new strains on the cohesion of the West, especially if a united Germany assumes a leading role in Europe. Fears that Germany may distance itself from the West, however, are surely unfounded. To begin with, Germany's strong political, economic, and cultural ties to Western Europe will not diminish; in fact, they are likely to be strengthened. And to the extent that the "West" denotes those countries that are democratic and capitalist, it has now expanded to include "Eastern" Europe as well. Most important, Ger-

---

2   During the years between World Wars I and II, France headed an alliance system known as the "Little Entente," linking it to Czechoslovakia, Romania, and Yugoslavia. The common bond was opposition to Hungarian expansion. The result was to push Hungary into alliance with Germany. See Chapter 2, "A New American Role in Europe's Balance of Power." France also established an anti-German alliance with Poland during this period. The German attack on Poland produced a French (and British) declaration of war.

The New Political Landscape in Europe

many would have little to gain, and much to lose, were it to loosen its ties to its Western allies in return for better relations with a bankrupt and disintegrating Soviet Union. Bonn consistently has rebuffed Soviet overtures designed to separate it from its Western allies, such as Stalin's offer in 1952 to allow German reunification in return for that country's neutrality.

EUROPEAN INTEGRATION

American troops in Europe have been the principal stabilizing force on the continent since World War II. The many changes in Europe, especially the likely decline of U.S. influence, threaten to undermine this secure arrangement. One of the most important replacements for the U.S. may be European integration.

The most important European institution is the European Economic Community (EC or Common Market). Founded in 1957 by the Treaty of Rome, the EC is primarily concerned with furthering economic integration in Europe. It, however, formally has been committed to political integration since it began, and even has established such political institutions as the popularly elected but largely powerless European Parliament.

Progress in political cooperation was slow until the ratification in 1987 of the Single European Act. This commits the EC countries to closer cooperation in foreign policy. It also adds some powers to the European Parliament, to which all citizens of all EC countries directly elect representatives. This Act accompanied a series of projects grouped under the heading "1992," whose aim is to achieve, by the end of 1992, the original EC goals of eliminating all trade barriers among member states, harmonizing economic regulations, and achieving a true free market for Western Europe.

Even as the "1992" project was being adopted, a far more ambitious agenda for European integration was put forward in 1988. Jacques Delors, the President of the European Commission, the principal executive body of the EC, has proposed building upon the momentum generated by the 1992 project to create a true economic union. In April 1990, the EC governments agreed that a new treaty of economic and monetary union (EMU) should be drawn up by an EC conference in December. This treaty should be ratified by the end of 1992. Among its major provisions will be the creation of a common currency for

Chapter 1

Europe, as well as a European central bank to coordinate economic and financial policy. While there are major disagreements over this sweeping proposal, several European leaders, such as France's Mitterrand, view EC integration as a means of helping to enmesh Germany in Europe politically and economically. This, according to them, would help contain Germany's growing economic influence. This is becoming particularly important as German unification approaches. West German Chancellor Kohl, Foreign Minister Hans-Dietrich Genscher, and other West German leaders express their strong support for integration.

European integration may be given a further boost this December when the EC countries will begin talks on amending the original Rome Treaty to create a political union. The extent of these amendments has not been agreed. Margaret Thatcher is opposing the surrender of national sovereignty to the EC, but Mitterand and Kohl issued a joint appeal in April for a strong "political union." Whatever the outcome of the negotiations, it is unlikely that institutions such as the European Parliament and the Commission will have been granted increased powers.

The revolutions of 1989 in Eastern Europe have added a new urgency to efforts for European integration. At Washington's urging, the EC has taken a leading role in providing Western assistance to Eastern Europe, especially by coordinating deliveries of food aid to Poland. The EC and its member countries have offered aid of several billion dollars, and the EC has pushed creation of the European Bank for Reconstruction and Development, which is being established to provide capital for Eastern Europe's economic transformation.

Despite the EC's prominence, other pan-European economic institutions also may play a role in European integration. The European Free Trade Association (EFTA), which includes Austria, Finland, Iceland, Norway, Sweden, and Switzerland, has begun negotiations with the EC to increase economic coordination and remove trade barriers, eventually to result in what has been termed the European Economic Space. Although membership in EFTA has been proposed for some Eastern European states as an interim step to the EC, the highly developed capitalist states of EFTA are unlikely to want an economic union with the most economically backward countries in Europe.

The New Political Landscape in Europe

Rather than join the EC or EFTA, the countries of Eastern Europe may establish their own economic organization, one which would aim at coordinating their policies on several problems. These include a severe shortage of hard currency, a need to adopt market reforms, and increased access to Western markets. Such an organization could give the East European states collective bargaining power with the EC.

The Council of Europe, established in 1948 to promote European cooperation and human rights, is at present the only truly pan-European organization. Its membership is open in principle to all European democracies, East or West. Composed of representatives from the parliaments of the member states, the Council of Europe has no formal power. It does provide, however, a forum for legislators from member countries to meet and work on human rights, the environment, and other common issues.

Because they were not democracies, East European countries had been excluded from Council of Europe membership. Hungary and Poland, however, were given observer status in 1989. Both have applied for full membership and are certain to receive it once their democratic systems are firmly established. They are likely to be followed by Czechoslovakia and those East European states making the transition to democracy. The desire for membership in the Council of Europe is evidence of these countries' strong desire to establish formal connections with the rest of Europe.

The West European Union (WEU) is another European institution that could spur European integration. It was established in 1948 by the Treaty of Brussels signed by Belgium, Britain, France, Luxembourg, and the Netherlands, as a means of addressing the growing threat from the Soviet Union. West Germany was admitted in 1955; Italy, Portugal, and Spain later became members. Superseded by the establishment of NATO in 1949, the WEU languished in obscurity until it enjoyed an unexpected revival in the 1980s. Largely on French insistence, the WEU was brought back to life to promote discussion and cooperation on security issues among West Europeans outside the NATO network, with the U.S. pointedly excluded.

No other existing European institution is as well suited as the WEU for creating a European-wide military organization to exist alongside NATO. Because NATO includes the U.S. and Canada, it cannot readily be expanded to Eastern Europe without alarming the Soviet Union. The EC, meanwhile, cannot take on a military role because it includes

Chapter 1

neutral Ireland while excluding NATO members Iceland and Norway. And other organizations such as the Council of Europe shy away from military issues altogether. Expansion of WEU's membership to include the countries of Eastern Europe would be less troublesome than would be the case for NATO. Unlike NATO, the WEU lacks an operational military organization or command structure which would make taking on new members much easier.

Another forum for cooperation in the new Europe will be the Conference on Security and Cooperation in Europe (CSCE), which includes all European countries plus the U.S., Canada, and the Soviet Union. The CSCE was pushed by the Soviets in the early 1970s as a means for gaining Western acceptance of Eastern Europe's post-World War II boundary changes and of Soviet domination of these countries, as well as to improve economic cooperation. The price of Western participation, however, was Moscow's agreement to include human rights. The CSCE's major accomplishment was the so-called "Final Act," signed in Helsinki in 1975. In it, the signatory states commit themselves to a number of cooperative measures, including a respect for existing borders and a greater emphasis on human rights. Since then, the CSCE has held a number of review sessions, which have focused primarily on highlighting Soviet and East European human rights abuses. Moscow has proposed making the 35-nation CSCE a permanent mechanism for the discussion of the broad range of European security issues, as well as political, economic, and human rights questions.

At a time when America's strongest link to Europe, NATO, may be losing importance, CSCE could become more important as a means of maintaining U.S. influence in Europe. The scale and speed of the changes in Europe have prompted calls for a CSCE meeting in November 1990. There, it is proposed, the European states, along with the U.S. and Canada, could address the political, security, and economic issues.

EUROPE AS COMPETITOR

Even as a united Europe would serve American interests by reducing instability, it also could become a major competitor to America for global influence. With a population and economic potential far in excess of that of the U.S., a united Europe could emerge as a political and economic superpower. While a stable and democratic Europe

The New Political Landscape in Europe

would have broad similarities of interest with the U.S., there are a number of areas where the two could come into conflict. Economic and political differences between the U.S. and Western Europe have existed for years, but these have been largely repressed by the latter's dependence upon the U.S. to protect Europe from Soviet attack and intimidation. As the Soviet threat recedes, these differences are likely to become more prominent.

A major difference concerns the Middle East. West Europeans often have opposed U.S. policy in the region by refusing either to back such American clients as Israel and Egypt or to cooperate with Washington's efforts to isolate such anti-Western countries as Iran and Libya. European cooperation with the U.S. in the embargo against Iraq is an exception to this, but the desire for a steady energy supply from the Middle East at times has led France and West Germany to appease international terrorists and the states that support them. The Europeans also more strongly back the Arab countries in their struggle with Israel. French and British colonial ties explain much of this tilt, but the political and military importance of the Arab world, as well as its markets, are the principal considerations by the Europeans. This has obstructed U.S. policy, for example, as when Bonn hindered the U.S. resupply of Israel during the 1973 war by refusing transit to U.S. aircraft, and when France and Spain refused to allow U.S. aircraft to fly over their territories in the U.S. bombing of Libya in 1987.

West European countries also have opposed U.S. policies in Vietnam and Central America. France and Britain retained their economic and other ties with North Vietnam throughout the Vietnam War and have refused to cooperate in the longstanding U.S. economic embargo against Cuba. The American interventions in Grenada in 1982 and Panama in 1989 were condemned by most West European countries. Nicaragua's Sandinista regime long was supported by the Socialist International, the global organization of socialist parties, headed by former West German Chancellor Willy Brandt. In the early 1980s, in fact, Nicaragua received substantial economic assistance from West Germany's Social Democratic government. And Spain's Socialist government continued to provide the Sandinistas with economic support until 1988.

Such differences have extended to America's dealings with the Soviet Union. West Europeans have been hesitant to back U.S. efforts to deny Moscow advanced technology and credits. West European

Chapter 1

governments lent billions of dollars to East European regimes and to Moscow in the 1970s. They also balked at tough enforcement of export restrictions, imposed by the West's Coordinating Committee for Multilateral Export Controls (COCOM), on sales to the East of militarily useful technology. Although West Germany had numerous laws and regulations on the books restricting such sales, the lack of effective export controls made them meaningless.

Washington's attempts to embargo trade with the Soviet Union following Moscow's 1979 invasion of Afghanistan met with only limited cooperation from Western Europe. Most countries refused even to follow the U.S. lead on boycotting the Moscow Olympics in 1980; Britain and West Germany were the only prominent exceptions.

The West Europeans also have been responsible for spreading nuclear and other advanced military technology to the Third World, including to such openly anti-Western countries as Libya and Iraq. France and Italy helped build the Iraqi nuclear reactor at Osirak, which was being used for nuclear weapons research until it was destroyed by an Israeli air raid in 1981. Moreover, West German firms provided Iraq with the technology to develop chemical weaponry and ballistic missiles, which became an enormous concern after Saddam Hussein's August 1990 invasion of Kuwait. West German companies also were major participants in constructing the massive chemical weapons plant in Rabta, Libya, and have assisted Iraq in developing ballistic missiles.[3]

Significantly, these and other differences in policies between the U.S. and Western Europe occurred at a time when U.S.-European cooperation was at its height and when the U.S. continued to shoulder most of the burden of Western Europe's defense. As U.S. influence in Europe wanes, such differences will probably grow. Moreover, a united Europe would have the power to compete with the U.S. economically and politically around the world. It could exercise enormous political influence in areas such as the Third World or even East Asia by means ranging from arms sales to controlling access to the European market, which is the largest and richest in the world. The economic challenge to the U.S. would be far greater than that posed by Japan. Already, the nearly $5 trillion combined Gross National Products (GNP) of the EC

---

3 "Iraq's Arsenal of Horrors," *The Washington Post*, April 8, 1990.

The New Political Landscape in Europe

states alone dwarf Japan's GNP of $2 trillion and approaches America's $5.2 trillion.

The economic challenge to the U.S is not competition; that is essential to a free market and an expanding economy. The danger is that Europe could turn its back on competition and, instead, try to manage trade to protect sectors of its economy. Many rightly fear that European integration could result in a "Fortress Europe" in which barriers to trade are erected to keep out or limit American and other non-European goods, services, and investment. For example, Europeans already severely restrict imports of Japanese cars, including those made in America.

A particular U.S. concern is EC government subsidies of high-technology industries to make them artificially competitive on international markets. Example: U.S. dominance of the world civil aviation market has been eroded by the Airbus consortium in Europe, ostensibly a private firm but one which would close its doors immediately if not for the enormous subsidies from European governments. A more ambitious project is Eureka. Billed as a counterpart to the U.S. Strategic Defense Initiative (SDI), Eureka was launched in 1984 as a cooperative effort among European governments to develop advanced technology for commercial use. The intent of this program is to assist in creating a high-technology sector of the European economy to compete with the U.S. and Japan for world markets.

The dangers to the U.S. of a united and competitive Europe are real, but they also are easily exaggerated. As long as both the U.S. and Europe remain democratic, there are few conceivable scenarios in which the two would wage war against each other. Economic and political competition may be intense, but both sides will have a strong interest in preserving the peace and probably also in maintaining a relatively free trading system.

The U.S., of course, has options for compensating for Europe's growing power. The U.S. and Canada already have signed an historic agreement which will create, by and large, a common market between the two countries by 1999. And the U.S. has begun exploratory talks with Mexico on a similar free trade area accord. A common market stretching from Canada to Mexico would create the world's most dynamic and innovative economy. Also possible are U.S. free trade agreements with the Republic of China on Taiwan, the Southeast Asian industrialized nations, South Korea, and even with Japan. The U.S.,

Chapter 1

also, will be able to maintain close bilateral ties with European countries, particularly Britain.

The task for American policy makers will not be to devise ways to counter Europe, but to secure access to its markets and its products and to cooperate with a larger and possibly more united Europe, which will still share many of its basic interests.

CHALLENGES FOR U.S. POLICY

Short-Term Goals

U.S. goals in Europe over the short term should focus upon completing the dismantling of the Soviet empire in Eastern Europe and ensuring stability on the continent. To do this, the U.S. should: 1) support the democratic revolutions in Eastern Europe; 2) promote economic reform in Eastern Europe and the integration of these economies into the West; and 3) use its influence to ensure that Soviet decolonization proceeds peacefully and orderly.

To accomplish these goals, Washington should:

♦ ♦ **Support democratization and develop a foreign aid strategy that promotes free market reforms in Eastern Europe.**

1990 is the year in which the East Europeans must lay the foundation for establishing democracy and prosperous market economies. Although the danger of political instability within the East European countries is quite real, the far greater potential danger comes from the Soviet Union, which continues to station over 500,000 occupation troops in Eastern Europe. The U.S. should make clear to Moscow that any attempt to use these forces to retard or repeal the democratic revolution in Eastern Europe will repeal improved Soviet ties to the West.

Once freely elected governments safely are in place in Eastern Europe, the U.S. should remove trade restrictions on these countries. They should be granted Most-Favored-Nation status, and even offered the possibility of free trade agreements. Though the U.S. should offer the European democracies foreign aid, the amounts should be limited and given only to the private sector or to promote free market reforms. Foreign assistance given directly to governments will slow economic reforms and distort the functioning of the market in these countries.

The goal of U.S. assistance should be to encourage the East European states to move quickly toward dismantling the Stalinist

The New Political Landscape in Europe

economic systems imposed by the Soviet Union and creating free-market systems. U.S. assistance can be an important catalyst and also help to smooth economic transition.

The basic points of reform the U.S. should advocate include the establishment of secure property rights and an independent judiciary to protect them; the removal of government-imposed restrictions on the private sector, such as limits on the number of employees an enterprise can have; the sale to the private sector of state-owned economic enterprises; the end of government monopolies; the elimination of wage and price controls; the establishment of a convertible currency; and the removal of restrictions on trade and foreign investments.

U.S. assistance can be an important source of capital to the emerging private sectors in these countries. The government-controlled financial institutions have little experience with, or interest in, serving the private sector; and the growth of free enterprise is hampered by a severe lack of capital. The U.S. must not give money to the governments or state-owned economical enterprises. These have borrowed billions in the past and have squandered them. Worse, such assistance could delay necessary reform by reducing the economic pressures on the governments. Thus, the U.S. must encourage the creation of private banking systems in these countries as a means of channeling assistance to the private sector.

More important than financial aid, however, is technical assistance. Most of the East European countries have had only a very limited experience with free-market economies since the Soviet takeover and would benefit from programs designed to address this need.

An area where the U.S. is well-positioned to assist democratization and economic reform is in economic and business education. The U.S. should launch a broad educational assistance program to establish business schools in these countries, to train business teachers and students in U.S. business schools, and to bring large numbers of students to American universities, as occurred with the mainland Chinese students in the 1980s. These programs should be funded and run largely by the private sector, with government support limited to defraying initial costs and coordinating efforts.

♦♦ **Support a peaceful and negotiated process of Soviet decolonization.**

Chapter 1

One of the most important factors determining the future of Europe is Soviet decolonization. The dissolution of Moscow's control over the western areas of the Soviet Union — the Baltic states, Byelorussia, Ukraine — would diminish Soviet power in Europe dramatically. There also is a growing potential for extensive conflict within the Soviet Union as Moscow attempts to reassert control.

Soviet decolonization is driven by the increasing demands for greater self-determination and even independence by the non-Russian peoples who together comprise half the Soviet population. The Baltic states of Estonia, Latvia, and Lithuania have been the first to move to independence. Azerbaijan, Georgia, Ukraine, and some others surely will follow.

These nationalist movements already are too strong for Moscow to suppress permanently; the process of imperial dissolution will proceed either peacefully or violently. Moscow's resort to force likely would result in widespread bloodshed and chaos. More important, such conflict could spill into Eastern Europe or the Middle East and even could threaten the loss of Moscow's control over thousands of Soviet nuclear weapons.

U.S. interests strongly favor a peaceful and negotiated resolution of the problems posed by Soviet decolonization. The U.S. can help this process by creating incentives and disincentives designed to promote peaceful change. Washington should warn Moscow that using force against breakaway republics inevitably would worsen U.S.-Soviet relations and should declare publicly that the U.S. will not support violence by any group. Once a republic declares independence from the U.S.S.R., Washington should include these new states in the U.S. foreign assistance program for Eastern Europe.

The U.S. should also seek to internationalize the problem of Soviet decolonization by involving the West as a whole and by raising the issue in such fora as the Conference on Security and Cooperation in Europe and at the United Nations. In these discussions the broad range of political, security, and economic concerns of the many actors involved could be addressed and compromises reached free of coercion.

♦ ♦ **Establish relations with each of the European republics of the Soviet Union.** Given the growing importance of the European republics of the Soviet Union, the U.S. should establish direct relations with their governments, whether or not they are committed to independence. Such ties are permitted under Article 80 of the current

The New Political Landscape in Europe

Soviet constitution, which states that "A Union Republic has the right to enter into relations with other states, conclude treaties with them, exchange diplomatic and consular representatives, and take part in the work of international organizations." In the past, Moscow forbade such contacts, but its new policy of greater respect for the rights of the republics should be put to the test. There is a precedent: Byelorussia and Ukraine have been members of the United Nations since 1945.

Opening relations with these republics need not imply official U.S. recognition of independence. However, should a democratically elected government come to power in any of these republics and declare independence, the President should grant it diplomatic recognition, provided doing so advances U.S. interests and does not contribute to violence within the Soviet Union. The U.S. has never recognized the incorporation of the Baltic states into the Soviet Union, but none of the other republics voluntarily joined the Soviet Union; all were forcibly annexed. Thus, the U.S. should look sympathetically upon the reassertion of their independence.

♦ ♦ **Use the CSCE meeting to push for peaceful change in Europe.**

At the fall 1990 meeting of the Conference on Security and Cooperation in Europe, the U.S. should press for the removal of the remaining Soviet forces from Eastern Europe; promote security cooperation among European states, especially between the NATO countries and the newly freed states in Eastern Europe; address the concerns of Poles and others over German unification, especially by guaranteeing Germany's borders; craft a common approach to the problem of Soviet decolonization that addresses the security and other concerns of all parties and allows the process to proceed peacefully; and push for reducing economic barriers between states.

The U.S. should press at the CSCE meeting for the recognition of the right of every country in Europe freely to join or leave any international organization. This would hasten the demise of the Warsaw Pact and COMECON because it is very unlikely that any democratically elected government voluntarily would remain in these Soviet-dominated organizations. The U.S., too, should press for a renewed CSCE commitment that all changes in borders must be peaceful and that the rights of minorities be guaranteed by all signatory states, including the right of emigration.

Since CSCE brings together all European states plus the U.S., and Canada, and its mandate covers the broad range of economic, political,

Chapter 1

and security issues, the U.S. should press for inclusion of the Baltic states in the CSCE meeting.

The CSCE meeting should address economic issues, including assistance to Eastern Europe and a commitment to free trade. The Soviet Union should be pressed to provide economic assistance to Eastern Europe in partial compensation for the economic failures it has been responsible for there. Its imposition of Stalinist command economies in these countries and their forced membership in the Soviet-dominated economic organization COMECON has impoverished them. And by cutting many of their ties to Western Europe and the world, the Soviet Union ensured that the East European economies became increasingly obsolescent and uncompetitive. Now these countries are struggling with difficult economic reforms and would be greatly helped by a cooperative attitude by Moscow in such areas as renegotiating the terms of trade imposed in the past. At a minimum, the Soviet Union should write off that portion of Eastern Europe's hard currency debt owed to Moscow, such as the approximately $2 billion owed by Poland.

Long-Term Goals

Over the long term, American interests require that no single hostile power dominate the continent of Europe. U.S. long-term policy should: 1) promote European stability; 2) keep Europe's markets open to American products; and 3) cooperate with the European states to advance Western interests around the world. To accomplish these goals the U.S. should:

♦ ♦ **Remain bilaterally and multilaterally actively involved in Europe.**

For over four decades U.S. involvement in NATO and similar organizations has given Washington a major voice in shaping events in Europe. Now those organizations have begun to change. NATO inevitably will weaken as the Soviet threat recedes. The military organization – the "O" in NATO – likely will diminish in importance. Yet the underlying North Atlantic Treaty should be preserved, especially the joint commitment by signatory states to cooperate against an armed attack and the joint military command structure. The importance of this commitment could be reinforced by a symbolic new signing, as a demonstration of a continuing American involvement in Europe.

The New Political Landscape in Europe

The U.S. also should consider creating a new North Atlantic Conference, a political organization to continue the political consultative functions of NATO and provide an institutional link between the U.S., Canada, and Europe. All European democracies, East and West, could join. It would have no formal power but would underscore the trans-Atlantic connection during a time when this tie may face many new strains. This organization would focus on strengthening trans-Atlantic ties and would be open only to the democracies of Europe, plus the U.S. and Canada. The republics breaking away from the Soviet Union, too, if democracies, could participate.

♦ ♦ **Support the creation of European political and security organizations to provide stability.**

The stability that Europe has enjoyed for over four decades may be undermined by the decline in U.S. influence in Europe. To prevent a return of instability, especially that stemming from Germany's unification, the U.S. should support European integration, especially the creation of European organizations that will promote political and security cooperation.

These institutions should be built around existing organizations such as NATO, the EC, and the Western European Union. The U.S. also should insist that European organizations include the East European states and those European areas of the Soviet Union that manage to establish their independence. Whatever European political and security organization emerges, the U.S. should maintain a formal presence in Europe, through a reformed NATO, CSCE, and a new trans-Atlantic organization of democratic states.

CONCLUSION

For almost half a century, America has had its troops on the continent of Europe, first during World War II and later during the Cold War. Even as it concentrated on defending Western Europe, the U.S. transformed the continent. Western Europe was revived economically and embarked on a course of international cooperation unprecedented in modern European history. The U.S. presence also guaranteed the peace and security of Western Europe, and even age-old enemies France and Germany came to accept cooperation as the norm.

This post-war order now has been swept away by the 1989 revolutions in Eastern Europe. The West's peaceful victory over the Soviet

Chapter 1

Union has transformed Europe and outpaced the ability of governments to control events. Even as the collapse of the Soviet empire in Eastern Europe vastly reduces the Soviet role in Europe, it also will erode U.S. influence as the need for U.S. protection declines. The revolution of the European state system, an enormous victory for the Western policy of containment, thus also will usher in a new system in which the stability provided by a large U.S. military presence will be gone.

In response to this, the U.S. should not withdraw all of its troops from Europe. Nor it should not retreat to a Fortress America. The U.S. has vital interests in Europe. These include preventing the domination of the continent by a single power, especially one that is anti-U.S.; the avoidance of major wars; the survival and expansion of democracy; and keeping Europe's markets open to the U.S. Twice in this century the U.S. was forced to intervene in wars in Europe, at a cost of hundreds of thousands of American lives. Only by remaining in Europe can the U.S. prevent events that could require a third U.S. intervention.

The forms of U.S. involvement will change. Familiar organizations such as NATO will decline in importance as America's allies will become increasingly independent once they are free from the Soviet threat.

To ensure that American political, economic, and security interests are furthered in the new Europe, the U.S. should support democratization in Eastern Europe and develop a foreign aid strategy that promotes free market reforms there; support a peaceful and negotiated process of Soviet decolonization; and use the CSCE meeting this autumn to push for peaceful change in Europe.

While NATO may continue to have some military utility for a time, its exclusion of the East European states limits its value in matters relating to the entire continent. The U.S. therefore should advocate a standing North Atlantic Conference, bringing together all the democracies of North America and Europe in a permanent forum for advancing common interests and addressing common problems. The U.S. should also seek to remove trade barriers between North America and Europe. Washington can take the first bold and imaginative steps toward this by calling for a U.S.-European free trade area.

In coming years, Europe will change in ways that cannot now be predicted with any certainty. It is certain, however, that the New World will continue to have an abiding interest in the affairs of the Old. By

The New Political Landscape in Europe

remaining involved in Europe, even as its role there changes dramatically, the U.S. will be well positioned to help ensure that the European peace and prosperity it has been so instrumental in creating will be safeguarded into the unforeseeable future.

Chapter 2

A New American Role in Europe's Balance of Power

Jay P. Kosminsky

Europe today is changing in the ways sought decades ago by Dean Acheson, George Marshall, John Foster Dulles, and the other architects of America's European security policy. The Soviet empire is collapsing beneath an onslaught of revolutionary democracy and the Soviet Union itself may be on the brink of political and economic disintegration. The states of Western Europe have developed into economically powerful and politically stable players on the European scene. A united Germany is emerging as a strong and confident democracy in the heart of Europe, firmly anchored in the West.

Americans can take a great deal of credit for Europe's transformation over the past four decades, which by and large was made possible by America's firm commitment to containing Soviet expansionism. With the East European revolutions of 1989, containment at long last has led to the rollback of Soviet power in Europe.

The United States' last great diplomatic challenge of the 20th Century will be to follow this triumph with policies designed to create a just and lasting European order in which its interests are supported.

As Soviet power in Europe recedes, the U.S. will be able to withdraw the bulk of its own forces from Europe, their main mission having been accomplished. The U.S. then will have to find a new place for itself in

Chapter 2

Europe's security order. If it fails to do so, and retreats to isolationism, it will risk creating the impression, and perhaps the reality, of an America without the will or ability to defend its vital interests in Europe. During Europe's uncertain transition, the U.S. should:

1) Establish objectives for a new European security system.

In looking toward a new Europe, the U.S. first should establish its objectives, and then design strategies, forces, and institutions to attain and uphold them. U.S. objectives should be to:

♦ ♦ **Roll back Soviet military power in Europe and ensure that all Soviet forces are withdrawn to within their own territory.**

♦ ♦ **Balance residual Soviet conventional and nuclear power.**

♦ ♦ **Resolve the "German question" by reassuring Germany and its neighbors of their security.**

♦ ♦ **Reduce the costs and risks of U.S. involvement in Europe.**

♦ ♦ **Protect and expand democracy in Europe including the Soviet Union.**

♦ ♦ **Establish the independence and sovereignty of all states in the European system.**

♦ ♦ **Contain regional conflicts and prevent them from spreading into European-wide wars.**

2) Support peaceful and rapid change, not stability.

Change in Europe so far is running unambiguously in favor of the West. The Warsaw Pact is breaking up, Soviet forces are withdrawing from Eastern Europe, and Germany is uniting peacefully within a democratic framework. American policy should be geared toward maintaining the momentum of the Soviet retreat from Europe and the peaceful democratization and decolonization of the Soviet Union.

3) Support strong military ties between Germany and its Western allies.

While it now seems a united Germany will remain in NATO, Moscow is liable to continue pressuring Germany to weaken its alliance ties through such means as an anticipated Soviet-German Non-Aggression Treaty. Western diplomatic strategy should be aimed at ensuring that Germany retains the right to: continue stationing foreign troops on its soil; remain in NATO's unified military command; and station NATO nuclear weapons on its territory.

A New American Role in Europe's Balance of Power

4) Proceed with caution on conventional arms control.
The Conventional Forces in Europe (CFE) negotiations are nearing completion. If signed and ratified, a CFE accord will set absolute limits on tanks, artillery, armored fighting vehicles, aircraft, and helicopters that NATO or Warsaw Pact countries can station in Europe. But there are problems with CFE. Most significantly, in the course of CFE negotiations Moscow withdrew much of its military equipment in Europe to behind the Urals, where it would not be counted under a CFE accord. This display of bad faith by Moscow, coupled with rapid change in Europe – including the potential breakup of the Soviet Union – counsel caution on conventional arms control. Specifically, the U.S. should:

♦♦ **Require destruction of Soviet equipment withdrawn to behind the Urals since the CFE negotiations got underway in March 1989.**

♦♦ **Pause for at least two years after a CFE accord before entering into follow-on conventional force negotiations.** This will allow time to evaluate Soviet compliance with CFE and take into account coming political changes in Europe.

5) Withdraw gradually most U.S. military forces from Europe while remaining an offshore European power.
If Soviet power in Europe is diminished substantially, the U.S. should:

♦♦ **Over the next five years reduce U.S. ground forces in Europe to about 50,000 troops.**

♦♦ **Demobilize at least half of the U.S.-based troops available for rapid reinforcement of NATO allies, while continuing to provide reserve manpower.**

♦♦ **Maintain naval capabilities sufficient to keep the North Atlantic open for the transport of reserve forces to Europe.**

♦♦ **Keep up to six U.S. tactical air wings in Europe with the agreement of allies.**

♦♦ **Retain a credible U.S. nuclear deterrent force in Europe.**

6) Preserve and transform NATO.
Even if the Soviet Union withdraws its forces to within its own borders, NATO will remain essential, at least for the time being, to balance residual Soviet power in Europe. Nonetheless, NATO will

Chapter 2

have to adapt to changing historical circumstances. Premises to guide U.S. policy toward NATO include:
♦ ♦ **Strengthen NATO's European component.**
♦ ♦ **Revise NATO's strategy and structure to account for German unification and the likely withdrawal of Soviet forces from Eastern Europe.**
♦ ♦ **Modify NATO nuclear strategy; resist pressures to adopt a "no first use" nuclear doctrine.**

7) **Support European solutions to European security issues.**
To encourage a broader European defense role, the U.S. should:
♦ ♦ **Back a stronger military role for the West European Union (WEU).**
♦ ♦ **Gradually expand WEU membership to include such East European countries as Czechoslovakia, Hungary, and Poland.**
♦ ♦ **Encourage regional alliances among East Europeans to defend themselves against a revived Soviet threat.**
♦ ♦ **Limit the East-West security role of the Conference on Security and Cooperation in Europe.**
♦ ♦ **Use European organizations, including the CSCE, to address regional conflict.**

8) **Find new ways to keep America involved in Europe.**
While the need for a powerful U.S. military role in Europe may be declining, America's interests in Europe are enduring. As the role of NATO moves from the center to the periphery of America's European policy, there will be a need to reinforce the American presence in Europe in other ways. These include:
♦ ♦ **Establish a new Atlantic Conference composed of North American and European democracies.**
♦ ♦ **Emphasize bilateral U.S. defense relationships, particularly with Germany and Great Britain.**

9) **Maintain a balance of power as Europe moves toward a new order.**
Timing is essential in the creation of a new European security system. If Europe jumps the gun and leaves the secure chrysalis of NATO before a new order has developed sufficiently, peace will be in jeopardy.

A New American Role in Europe's Balance of Power

AMERICA AND THE COLD WAR EUROPEAN SECURITY SYSTEM

Stretching from the Atlantic Ocean to the Ural Mountains in central Russia, Europe is the world's greatest strategic prize. Its 820 million people inhabit the world's industrial heartland, producing just about 50 percent of the entire world's economic output, compared to roughly 30 percent for the U.S. The continent counts among its states some of the most technologically advanced in the world. Europe dominates the main maritime approaches to the oil-rich Middle East.

American Interests in Europe

Given its tremendous population, wealth, and technology base, Europe potentially is either America's greatest global ally or its most dangerous rival.

The potential benefits of the U.S.-European relationship are captured in the 1949 North Atlantic Treaty establishing the NATO Alliance, which binds the U.S. and its West European allies jointly to safeguard the "freedom, common heritage and civilization of their peoples." If all Europe from the Atlantic to the Urals were united in its commitment to uphold these Western ideals, Europe and America together could secure a global peace that could last for generations. In such a world, there would be no major threats to America's most basic security interest — the freedom of its citizens to pursue life, liberty, and happiness free from the threat of war or foreign domination.

But if Europe's wealth and technology were united under a hostile power, it would have the military potential to wage a global struggle against America, isolate it from potential allies and trading partners, and perhaps eventually overwhelm the U.S. militarily. For this reason, America's paramount global security interest is to prevent an expansionist European power from gaining continental dominance.[1]

---

[1] The best exposition of America's security interests in Europe remains Nicholas J. Spykman, *American Strategy and World Politics: The U.S. and the Balance of Power* (Archoni Press, 1970) reprint 1942, which stressed the defense of the Eurasian "rimland," against such "heartland" powers as the Soviet Union or Germany.

Chapter 2

In its early years as a republic, America for the most part was able to ignore the affairs of Europe while still enjoying close to perfect security. As American strategist Robert Komer argues, this policy was made possible by an enormous geopolitical advantage:

> ... [T]he United States was protected from hostile pressure or involvement in great power quarrels by two broad moats, the Atlantic and Pacific oceans. [The policy] was also greatly facilitated both by a stable balance of power in Europe and by Britain's mastery of the seas throughout the nineteenth and early twentieth centuries.[2]

America's relative isolation from global affairs ended, of course, in the early part of this century when a mainly European affair, World War I, led to the sinking of American ships on the high seas in 1916. Washington's leaders eventually felt compelled to commit U.S. expeditionary forces to Europe. Their aim: to prevent a single power — the expansionist German empire of Kaiser Wilhelm II — from tipping the European balance of power and controlling the continent. After withdrawing from Europe once it had assured an allied victory, America was back a quarter-century later to prevent a second, even more threatening, German attempt to dominate Europe.

Dwight D. Eisenhower sent American forces ashore at Normandy in June 1944, with the intention not only of ending the war and liberating Europe from Nazi domination, but of forging a new European order based on the vision of the Atlantic Charter, signed by Franklin D. Roosevelt and Winston Churchill in August 1941: a Europe of free and democratic states liberated from foreign occupation.[3] Instead, after the destruction of Hitler's armies, the U.S. found itself struggling

---

2 Robert Komer, *Maritime Strategy or Coalition Defense?* (Cambridge: Abt Books, 1984), p. 1.
3 Soviet Ambassador in London Ivan Maisky announced official Soviet support for the Atlantic Charter on September 24, 1941; Stalin also signed on to its contents as part of the Yalta Accords' "Declaration on Liberated Europe" in February 1945. See Herbert Feis, *Churchill, Roosevelt, Stalin: The War they Waged, the Peace they Sought* (Princeton: Princeton University Press, 1957), pp.23-24.

A New American Role in Europe's Balance of Power

unsuccessfully to prevent its erstwhile ally, the Soviet Union, from establishing its own empire over half the continent. Having twice intervened in European wars of expansion after they had begun, the U.S. this time remained in Europe to prevent an imperial Soviet Union from making its own run at continental supremacy.

America and Europe's Balance of Power Since World War II

U.S. Ambassador to Moscow George Kennan's famous "long telegram" to the State Department in February 1946 marked the beginning of America's realization that its wartime goal of a liberated Europe was not to be reached in the near term.[4] Stalin, Kennan wrote, did not and never had shared U.S. war aims, and moreover was impervious to any inducements or pressure that the U.S. was likely to muster to drive his armies from their new lodgment in Eastern Europe. The result: self-government and sovereign rights were not to be realized throughout Europe as promised in the Atlantic Charter. The peace would not be enforced by "four policemen" — the U.S., Britain, the Soviet Union and China — as Roosevelt had hoped. Much of Europe liberated from Nazi domination by Soviet forces, Kennan wrote, was doomed for many years at least to remain under Moscow's dominion.

Still, Kennan warned, this was not the worst of it. Not only were America's maximal goals beyond reach for the time being, but unless the U.S. acted quickly and decisively it was apt to lose through intimidation, subversion, and perhaps outright invasion the ground it had liberated in Europe through years of hard fighting. If America's interests in Europe were to be protected, the U.S. would have to engage in a concerted effort to shore up the political, economic, and military security of Western Europe. Unlike the years following World War I, the predominance of Soviet power on the continent left little hope that Europeans themselves quickly could restore a balance of power. Kennan's arguments helped persuade Harry Truman and a reluctant Congress that U.S. interests in Europe could be met only by a U.S.

---

4   See John Lewis Gaddis, *Strategies of Containment* (Oxford University Press, 1982), Chapter 1, and Kennan's famous "Mr. X" article, "The Sources of Soviet Conduct," *Foreign Affairs*, July 1947, p.582.

Chapter 2

policy of, in Kennan's words, containing Soviet power through economic, political, and military means.

By the late 1940s, Washington was pursuing a policy of containment. Secretary of State James Byrnes announced on September 6, 1946, that America intended to station troops in Europe for an indefinite period and he recommended an economic merger of Western occupation zones in Germany.[5] In the wake of the harsh European winter of 1946-1947, during which Europeans faced nationwide strikes and desperate shortages of such basic items as food and shelter, the need became apparent to Secretary of State George C. Marshall, Kennan, and others that political and military stability could not be achieved without economic reconstruction.[6] The U.S. response was the $12.5 billion (about $65 billion in today's dollars) European Recovery Program, or Marshall Plan, which along with German free market reforms ignited the growth of the devastated West European economies.

Still, containment lacked an effective military enforcement arm. The North Atlantic Treaty was signed on April 4, 1949, with one "dominant and overwhelming purpose," according to Secretary of State Dean Acheson: "deterrence" of Soviet aggression in Europe by formally committing U.S. military power to West European defense.[7]

Before 1950, little thought was given to what military forces would be needed to meet Soviet aggression. Even NATO as first constituted was little more than a U.S. commitment to defend Europe rather than a framework for effective common defense. It entailed no unified military command structure or specific military commitments by its

---

[5] Speech by Secretary of State James Byrnes at Stuttgart, U.S. occupation zone in Germany, September 6, 1946.
[6] See Marshall's Harvard University commencement address, June 5, 1947.
[7] Original signatories to the North Atlantic Treaty were the U.S., Belgium, Britain, Canada, Denmark, France, Iceland, Italy, Luxembourg, the Netherlands, Norway and Portugal. Greece and Turkey joined in 1951, Germany in 1955, and Spain in 1982.

A New American Role in Europe's Balance of Power

signatories. If NATO was to deter Moscow — more effectively, for example, than British and French guarantees to Poland had deterred Hitler and Stalin from carving up Poland in 1939 — the West would require more than solemn oaths and promises. It would require, in Acheson's words, "strategy and force."[8]

Prompted in part by dramatic events of 1949, including the communist coup in Czechoslovakia, the first Soviet atomic explosion, and the communist victory in China, the U.S. launched in 1950 its first national strategy review. It produced the milestone presidential national security document known as NSC-68, which remained secret until 1975.[9] NSC-68 concluded that the U.S. and its allies did not have the conventional military forces required to defeat a Soviet attack in Europe: NATO fielded about twelve scattered and undermanned divisions in Europe in 1949, only one of which was American. These troops faced about 25 Soviet Army divisions in Eastern Europe backed by roughly 175 more divisions in the Soviet Union.[10]

NSC-68 recommended a conventional military buildup, but recognized that politically it would be difficult for the West to pay for a force large enough to defend Western Europe with conventional weapons

---

8 Dean Acheson, *Present at the Creation: My Years in the State Department* (New York: W.W. Norton and Company, 1969), p. 637.
9 "A Report to the National Security Council by the Executive Secretary on United States Objectives and Programs for National Security, April 4, 1959." See the account by NSC-68's principal author Paul Nitze (and a second account by John Lewis Gaddis) in "NSC-68 and the Soviet Threat Reconsidered," *International Security*, Summer 1980, pp. 164-176. See also Samuel F. Wells, Jr., "Sounding the Tocsin," *International Security*, Fall 1979.
10 U.S. intelligence services at the time believed Moscow had 208 combat-ready divisions. Later estimates lowered this to about 175, not all of which were at full strength. See Mathew Evangelista, "Stalin's Postwar Army Reappraised," *International Security*, Spring 1983, p. 110. See also William P. Mako, *U.S. Ground Forces and the Defense of Europe* (Washington, D.C.: The Brookings Institution, 1983) and Samuel P. Huntington, *The Common Defense* (New York: Columbia University Press, 1961) for estimates of U.S. and Soviet ground forces in Europe in the post World War II years.

Chapter 2

alone. The report predicted, therefore, that U.S. nuclear weapons would be needed to stop a Soviet advance in Europe.[11]

The U.S., however, did take important steps to strengthen NATO's conventional capabilities. Despite Acheson's testimony to Congress in 1949 that the U.S. would not send large-scale ground forces to Europe, the Truman Administration two years later convinced Congress to station six U.S. Army divisions on the continent.[12] Also, the U.S. took steps to improve NATO's conventional defense capabilities by arming West Germany. After years of struggling with Britain, France, and other allies hesitant to rearm their nemesis in two world wars, the U.S. pushed through a plan for West German rearmament in 1955; that same year West Germany joined NATO.[13] West Germany's first Chancellor, Konrad Adenauer, committed twelve West German Army divisions to NATO to defend the East-West German border.[14] Within eight years, the size of West Germany's armed forces surpassed the nearly 400,000 U.S. forces then in Europe.[15]

By 1955, the last elements of Europe's post-war balance of power were pretty much frozen in place, pitting the ground forces of the Soviet empire against NATO's maritime coalition of states. Moscow's empire straddled the entire area that legendary strategist Sir Halford Mackinder called the geographical "pivot of history" — stretching from the Ural Mountains westward into the heart of Prussia (now Western Poland and East Germany). The U.S.S.R.'s standing armies outnumbered and outgunned all its European neighbors combined. Its

---

11 In February 1952, at a Lisbon meeting of NATO's highest decision-making body, the North Atlantic Council, the Alliance set ambitious requirements for 40 combat-ready NATO divisions, 56 reserve divisions, and 1,000 aircraft to counter the Soviet conventional military threat. The Alliance never has come close to meeting the Lisbon goals. The assessment remained valid for four decades.
12 Acheson discusses the contradiction between his testimony and later policy in *Present at the Creation*, op. cit., p. 285.
13 The agreement is formalized in the London and Paris Accords of 1955.
14 See Alfred Grosser, *The Western Alliance: European-American Relations Since 1945* (New York: Vintage Books, 1982) for a good discussion of the early plans to arm West Germany and its admission to NATO. The best history of the building of the post-World War II West German army is Donald Abenheim, *Reforging the Iron Cross* (Princeton: Princeton University Press, 1988).
15 Sloan, *op. cit.*, p. 55.

A New American Role in Europe's Balance of Power

capacity to mobilize a large force was unsurpassed. The bulk of its best forces, armed with conventional and nuclear weapons, were deployed along the empire's westernmost fringe along the East-West German border. The Soviet empire in 1955 was organized militarily as the Warsaw Pact, whose non-Soviet armies were kept under Moscow's strict control via communist party cells within their ranks and by Soviet commanders. Gradually the Soviet military developed global reach, including the ability to launch intercontinental nuclear strikes against the U.S.

What had emerged to balance Soviet power on the continent was a coalition of mostly democratic North Atlantic states led by a non-European maritime power — the U.S. NATO's land power in central Europe was provided by an international army composed of American and West European forces stationed along the Eastern border of a substantially rearmed but non-nuclear West German state. NATO's ground forces in central Europe relied heavily on the reserve manpower and rapid reinforcement capability of the U.S. This reinforcement depended on U.S. naval control of the North Atlantic sea link between the North American and European members of the Alliance.

The U.S. also provided the bulk of NATO's nuclear firepower in the form of European-based weapons and those capable of striking Russian territory from North America or the sea. NATO's strategy envisioned the "forward defense" of West German territory at the border with the East. From the start, however, NATO conventional forces were not up to the task, and the Alliance remained dependent on the threat to use nuclear weapons to deter a Warsaw Pact advance.

Assessing the Cold War European Order

This new European system had advantages and disadvantages for U.S. and allied interests. It was relatively stable insofar as it avoided war among the major powers. The system achieved this stability mainly by providing an effective military counterweight, through NATO, to Europe's most powerful state, the Soviet Union. Although Moscow occupied much of Eastern and Central Europe, NATO's military power was sufficient to impose unacceptable costs and risks on any Soviet move to expand its empire westward.

By dividing Europe in two, with half remaining effectively under Soviet occupation, the post-war system implicitly eliminated two sour-

Chapter 2

ces of instability which had undone earlier European state systems: German expansion and regional conflict.

The German question was addressed, first, when the post-war occupying powers decided to reduce Germany in size at the 1945 Yalta and Potsdam conferences, by shifting its eastern border to the west and ceding to Poland and the Soviet Union the former German territories of East Prussia, Pomerania, and Silesia. Second, what remained of Germany was divided — officially in 1949 with the establishment of the two German states — with East Germany remaining under Soviet military occupation and a Moscow-controlled puppet regime. Even the West German state, while essentially sovereign, continued to operate under certain military restrictions: its army, established in 1955, remained under NATO command, and the Bonn government agreed to limit its armaments, including the renunciation of atomic, biological, and chemical weapons. Given these conditions of the Cold War European security system, it was inconceivable that either or both Germanys could become a threat to their European neighbors; Germany was contained. At the same time, West German territory was well defended against the Soviet Union. This ability to protect West Germany against Soviet power was as important for West Germany's NATO allies as for the West Germans themselves, since a secure West Germany was all that stood between them and the Red Army in Central Europe.

Regional conflict, which contributed in particular to the outbreak of World War I, also ceased to pose a threat to continental peace in the new system. Areas most prone to regional and ethnic conflict, such as the Balkans, were under Soviet or Yugoslav communist control. While brutal, the Soviet occupation and monopoly on military force effectively kept a lid on regional conflicts which might otherwise have erupted, for example between Hungarians and Romanians or Germans and Poles. While regional conflicts did occur, they generally involved attempts by Moscow to reassert its own control over rebellious parts of its empire, as in East Germany in 1953, Hungary in 1956, or Czechoslovakia in 1968. While these conflicts were repressive and brutal, the relative balance of power between East and West blocked Moscow from using them as a pretext for a broader war.

Purely from the standpoint of American interests, the Cold War European system also had some advantages. Washington's new role as peacetime participant in Europe's balance of power system gave

A New American Role in Europe's Balance of Power

Washington a new element of control over European affairs. The U.S. was on the sidelines in 1914 and 1939 as Europe slid toward wars in which Americans eventually would lose their lives. America's new role as military balancer and Alliance leader gave it the ability to influence events that threatened to upset the European balance and lead to war, when, for example, Stalin tried to blockade Berlin in 1948, or when Nikita Khrushchev built the Berlin Wall in 1962.

Nonetheless, the post-war European security system was deeply flawed. While the East-West military standoff in Central Europe made the chances of a major war remote, the heavy concentration of nuclear and conventional weapons held by the potential combatants ensured that the consequences of war, had it occurred, would have been devastating for all states involved.

Moreover, for the U.S. in particular the post-war European order held high costs and risks. According to the Pentagon, costs directly related to NATO defense today amount to about 60 percent of a nearly $300 billion defense budget. Since 1949, measured in today's dollars, the U.S. has spent some $5 trillion fulfilling its commitment to NATO.[16] Further, NATO strategy requires that U.S. forces be on Europe's front lines, ensuring early American involvement in a war; this is NATO's famed "trip wire." NATO's nuclear strategy of "flexible response," adopted in 1967, commits the U.S. to put its own territory at risk by using nuclear weapons in the event that NATO's insufficient conventional defenses were to fail to hold back a Soviet assault.[17] An unintended, though predictable, consequence of America's strong military presence in Europe has been the emergence of a culture of military dependency among the European allies. As a result, the U.S. has had to bear a disproportionate economic burden for Western defense; long

---

16 This assumes roughly 50 percent of the approximately $10 trillion spent on defense since 1949 has been NATO-related.
17 For more on "flexible response," see Jay Kosminsky, "European Nuclear Security," in Stephen J. Flanagan and Fen Osler Hampson, eds., *Securing Europe's Future* (London: Croon Helm, 1986).

Chapter 2

after European allies recovered from the economic devastation of World War II, the U.S. still spends more than twice proportionally what its NATO allies spend for Western defense.[18]

The most glaring drawback of the post-war European security system, of course, has been its injustice. For half of Europe, liberation from Nazi domination in 1945 meant deliverance into the hands of an equally brutal totalitarian power, the Soviet Union. America has stayed in Europe since World War II not only to balance Soviet power, but to maintain freedom and democracy in the West, and ultimately to realize Churchill's and Roosevelt's dream, embodied in the Atlantic Charter, of a Europe whole, free, and at peace. Today, for the first time since 1945, this dream seems within America's grasp.

EUROPE'S CHANGING SECURITY ORDER

The collapse of the Soviet Union's East European empire is transforming Europe's security order. If the Red Army continues its retreat from Eastern Europe, the military threat to Western Europe will ease, and the countries of Eastern Europe will regain fully the sovereignty they were denied after World War II. Unless the Soviet Union breaks apart, however, it is likely to remain the continent's dominant land power and its only nuclear superpower, and still in need of balancing. Moreover, problems long suppressed by the Soviet presence in Eastern Europe again are emerging, including the German question, and regional and ethnic conflict in Central and Eastern Europe. Even as the superpower-dominated military standoff dissipates, the U.S. and Europeans can build on existing institutions and alliances, and in some instances create new ones, to lay the foundation for a new, stable, and more just European order to replace the deadlock of the Cold War.

Declining Soviet Power in Europe

The fact of Soviet military power, and the need for it to be balanced so that it does not give Moscow continental hegemony, has been the

---

18 U.S. Secretary of Defense, *Report on Allied Contributions to the Common Defense*, April 1990, p. A/7. See also Jay Kosminsky, "A Ten-point Program for Increasing the Allies' Share of Defense Costs," Heritage Foundation *Backgrounder* No. 686, January 17, 1989.

A New American Role in Europe's Balance of Power

central feature of Europe's security landscape since the end of World War II. Already, Soviet leader Mikhail Gorbachev's reform of the Soviet military and his decision to grant political autonomy to Eastern Europe have eroded Soviet military power in Europe significantly. How far this erosion will go, and whether it can be reversed, remain open questions. But there can be no doubt that a fundamental revolution is underway in Europe that affects the basic assumptions of four decades of American military policy in Europe.

The first indication of significant change came in the December 7, 1988, speech at the United Nations in which Gorbachev announced he would withdraw 5,000 tanks and 50,000 men from Eastern Europe, and reduce total Soviet forces West of the Ural Mountains by a total of 10,000 tanks, 8,500 artillery systems, and 800 combat aircraft.[19]

Some of these promises are being kept, others apparently are not. As of spring 1990, about half the announced tank withdrawals and three-quarters of the artillery and combat aircraft reductions had been completed.[20] Many of these weapons, according to Pentagon and congressional experts, however, are being stored in the Soviet Union rather than being destroyed or converted to civilian use as promised by Gorbachev in his U.N. speech. Much of this equipment is being removed to behind the Ural Mountains, where it will escape being counted if agreement is reached in the ongoing Conventional Forces

---

19 Gorbachev's speech reprinted in *The Washington Post*, December 8, 1989, p. 32.
20 U.S. Congress, Joint Economic Committee, Statement by Dennis M. Nagy, Acting Deputy Director for Foreign Intelligence, Defense Intelligence Agency, April 20, 1990, p. 1.

Chapter 2

in Europe (CFE) negotiations in Vienna.[21] Moreover, pullbacks from Eastern Europe reportedly slowed in spring 1990 and withdrawals from East Germany may have stopped altogether.[22]

Other combat equipment, such as armored Infantry Fighting Vehicles, anti-tank guns, artillery, and air defense guns associated with the tank regiments withdrawn from Eastern Europe are being reassigned to other divisions in Western Europe and the Soviet Union.[23] Before the unilateral withdrawals, Moscow fielded ten tank and nine "motorized rifle divisions" (MRD) in East Germany. A motorized rifle division is roughly equivalent to a U.S. "mechanized" division and contains tanks and armored Infantry Fighting Vehicles. Each tank division fielded about 322 tanks and each MRD about 271. Moscow has been reorganizing these divisions: tank divisions now will hold about 234 tanks and MRDs about 177. Each will be augmented, however, with additional air defense weapons, anti-tank weapons, artillery, and armored Infantry Fighting Vehicles.[24] Because of this reorganization, analysts predict that these unilateral reductions will result in a decrease in Soviet combat power of only about 10 percent instead of the 20 percent initially predicted to result from the withdrawals.[25] This reduction, according to the Pentagon, will bring Soviet combat power in Europe down to about what it was when Gorbachev took office in 1985.

---

21 See U.S. House of Representatives, Committee on Armed Services, "Status of the Soviet Union's Unilateral Force Reductions and Restructuring of its Forces," October 16, 1989, p.7: "Despite some earlier statements that the tanks being removed from Eastern Europe would be destroyed or converted, it now appears that the withdrawn tanks — mostly T-64s ... will replace older equipment in units in the Soviet Union (perhaps on both sides of the Urals) and may even go into storage in the interior of the Soviet Union." See also James Kinnear, " Soviet Army Weapons Disposal — An Overview," *Jane's Soviet Intelligence Review*, January 1990, pp. 32-36.
22 Author's discussion with senior Pentagon military analyst.
23 *Jane's Defense Weekly*, October 14, 1989, p. 785.
24 For the makeup of new Soviet tank and motorized rifle divisions see International Institute for Strategic Studies (IISS) *The Military Balance, 1989-1990*, p. 5.
25 Statement of Ted Warner, RAND Corporation, to the Senate Armed Services Committee, January 24, 1990.

A New American Role in Europe's Balance of Power

Soviet forces are likely to be reduced much further through the CFE negotiations, which began in Vienna in March 1989. A CFE agreement would give NATO and the Warsaw Pact equal numbers of tanks, armored troop carriers, aircraft, and artillery in a region stretching from the Atlantic Ocean to the Ural Mountains, at levels roughly 10 percent below current NATO levels. This would require the Warsaw Pact to withdraw and dismantle roughly 30,000 tanks, 25,000 armored troop carriers, and between 20,000 and 30,000 artillery pieces in return for much smaller cuts by NATO. It also would result in the withdrawal of about 385,000 of the roughly 580,000 Soviet troops now stationed in Eastern Europe.[26]

Falling Soviet Military Spending and Production

Soviet military spending in 1989 began to reflect the restructuring promised by Gorbachev. After increasing military spending by an average of 3 percent during his first four years in office, Gorbachev cut Soviet military spending in 1989 by between 4 and 5 percent; spending on weapons procurement was down by between 6 and 7 percent.[27]

Soviet military production also is down in some key areas, but up in others. Moscow began slowing tank production in 1989; in 1988 it had reached a post-World War II high of 3,500 tanks per year, falling to 1,700 in 1989. Field artillery production also is down — from 2,500 tubes in 1988 to 1,850 in 1989. But rates for other equipment are up, including armored combat vehicles and anti-aircraft weapons. Production of short-range missiles, such as the 75-mile range SS-21, increased

---

26 See Jay Kosminsky, "A U.S. Agenda for the Conventional Forces Reduction Talks," Heritage Foundation *Backgrounder* No. 725, September 1, 1989.
27 U.S. Congress, Joint Economic Committee, *The Soviet Economy Stumbles Badly in 1989*, paper presented by the Central Intelligence Agency and Defense Intelligence Agency, April 20, 1990, p. 11.

Chapter 2

from 650 in 1988 to 700 in 1989.[28] Over the past five years, Moscow has produced about 3,050 short-range missiles while the U.S. has produced none. In other areas of military production, including strategic nuclear forces and naval shipbuilding, major modernization and production programs are continuing apace. For example, the Soviet Navy in 1989 accepted delivery of a higher tonnage of new combatants than anytime in the past twenty years.[29]

The Collapsing Warsaw Pact

The impact of Gorbachev's unilateral troop cutbacks and military spending cuts rapidly are being overshadowed by the collapse of the Warsaw Pact, the military arm of Moscow's East European empire. The East European revolutions of 1989 laid the groundwork for freely-elected regimes which are challenging the Soviet military presence on their territory and taking control of their own armed forces.

The Soviet Union signed an agreement with Czechoslovakia in February 1990 to withdraw its 70,000 troops from Czech territory within two years; it reached a similar agreement with Hungary in March 1990 to withdraw 65,000 Soviet troops from that country. The Soviet troops in Czechoslovakia force NATO to defend southwestern West Germany, diverting important resources from the central front along the East-West German border. Red Army troops in Hungary could move into neutral Austria during wartime, cutting NATO's lines of communication between forces on the central front in Germany and the southern flank in Italy and the Mediterranean.[30]

The departure of Soviet troops from Czechoslovakia and Hungary will reduce Soviet capabilities in Europe only marginally. By contrast,

---

[28] Figures released by Under Secretary of Defense Paul Wolfowitz at a February 28, 1990, hearing before the House Armed Services Committee.

[29] See statement of Central Intelligence Director William Webster before the Senate Armed Services Committee, January 23, 1990. For a detailed analysis of changing Soviet military capabilities see "The Fading Threat: Soviet Conventional Military Power in Decline," report of the Defense Policy Panel, House Armed Services Committee, July 9, 1990.

[30] The U.S. responded to the new threat posed by Soviet forces after they invaded Czechoslovakia in 1968 by sending two additional brigades of about 10,000 combat troops to bolster NATO forces in West Germany in the early 1970s.

A New American Role in Europe's Balance of Power

the departure of most or all of the 380,000 crack Soviet forces in East Germany, will remove Moscow's key lever for applying military pressure on Western Europe. The July 16, 1990, agreement between West German Chancellor Helmut Kohl and Mikhail Gorbachev in Zheleznovodsk, in the Soviet Union, paves the way for the withdrawal of these troops within three to four years. If this agreement holds — and is ratified by the World War II powers at the Two Plus Four talks over German unification and by the Conference on Security and Cooperation in Europe later this year — Soviet troops will be on their way out of a united Germany. At that point, the European security situation will have been transformed fundamentally.

Even if Moscow were to try to reverse course and go back on these agreements, it is difficult to conceive of the Warsaw Pact being reconstituted. About one-third of the Warsaw Pact troops facing NATO in Europe belong not to the Soviet Union, but to Czechoslovakia, East Germany, Hungary, Poland, and other putative Soviet allies. None of these forces could be counted upon by Moscow in the event of war. To be sure, Moscow never has relied on the active participation of these armies in an offensive against NATO. Now, however, Moscow must contend with the likelihood that in the event of war these armies would be deployed against the Soviet Union. At the very least, Moscow cannot count on secure lines of communication and supplies in Eastern Europe in wartime.

In Czechoslovakia, Hungary, and Poland, governments began breaking up communist party cells within the military in 1989, thereby denying Moscow its chief means of control over these armies. Czechoslovak and Hungarian leaders have not hesitated to distance themselves from Soviet military policy. In a June 12-15, 1990, meeting, Pact leaders agreed to transform the organization into a "political" grouping that fully respects the sovereignty of its seven member states. On June 26, the Hungarian parliament voted to suspend its military participation in the Warsaw Pact and pressed its intention to withdraw completely at a later date.[31] Czechoslovakia, meanwhile, began dismantling its

---

31 See "Hungary Votes to Quit Warsaw Pact," *Washington Post*, June 27, 1990, p. 24.

Chapter 2

border fortifications along the border with West Germany in January 1990, and has adopted a new policy of "homeland defense," to defend against attacks from West — or East.[32] Poland has announced deep cuts in military spending and deployments, and in East Germany the army has been plagued by desertions and a breakdown in discipline and in all likelihood will cease to exist when German unification takes place later this year.[33]

The cumulative effects of these developments on Europe's balance of power already are evident. NATO's probable warning time before a Soviet attack in Europe now is estimated to be between two and three months; in early 1989, warning was two weeks. This is the time it now would take for Moscow to mass sufficient numbers of well-trained troops for an attack against NATO. As a result of increased warning, according to the Joint Chiefs of Staff, NATO's earlier assumption that it probably would have to resort to nuclear weapons to stop a Soviet attack in Europe no longer is valid. Perhaps for the first time in its history, NATO's conventional forces are considered sufficient to stop a Soviet advance.[34]

For the time being at least, NATO's main defense dilemma in Europe, its overreliance on nuclear weapons to counter a sudden Soviet attack, has been resolved.

An Unpredictable Soviet Future

If the Soviet Union manages to hold together, it will remain the single most powerful conventional military force in Europe and the continent's only nuclear superpower. Under these conditions, even if a CFE agreement is signed and Soviet troops are withdrawn from

---

[32] Radio Free Europe Background Report, "Major Reorganization of Hungary's Military Establishment," December 29, 1989.
[33] Poland, for example, will have cut the size of its armed forces by about 10 percent by the end of 1991. See "Polish Reforms to Disband 57 Units," *Jane's Defense Week*, January 27, 1990, p. 143.
[34] According to Representative Les Aspin, who referred to a classified report to Congress from the Joint Chiefs of Staff. See Peter Almond, "Declining threat leaves NATO with response time to spare," *Washington Times*, March 14, 1990, p. 7.

A New American Role in Europe's Balance of Power

Eastern Europe, Moscow's military power still will require balancing. Moscow still would have 49 army divisions with 11,500 tanks east of the Ural Mountains in the Asian part of the U.S.S.R.[35] While most of this equipment is on the Chinese border, much of it could be shifted to Europe in a crisis. In addition, neither Moscow's military production nor the storage of military equipment east of the Urals would be limited by any arms control agreement now being negotiated.

Given the Soviet Union's huge population, much of it with military training, Moscow's military potential after mobilization and a transfer of forces to the west would be formidable. While this mobilization would be time-consuming and logistically difficult, it could tip the European balance, in the absence of reinforcement from the U.S. Europeans would not have the means on hand to match the buildup since their own stocks of military equipment, unlike Soviet stocks, would be fully constrained by a CFE treaty. The reason: all of their territory would be covered by a CFE treaty, while only Moscow's territory from the Soviet-Polish border in the west to the Ural Mountains in the east would be affected by CFE reductions.

The Soviet Union also will continue to be Europe's only nuclear superpower into the foreseeable future. In addition to land-based intercontinental missiles, submarine-based missiles, and long-range bombers capable of striking the U.S., Moscow also deploys a battlefield nuclear weapons force that includes about 10,000 nuclear artillery shells, short-range missiles, and air-launched missiles and bombs. Even if these are reduced through arms control, verification would be virtually impossible for nuclear artillery shells and bombs, which easily are hidden. And Moscow certainly will want to keep its forces on the Chinese border equipped with battlefield nuclear weapons, which always could be transferred to the Soviet Union's European frontier.

Another possibility, of course, is that the Soviet Union will disintegrate in coming months and years. This process already has begun, with most of the European republics of the Soviet Union, including the Baltic states, Ukraine, and the Russian Republic, having declared

---

35 International Institute for Strategic Studies, *The Military Balance, 1989-1990* (London, 1990).

Chapter 2

independence or sovereignty from central authorities in Moscow.[36] If this process proceeds peacefully, resulting in the decolonization and democratization of the European areas of what now is the Soviet Union, the main threat to European security since the end of World War II will have been removed.

A violent breakup of the Soviet Union, on the other hand, could increase the risk of war. Armed conflict in the Soviet Union could take several forms, including civil war between central authorities in Moscow and a seceding republic. Ukraine, for example, in its July 18 declaration of sovereignty, asserted its right to form an army, raising the specter of just such a confrontation.[37] Another possibility is that the Soviet situation will degenerate into a general civil war among a variety of national, political, and institutional factions, as happened during the four years following the Bolshevik takeover in 1917.

Armed conflict within the Soviet Union could spread beyond Soviet borders if nationalities were to receive outside support. Example: support from Romania for a Moldavian secession attempt.[38] Even if outside powers did not interfere in a Soviet civil war, a military or hard-line communist government in Moscow could use the specter of outside interference as a pretext to move armies back into parts of Eastern Europe. A further danger of widespread conflict in the Soviet Union is that central command over the Soviet nuclear arsenal could be lost as factions within the army, the secret police, or even the national movements sought control over nuclear weapons to strengthen their position.

The Re-emergence of the German Question

As the Soviet empire collapses, and the post-war European security system along with it, so are the structures which since 1945 had resolved

---

36 See Chapter 1 in this volume.
37 See *Declaration on Ukranian State Sovereignty*, copy available from Popular Front of Ukraine.
38 Alternative scenarios are presented in John A. Battilega, "Soviet Alternative Futures," SAIC Foreign Systems Research Center, May 21, 1990.

A New American Role in Europe's Balance of Power

"the German Question" in Europe. As Germany's division ends and a united German state reappears on the historical horizon, the U.S. and other European powers must deal with the dual question raised by the prospect of German unification: how to reassure Germany's neighbors against a resurgence of German power, and at the same time, how to reassure Germany — and therefore the rest of Central Europe — against residual Soviet power.[39]

German unification will recreate in the heart of Europe a somewhat smaller version of what was, through the first half of this century, Europe's strongest and most reckless military power. It also, however, expands eastward a West German state which, through the second half of this century, has been a model of political stability and democracy. Whether the new Germany eventually becomes a menace to Europe or a force for peace in large measure will be determined by how satisfied Germans and their neighbors are with the specific terms of unification.

Either way, Germany will have the potential to be a major European military power. A united Germany's population will be 78 million, about 25 percent greater than West Germany's 61 million. Its gross national product (GNP) immediately will be about $1.2 trillion or $1.3 trillion, about one-tenth greater than West Germany's $1.1 trillion, although what is now East Germany's economy should expand quickly as it converts to a free market.

These developments will put united Germany far ahead of its closest West European competitor, France, which has a population of about 56 million and GNP of about $900 million. The Soviet Union, which has a GNP estimated at somewhat over $1.3 trillion and a population of close to 290 million still leads a united Germany in those indicators of military potential, but lags far behind in technology.[40]

---

39 The author thanks Ivo Danlder of the University of Maryland for his thoughts on the German Question.
40 Figures from International Institute of Strategic Studies, *The Military Balance, 1989-1990* (London).

Chapter 2

In the July 16 Kohl-Gorbachev agreement at Zheleznovodsk, and in a July 18 Polish-German accord in Paris, Germany accepted a series of measures designed to reassure its neighbors over impending unification. These include: 1) accepting Germany's border with Poland as permanent; 2) renouncing atomic, biological, and chemical weapons; and 3) limiting the size of united Germany's armed forces to 370,000, pending the signing of a CFE accord.[41] Kohl also told Gorbachev that no troops under NATO command would be stationed in what is now East Germany until 1994, when all Soviet troops are scheduled to be out of Germany. Thereafter, no NATO nuclear weapons or foreign troops would be stationed on former East German territory. These concessions by Kohl to Gorbachev were broadly consistent with the U.S. plan, presented at the May 30-June 2 Bush-Gorbachev summit, to reassure Moscow over a reunited Germany in NATO.[42]

Addressing the legitimate security concerns of Germany's neighbors is the easier part of the German question to resolve. The more difficult question is how to ensure that Germany itself continues to be militarily reassured against what remains of Soviet power in Europe. As the Western allies understood when they rearmed West Germany in 1955, a weak Germany unable to turn to its allies for protection and disarmed below levels needed for self-defense would leave all of Europe dangerously exposed to Soviet military coercion. Because of Moscow's strategic nuclear power and tremendous mobilization potential, this axiom will remain true even if the Soviet Union withdraws all its forces to within its own borders.

Ensuring German security — and therefore European security — within the framework of agreement reached at Zheleznovodsk will be one key to future European stability. This task will be made easier, but not assured, by Moscow's main concession – acquiescence to a united Germany in NATO.

---

[41] See text of Kohl-Gorbachev press conference, July 16, 1990, reprinted in *The New York Times*, July 17, 1990, p. A8.
[42] For the U.S. nine-point plan to reassure Moscow on German unification, see Thomas L. Friedman, "U.S. Will Press Soviets to Accept Plan on Germany," *The New York Times*, June 5, 1990, p. 17.

A New American Role in Europe's Balance of Power

One potential problem is that German armed forces, limited to 370,000, are likely to be dwarfed by Soviet military manpower, which now numbers nearly five million and will remain unrestricted by the CFE agreement now being negotiated. This could increase Germany's reliance on foreign troops stationed on its territory at a time when U.S. forces in Germany will be cut to at most 195,000, the 55,000-strong British Army on the Rhine (BAOR) is scheduled to be halved, and other NATO members are looking to cut back on military costs and manpower.

German nuclear security also will be an issue. While Gorbachev was unable to force Kohl into a formal ban on the deployment of NATO nuclear weapons in a united Germany, Kohl is refusing to commit Germany to such deployments. Example: West Germany pushed hard at a June NATO foreign ministers' meeting in Turnberry, Scotland, to bar deployment of the new Tactical-Air-to-Surface nuclear missile in Germany, opting instead for storing the missile in the U.S., to be deployed to Germany "in crisis only."[43]

Finally, Kohl's announcement on July 15 that Germany expects a wide-ranging "non-aggression" pact with Moscow in 1991, leaves open the possibility that Germany will accept further measures to limit German military capabilities.[44] The danger in these moves is that Germany eventually will come to rely too heavily on its political and economic relationship with Moscow, while overlooking the military imbalance between them. If the political relationship were to sour in coming years, Germany suddenly could find itself vulnerable and without sufficient military links to its allies.

Military vulnerability could lead to political instability in Germany, or it could lead a cornered Germany to take unilateral steps to guarantee its sovereignty. This could take the form of rapid conventional rearmament, or even the development of German nuclear weapons. Even if Germany's intent were entirely defensive, such moves could have dire consequences if the Soviet Union, or any of Germany's other World War II enemies, chose to respond militarily.

---

43 See "TASM deployment in crisis only," *Jane's Defense Week*, July 14, 1990, p. 37.
44 See "Soviet-German treaty planned," *Financial Times*, July 18, 1990, p.1.

Chapter 2

A renewal of German militarism arising from terms of unification that are too generous is not likely to threaten European security. On the contrary, the threat is that Russia will offer, and Germany will impose on itself, harsh terms that will make Germany dangerously vulnerable to Soviet power.

Resurgent Regional Conflicts

If Moscow truly has decided to relinquish its empire in Europe, the major source of European conflict will have been removed, since all Europe's cross-border wars since World War II have involved Soviet attempts to reimpose control over its empire. But as Eastern Europe regains its freedom, latent ethnic and border disputes suppressed by Moscow or other communist governments are sure to emerge — as some already have. Some involve the breakup of ethnically diverse states, like Yugoslavia with its Albanians, Croatians, Serbs, and Slovenes. Others involve suppression of ethnic minorities, like the Turks in Bulgaria. Still others combine ethnic hatred with territorial disputes, like the Hungarians living in territory that Hungary lost to Romania after World War I, or like the Germans living on land that Germany lost to Poland after World War II.[45]

Whether regional confrontations spread to European-wide conflict will depend on whether any of Europe's major powers seek to use these conflicts to increase their power within the European state system, and whether the balance of power enables them to pursue these ambitions. If so, minor disputes among smaller European powers could become pretexts for the Soviet Union or any other major power in Europe to advance its own agenda, as happened in the events that ignited World War I. By contrast, if regional conflicts occur within a system which otherwise is stable and marked by an effective balance of power, they need not erupt into broader wars.

Security Institutions in the New Europe

To be stable, Europe's emerging security order must balance residual Soviet power, provide for a resolution of the "German Ques-

---

[45] See Chapter 1 for a detailed description of these disputes.

A New American Role in Europe's Balance of Power

tion" that leaves Germany and its neighbors secure, and cope with the possibility of regional conflict. Several institutions and organizations have been proposed as the foundation for such an order, including NATO, such West European institutions as the European Community (EC) or West European Union (WEU), and the Conference on Security and Cooperation in Europe (CSCE).

NATO

The U.S. and its allies, particularly Britain's Margaret Thatcher, consistently stress the continuing role of NATO as the cornerstone of European security. Kohl also has demonstrated substantial fealty to the Alliance, most recently by standing firm against Soviet pressure to decouple united Germany from NATO. Even with the Soviet threat on the wane, NATO leaders are in agreement that NATO will remain the only institution capable of assuring their security, at least until Moscow withdraws its forces from Eastern Europe and restricts those forces through arms control. Beyond this, however, there is little consensus regarding the future political or military role of the Alliance except for the widely-shared perception that changes will be necessary.

The June 4-6 summit of Alliance leaders in London provided a few hints of how the new NATO might shape up. In their London communique, NATO leaders agreed to several measures, including: officially designating nuclear weapons as "weapons of last resort"; a decision to shift NATO's conventional strategy from "forward defense at the inner-German border" toward a more mobile strategy relying on smaller forces based further to the rear; reductions in training and exercises for NATO troops; support for negotiations to eliminate nuclear artillery shells from Europe; and an invitation to Gorbachev to address the NATO leadership.[46]

Still, NATO faces difficulties over the longer term. U.S. Secretary of State James Baker and others have argued that as NATO's military role decreases, the Alliance will have to adopt a more political character.[47]

---

[46] Text of the London NATO summit final declaration.
[47] See James Baker, "A New Europe, A New Atlanticism: Architecture for a New Era," Speech to the Berlin Press Club, Berlin, December 12, 1989.

Chapter 2

But this is difficult to define. In fact, a NATO working group tasked with finding practical ways to expand allied political cooperation met for over a year between 1989 and 1990, and was unable to make any decisive recommendations.[48] Baker's favored option, an expanded NATO military role outside of Europe, in so-called "out of area" operations, did not make it into the June 1990 London summit communique due to European opposition.

Germany's future role in the Alliance poses another set of questions for NATO. Even with German-American relations at a high-water mark, polls reveal that not all Germans are convinced of the need for NATO or an American military presence on their territory: 56 percent of all Germans would welcome the withdrawal of all U.S. troops from Germany.[49]

If a Social Democratic government comes to power in Germany, it could well demand the removal of NATO nuclear weapons. Steps which even a conservative German government might take to strengthen support for NATO within Germany (examples: cancelling major military exercises or banning "low-flying" NATO aircraft) are likely to be viewed in Washington as Bonn shirking its Alliance responsibilities. This will increase pressure over time for the U.S. to distance itself from the Alliance.

For now, given existing Soviet conventional and nuclear military capabilities in Europe, NATO remains the only institution capable of reassuring West Europeans, particularly Germans, of their security. But if coming years see a complete pullout of Soviet forces from Eastern Europe and significant Soviet arms cuts, NATO's future becomes problematic.

West European Organizations

Increasing West European political and military integration, gradually expanding to include the new democracies of Eastern Europe, is one alternative to a European security structure anchored in NATO. During the 1980s, West Europeans led by France and

---

[48] Author's interviews with U.S. State Department officials.
[49] Friedrich-Naumann Stiftung, *Public Opinion in the U.S.A. and the Federal Republic of Germany: A Two Nation Study*, based on March 1990 polling data.

A New American Role in Europe's Balance of Power

Germany sought to develop a "defense identity" of their own. Then, with a clear cut Soviet threat and a strong American commitment to the Alliance, this "defense identity" became strong enough to allow Europeans a measure of independence from Washington, but never so strong as to tempt the U.S. to pack up and go home. Today, with Soviet power in decline and the prospect of major American withdrawals on the horizon, European defense efforts are likely to become more serious.

The European Community (EC) has struggled with the question of expanding its role in the defense field. One reason: the 1956 Treaty of Rome establishing the community bars a direct military role. Nonetheless, France in particular has pressed for an expanded defense role for the EC. The President of the EC's governing European Commission, Jacques Delours, in 1989 promoted EC participation in arms reduction talks, treaty verification, and even German unification.[50] At an April 19 meeting in Paris, French President François Mitterrand and Chancellor Kohl endorsed a stronger security role for the EC. And Kohl, while backing NATO, has expressed his support for embedding a unified Germany within an increasingly unified Europe.[51]

One of the most important efforts to integrate West European defense policies in the 1980s was the revival in 1984 of the West European Union (WEU), a long-dormant European defense organization with its origins in the 1948 Brussels Pact between Britain, France, and several smaller West European powers, to which Germany and Italy were added in 1955. The pact commits members automatically to come to one another's defense in the event of attack. The WEU's assembly of parliamentarians in July put forward proposals for strengthening the organization through such means as a WEU-based European treaty verification organization. In August, the WEU served as a coordinating body for the deployment of West European forces to the Persian Gulf after Iraq's invasion of Kuwait. One hurdle the WEU

---

50 See statements by Delours and Giovanni Jannuzzi, Secretary General of the EC's European Political Cooperation Secretariat in Theresa Hitchens, "EC Eager to Play Key Role in Arms, Security Policy," *Defense News*, March 5, 1990, p. 1.
51 See Helmut Kohl, "Europe — Every German's Future," speech at the World Economic Forum, Davos, February 3, 1990, p. 5.

Chapter 2

will have to overcome is that its political bodies were constituted in 1955 to help reassure France and Britain over West German rearmament by giving them special responsibilities, through WEU, for overseeing limitations on the West German military. While these powers are largely dormant, Germans have reservations about the symbolism of reinvigorating the WEU just as Germany is moving toward full sovereignty and unification.

Through the EC and WEU, institutional arrangements already are in place for an expanded West European role in Europe's new security order. Over time, these institutions perhaps could be expanded to include the new democracies of Eastern Europe as was suggested in July by Sir Dudley Smith, chairman of the WEU assemby's defense committee. Incentives for Europeans to expand their cooperation will include the ongoing threat to their security posed by residual Soviet power in Europe and the likelihood of substantial withdrawals of U.S. forces. Further, with a united Germany emerging as a potential European superpower, such countries as Britain and France will be inclined to tie Germany's defense activities to their own in order to maximize their influence over German defense policy. A likely impediment: a sovereign, united Germany is sure to insist that influence run both ways.

The Conference on Security and Cooperation in Europe (CSCE)

Gorbachev and German Foreign Minister Genscher, among others, have proposed that the 35-nation CSCE form the foundation for a new "collective security" system in Europe, in which differences would be resolved through consensus. The CSCE includes the U.S., Canada, the U.S.S.R. and all European states. It has been associated mainly with the 1975 Helsinki Agreement, a wide-ranging but largely symbolic accord which recognized the inviolability of European borders and committed its signatories to such human rights provisions as the free flow of information across borders, which widely were ignored by the East bloc.

NATO gave limited endorsement to CSCE in its 1990 London Summit Communique, which called for yearly meetings between CSCE heads of State and establishment of a permanent CSCE secretariat. A far more ambitious agenda for CSCE has been proposed by those favoring a "collective security" solution to European security issues.

A New American Role in Europe's Balance of Power

These include Gorbachev's idea for a "common European home," in which the CSCE would replace existing alliances, and Genscher's "pan-European order," in which such alliances as NATO and the Warsaw Pact would continue to exist during an extended transition to a CSCE-based security system.[52] In both, CSCE would become the main organization responsible for maintaining peace in Europe.

While CSCE has advantages as a forum for discussing and mediating some European security issues because of its broad European and North Atlantic membership, CSCE has serious deficiencies as a collective security organization. First, it operates by consensus. Second, it includes the Soviet Union.

Consensus may not always be possible when basic national security interests among states diverge. None of the "collective security" proposals now being suggested for CSCE seriously addresses the question of what would happen if consensus is not possible. CSCE has no military enforcement arm should consensus fail. Decisions reached at CSCE therefore would be influenced by and ultimately subject to Europe's underlying balance of power. In the absence of NATO or other defensive alliances capable of upholding a balance, the influence of the Soviet Union – Europe's dominant power – would be vastly enhanced in a CSCE-based European security system.

CSCE can be an important supplement to such organizations as NATO and the WEU in maintaining peace. If too much is expected of CSCE, however, its future is likely to parallel that of the League of Nations, Europe's post-World War I collective security organization, which failed even to stop the 1935 Italian invasion of Ethiopia, much less the outbreak of World War II.

RECOMMENDATIONS FOR AMERICAN POLICY

1) Establish objectives for a new European security system.

In looking toward a new Europe, the U.S. first should establish its objectives, and then design strategies, forces and institutions to attain and uphold them. U.S. objectives should be to:

---

52 Genscher outlined his ideas for an expanded CSCE in his "Speech to the Special Session of the West European Union Assembly," Luxembourg, March 23, 1990. See Chapter 4 in this volume for more on Gorbachev's "common European home."

Chapter 2

◆ ◆ **Roll back Soviet military power in Europe and ensure that all Soviet forces are withdrawn to within their own territory and limited through conventional arms control.**

◆ ◆ **Establish the sovereignty of all states in the European system.** All states in the European security system, including all East European countries and a united Germany, should have the sovereign right to seek their own security arrangements. This would include the right to seek allies of their choosing and to request or reject the stationing of foreign forces on their own territory.

◆ ◆ **Balance Soviet conventional and nuclear power.** As long as it manages to hold together under Moscow's domination, the Soviet Union is likely to remain the most powerful state on the continent because of its tremendous military mobilization potential and its strategic nuclear forces, even if it withdraws all its forces to within its own borders. Effectively balancing this power to prevent Soviet expansion or political coercion against European democracies will remain the top concern of the U.S. and its allies in Europe in the post-Cold War era, although the military requirements for doing so should be substantially reduced.

◆ ◆ **Resolve the "German question" by reassuring Germany and its neighbors of their security.** The Cold War European security system temporarily solved the "German question" by dividing Germany and integrating half into the Soviet empire and half into the NATO alliance. In the new European system, means still will have to be found to reassure Germany's neighbors against a resurgence of German power. As important, it will be necessary to reassure a united Germany — just as West Germany has been reassured in the post-war era — of its ability to protect itself with help from its allies.

◆ ◆ **Reduce the costs and risks of U.S. involvement in Europe.** One of the major deficiencies of the Cold War European order was the cost and risk to the U.S. of defending it. The new European order should permit the U.S. to reduce its military role in Europe and to transfer many of the costs and military risks of European defense to Europeans.

A New American Role in Europe's Balance of Power

♦ ♦ **Protect and expand democracy in Europe, including the Soviet Union.** Democracy ultimately is the best guarantee of peace and security among states.[53] Its expansion therefore is in America's national security interests, in addition to being an intrinsically worthy goal of U.S. policy. Democracies share common values and interests and generally seek to resolve their differences peacefully through negotiation. The expansion of democracy into Eastern Europe already has ensured that East German, Czech, Hungarian, and Polish armed forces no longer will threaten U.S. allies. The expansion of genuine democracy into the Soviet Union will lead to Soviet decolonization, as such captive "republics" as the Baltic states, Georgia, Ukraine, and others seek freedom from Moscow's control. If this process of decolonization and democratization proceeds peacefully, it could lay the foundation for a just and lasting European peace.

♦ ♦ **Contain regional conflict.** Since the chance of regional conflicts will increase as the Soviet empire is rolled back in Europe, the emerging European security order will have to find ways to help prevent them, or at least to prevent them from spreading into European-wide wars.

2) Press for rapid and peaceful change in Europe.
The East European revolutions of 1989 and the political and economic crises of the Soviet Union have set in motion the collapse of the Soviet empire and the retreat of Soviet power from Europe. It is in American and allied interests to keep this revolutionary process moving through such measures as supporting quick German unification, strengthening the new democracies of Eastern Europe, backing negotiated independence for rebellious Soviet republics, and pursuing an arms control negotiating strategy aimed at radically reducing Soviet military power and keeping it reduced.

---

53 This hypothesis was tested and convincingly demonstrated to be true historically by Michael W. Doyle in "Kant, Liberal Legacies, and Foreign Affairs," Pts. I and II, *Philosophy and Public Affairs*, Vol. 12 (1983), Nos. 3 and 4.

Chapter 2

Some policy makers in the U.S. and Europe, particularly France, urge going slow on such changes as the breakup of the Soviet Union because they are concerned about European "stability."[54] They miss the point.

While Europe has not suffered a major war since World War II, it has lived in a warlike state on the brink of conflict. Its peace has been unjust, founded on a brutal Soviet military occupation of Eastern Europe. It also has been tenuous, requiring constant Western vigilance to block further Soviet expansion. And it has been costly to Europeans, and more so to the U.S. If the Soviet threat can be removed — be it through reductions in the size of Soviet forces, withdrawal of the Red Army from Eastern Europe, or perhaps the democratization and breakup of the Soviet Union itself — Europe at last will have a chance, with U.S. participation, to establish a genuine peace based on cooperation among free and sovereign states. A misplaced longing for the false security of the Cold War only diverts the West's attention from these tremendous opportunities.

3) Promote strong military ties between Germany and its European and North American allies.

The July 16, 1990, Kohl-Gorbachev agreement at Zheleznovodsk paved the way for a unified Germany in NATO. Nonetheless, Moscow still will use such means as the proposed Soviet-German "non-aggression" treaty, expected in 1991, to pressure Germany to loosen its security ties to its allies. If Moscow were to succeed in these efforts, Germany over the longer term could become unduly subject to Soviet political and military pressure, and therefore insecure. Unilateral steps which Germany might take to provide for its security under these conditions, such as developing weapons of mass destruction or breaking out of agreed conventional arms limitations, would lead to insecurity among Germany's neighbors. Providing for German security in the face of Soviet power therefore will remain integral to a long-term resolution of the "German question."

---

54 George Kennan, for example, has argued for a several-year "moratorium" on change in Europe's security structures. Also, author's background discussions with French Defense Ministry officials and U.S. Department of Defense officials.

A New American Role in Europe's Balance of Power

Ensuring that Germany remains secure in coming years will require that Germany retains the right to: 1) continue stationing foreign troops on its soil; 2) remain within NATO's unified military command; and 3) station NATO nuclear weapons on its territory.

There can be no guarantees that Germany will continue to choose a close military relationship with its allies. This is an unavoidable price of a diminishing Soviet threat and the establishment of a sovereign, unified Germany. In fact Germany already has taken steps — such as consenting in the Kohl-Gorbachev agreement to limit its armed forces to 370,000, without requiring reciprocal limits on Soviet forces — which could weaken NATO's long-term ability to defend Europe. The U.S. can, however, continue as it has throughout the Two Plus Four negotiations, to resist any Soviet attempts to dictate Germany's security status against the will of Germans and other Europeans.

4) Proceed with caution on conventional arms control.

Secretary of State James Baker and Soviet Foreign Minister Eduard Shevardnadze in New York on October 3 announced agreement on the major outlines of a Conventional Forces in Europe (CFE) agreement. These include absolute limits on tanks, artillery, armored fighting vehicles, aircraft, and helicopters that either NATO or the Warsaw Pact can station in Europe, from the Atlantic Ocean to the Ural Mountains. It also prohibits any country from possessing more than two-thirds to three-quarters, depending on the item, of the military equipment allocated to each alliance. But problems remain. Most significantly, during the CFE negotiations Moscow withdrew much of its military equipment in Europe to behind the Urals, where it would not be counted under CFE and therefore would not be subject to destruction under a CFE treaty. This display of bad faith by Moscow, coupled with rapid change in Europe — including the potential breakup of the Soviet Union — counsel caution on conventional arms control. Specifically, the U.S. should:

Chapter 2

♦ ♦ **Require destruction of Soviet equipment withdrawn to behind the Urals since the CFE negotiations got underway in March 1989.** During the course of the CFE negotiations, scattered reports indicated that Moscow was withdrawing tanks and other equipment to behind the Urals, where it would not be counted under CFE limits.[55] Only in October 1990 did the magnitude of this withdrawal become apparent. From the time negotiations began in March 1989 until October 1990, Moscow withdrew to behind the Urals between 7,000 and 10,000 tanks, 12,000 artillery pieces, along with perhaps thousands of aircraft.[56] Unless this equipment ultimately is counted under an accord and destroyed, the purpose of CFE – a balance of military power in Europe – could be undermined; with this equipment exempted, Moscow would have a dangerous store of military equipment to bring to bear against Europe after a period of mobilization.

♦ ♦ **Pause after CFE. Even if a CFE agreement is signed and ratified, it will take about five years to carry out.** There are good political and military reasons to pause for at least two years before beginning follow-on CFE negotiations.

First, political change is outpacing the ability of negotiators to account for it. CFE itself rapidly was overtaken by political events in Europe: the NATO-Warsaw Pact framework for negotiations made little sense as the Warsaw Pact began to unravel, and one country that began the talks – East Germany – no longer existed as discussions drew to a close. Political change in Europe shows no sign of slowing down. The Warsaw Pact is liable to collapse entirely in coming months, and the Soviet Union may not be far behind. It makes little sense to negotiate until the pace of political change has slowed. After all, next year Lithuania, Latvia, Estonia, Ukraine, and other European republics of what now is the Soviet Union could join Moscow at the bargaining table.

Second, Moscow's decision to move military equipment from Europe to behind the Urals has poisoned the atmosphere for conven-

---

[55] See Jay Kosminsky, "Moscow Arms for Arms Control," Heritage Foundation *Backgrounder* No. 118, October 26, 1989.
[56] U.S. Department of Defense, *Soviet Military Power 1990* (Washington, D.C.: U.S. GPO), p. 95.

A New American Role in Europe's Balance of Power

tional force negotiations. If a CFE treaty is signed and ratified, the West should wait to see how Moscow carries out its provisions before starting further negotiations. If it turns out that Moscow is determined to hold tremendous stores of military equipment behind the Urals, the deep reductions in European forces envisioned for "CFE II" would be out of the question, since smaller Western forces would be more vulnerable to Soviet equipment moved into Europe from behind the Urals.

5) Redefine the U.S. military role in Europe.

For now, Moscow continues to station over 500,000 well-armed troops in Eastern Europe. If most or all Soviet forces withdraw to their own territory and are constrained by CFE and other arms control accords, the current U.S. military role in Europe and the NATO strategy its supports will have become anachronistic. At that time, U.S. allies will be able to take over responsibility for their own ground defense without the presence of large numbers of American forces in Europe and without the need for substantial American rapid reinforcement. Freed of these requirements, the U.S. will be able to reduce dramatically its military role in Europe. If the Soviet pullback continues the U.S. should:

♦ ♦ **Reduce U.S. ground forces.** With the Red Army pulled back to Soviet territory and constrained through arms control, it will be very difficult for Moscow to mass its forces for an attack on NATO without extensive warning. Such a situation would allow the U.S. to withdraw the bulk of its 250,000 ground forces from Europe and turn over to the Europeans the main responsibility for their conventional defense. Almost 50,000 or so U.S. army troops could remain if desired by allies, or roughly one division plus support troops, largely as a symbol of America's continuing interest in maintaining Europe's peace and security. These forces could maintain U.S. equipment which remained stored in Europe for U.S. reinforcements and could work with Europeans to prepare to help receive and deploy U.S. troops that arrived in a crisis. Or they could be part of a mobile force which would help European armies bolster their defenses until reserves were mobilized and reinforcements began arriving from the U.S. and elsewhere in Europe. Given a CFE treaty and agreement on German unification in 1990, these cuts can be completed within the next five years.

Given a Soviet pullback, the U.S. also will be able to demobilize several of the ten heavy army divisions in the U.S. earmarked for rapid

Chapter 2

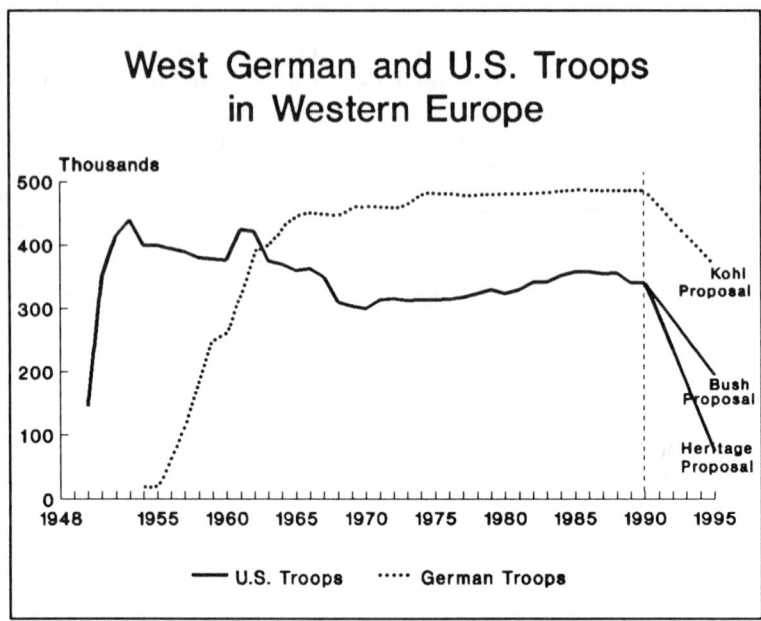

West German and U.S. Troops in Western Europe

[Line graph showing U.S. Troops (solid line) and German Troops (dotted line) in thousands from 1948 to 1995. U.S. troops rise quickly to about 430,000 by 1955, dip and peak again around 1960, then decline to about 300,000 by 1970, remaining around 300,000–350,000 through the 1980s. German troops rise from near zero in the mid-1950s to about 480,000 by the mid-1960s, staying near that level through 1990. Three proposals are labeled at 1990: Kohl Proposal, Bush Proposal, and Heritage Proposal.]

deployment in Europe. Depending on needs arising from other global requirements, the size of the U.S. army could be cut to between ten to twelve divisions from the current eighteen active divisions. The precise mix of these divisions would depend on potential missions in other regions besides Europe, but should include at least five mechanized and armored divisions, and sealift sufficient to transport them, in addition to airborne and other light divisions.

The primary U.S. role in Europe's ground defense then will be to dispatch Reserve and National Guard forces to counter a Soviet mobilization and transfer of forces to Europe from Soviet Asia. The size and capabilities of this U.S. force will have to be tailored carefully to match Soviet mobilization capabilities. For this, at least the current ten reserve army divisions are likely to be needed for the foreseeable future. The U.S. reserve role will be particularly important since arms control agreements are likely to limit strictly the amount of stored equipment, including tanks, that European allies will have available to arm their own reserves. With the U.S. playing largely a reserve role, the need for airlift planes such as the C-5 and proposed C-17, used to

A New American Role in Europe's Balance of Power

transport troops quickly to Europe, will not be as important as the need for sealift ships to move reserve forces.

♦ ♦ **Stress a continuing U.S. naval role. To transport the U.S. reserve force to Europe, the U.S.** still will need warships to defend the North Atlantic against the Soviet navy, particularly its submarines. Sealift ships to transport reserve forces and their equipment to Europe also will remain a priority. With the immediate Soviet threat in Europe greatly reduced, the U.S. Navy, like the Army, will be able to focus more on reserve capabilities. As former Navy Secretary John Lehman has suggested, naval forces can spend more time training in home waters and less time steaming in distant seas. The Navy also will be able to rely more heavily on reserves to man its ships since it will have a longer time to prepare for a major war. Given the ongoing need to project American power elsewhere in the world, as well as protect the North Atlantic sealanes in the event of a wartime return to Europe, naval power — including aircraft carrier battle groups — will remain the backbone of America's conventional defense.

♦ ♦ **Offer to provide airpower. U.S. airpower should remain in Europe if desired by allies.** Air power, along with naval power, traditionally has been a U.S. military and technological strength. The U.S. already is developing the next generation of stealth fighters and bombers — the Air Force's Advanced Tactical Fighter and Navy's Advanced Tactical Aircraft. Given America's comparative advantage in this field, airpower should become the principle means of maintaining a U.S. military role in Europe.

The missions of U.S. tactical air forces in Europe would not change fundamentally: helping to gain control of the air over the battlefield, striking at such targets as command posts and ammunition depots, providing firepower for troops in combat, and conducting electronic warfare. However, the eight U.S. tactical air wings in Europe, each composed of about 72 planes, could be cut back to six following a CFE agreement, and perhaps further pending reciprocal Soviet cuts through follow-on arms control agreements. U.S. airbases in Portugal and Italy, which could be used to support U.S. military operations in the Mediterranean, still will be vital to protecting U.S. interests as long as Middle East conflict and anti-Western regimes continue to threaten the security of U.S. and European oil supplies.

Chapter 2

♦ ♦ **Retain a credible U.S. nuclear deterrent force in Europe.** Even in the wake of NATO's July summit decision to negotiate the withdrawal of nuclear artillery shells from Europe and Bush's unilateral decision on May 3 to forego modernization of the short-range *Lance* missile, NATO will remain dependent on U.S. nuclear weapons. Examples: except for small French and British arsenals, virtually all NATO's approximately 1,400 nuclear bombs for strike aircraft are U.S. weapons. This is another reason for keeping U.S. airpower in Europe.

For now, only the U.S. has the capability to deploy a battlefield nuclear force to counter Moscow's. Europeans eventually could develop one, perhaps under the auspices of the West European Union. However, strong emotional and political obstacles stand in the way of a joint European nuclear force, which likely will be the last aspect of European defense integration to fall into place. In the meantime, there is no reasonable alternative to an ongoing U.S. role in NATO nuclear deterrence, as long as the Soviet Union remains a nuclear superpower.

6) Preserve and transform NATO.

Even if the Soviet Union withdraws its forces to within its own borders, only the U.S. military alliance in the short term can reassure Germany and other European allies against residual Soviet military power, particularly its nuclear striking power. Nonetheless, NATO will have to adapt to changing historical circumstances, including a reduced military threat and a lack of public support either in the U.S. or Germany for what heretofore had been some of the more demanding responsibilities of common defense. Examples: For Germans, such large-scale military exercises as Reforger; for Americans, the high cost of fielding front-line and rapid reinforcement manpower for NATO defense. Steps NATO should take to adjust to the new environment include:

♦ ♦ **Strengthen NATO's European component.** The U.S. should convey to its European allies unambiguously that within five years they will assume primary responsibility for Alliance ground defense and rapid reinforcement missions, assuming continued pullbacks in Soviet forces from Europe. Plans to reduce U.S. ground forces in Europe to at most 50,000, along with the demobilization of several U.S.-based divisions slated for NATO rapid reinforcement, will help convey the message. Once these withdrawals are complete, the U.S. should con-

A New American Role in Europe's Balance of Power

sider turning over to a European the job of Supreme Allied Commander Europe (SACEUR), held by an American since NATO's inception. The position could rotate between an American and a European thereafter.

♦ ♦ **Revise NATO conventional military strategy to match new realities.** If the Soviet military threat to NATO continues to recede, NATO's military requirements for deterring attack will ease, and significant changes can be made in NATO strategy.

NATO's strategy of "forward defense" at the East-West German border makes little sense as this border disappears with unification and the withdrawal of Soviet troops from Germany. NATO will, however, face new problems. Germany is likely to insist that NATO plan to defend all German territory after unification, even though no foreign troops will be stationed in what now is East Germany. This means that NATO will have to prepare to move its troops forward from western Germany and elsewhere in Europe into eastern Germany during such an emergency as a Soviet mobilization and invasion of Poland. This will require a more mobile strategy heavily dependent on timely mobilization, clear communications among NATO forces, and improved "intra-theater," or short-haul airlift and other troop transport capabilities.

NATO countries under present doctrine are assigned different military sectors along the 500-mile inter-German border that they alone are responsible for supplying and defending. Preferably, under the new strategy NATO's divisions would fight side-by-side with common supply lines. This would entail much closer cooperation and standardization among NATO armies than exists today. The reason: various allied nations now use different military tactics, incompatible equipment such as radios that operate on different frequencies, and guns that use different ammunition.

Politically, achieving this level of coordination will be difficult. For example, it would require much closer and more open military cooperation between France and the rest of the Alliance. The U.S. cannot force this level of cooperation on its allies and should not attempt to do so, particularly if Washington is serious about limiting its role in NATO defense. If ground defense is to become a mainly European responsibility over the next few years, the impetus for closer cooperation will have to come from Europeans. If they are willing to take it, the U.S. by all means should participate in their efforts. If not, however, the U.S. should be prepared to design military forces, and a

Chapter 2

military doctrine, that will enable it to fight alongside, but largely independently, of its European allies. This fall-back strategy would rely most heavily on those countries that demonstrate a clear willingness to cooperate bi-laterally with the U.S.

♦ ♦ **Modify NATO nuclear strategy; resist pressure to adopt a "no first use" doctrine.**

If conventional military parity is established between NATO and the Soviet Union, NATO no longer will need a nuclear doctrine that assumes it will have to use nuclear weapons to defend itself on the battlefield. NATO will need a small battlefield nuclear force: 1) to deter Soviet use of nuclear weapons on the battlefield; 2) as a weapon of last resort in the unlikely event of an impending conventional military defeat, and 3) to make the prospect of war more frightening and uncertain to a potential aggressor, and therefore strengthen deterrence of a major war in Europe. These last two requirements only can be upheld if NATO reserves the option of using nuclear weapons first.

Given its nuclear capabilities on the ground in Europe, including about 4,000 nuclear warheads, there is no immediate need for NATO to decide on a new nuclear force posture. All that is necessary at the moment is to uphold the principle of nuclear deterrence and the sovereign right of Alliance members to station nuclear forces on their territory.

Once the dust settles in Europe, assuming that current negotiations lead to German unification and a CFE agreement, there will be time to decide on a deployment plan. Ideally this force would be centered on the planned Tactical Air-to-Surface Missile (TASM), an air-launched missile with a range of about 280 miles, in addition to the range of the aircraft which carries it. Example: if deployed on a European *Tornado* bomber, with a range of 2,800 miles, TASM would have an effective range in excess of 3,000 miles — more than enough to strike deep into Soviet territory from bases in Germany or elsewhere.[57]

U.S. nuclear protection for European allies could be bolstered by ensuring that the Air Forces of such allies as Germany are equipped to launch TASM, although the warheads themselves would be kept

---

57 IISS, *Military Balance*, 1987-88, p. 205.

A New American Role in Europe's Balance of Power

under American control. This would give the U.S. the ability in principle to transfer these weapons to its allies in the event of a Soviet nuclear threat against them. This would be consistent with current arrangements whereby such allies as Belgium, Britain, and West Germany possess the *Lance* missile, as well as artillery and aircraft, capable of launching nuclear warheads kept under U.S. control. TASM would be supplemented by nuclear-tipped cruise missiles and SLBMs on U.S. submarines, and by nuclear artillery shells, which would be stored in the U.S. and moved to Europe during a crisis.

♦ ♦ **Continue to emphasize NATO's military role.** NATO is a military alliance created, in Acheson's words, for "deterrence of aggression." While it would be dangerous to hasten NATO's demise as long as the Soviet military threat remains, there is no particular reason to try to expand NATO's function beyond its primary mandate: military deterrence of a major war in Europe. NATO is not well suited to the expanded political role suggested by Secretary of State Baker. NATO allies have had trouble cooperating on such issues as "out of area conflict," most notably in the Middle East.

Further, NATO does not include the new democracies of Eastern Europe, and therefore is not the ideal institution for expanding America's political role in Europe and its cooperation with continental democracies. While ways conceivably might be found to expand some of NATO's political councils to the East, the U.S. should not explicitly expand its defense commitments eastward at a time when it is reducing its military role in Europe.

7) Support European solutions to European security issues.

For the U.S. safely to diminish its own military role in Europe, European security institutions will have to be strengthened. Among steps the U.S. should encourage Europeans to take are:

♦ ♦ **Strengthen the West European Union (WEU).** The WEU is an in-place military alliance through which Europeans could begin to improve their military cooperation and coordination. Immediate steps to strengthen European defense planning should include creation of a standing WEU military planning committee of high-level officers and institutionalized meetings of WEU national military commanders. WEU should become the main forum for West European coordination on defense planning and cooperation. This would have several advantages. First, it might provide a politically more acceptable way for

Chapter 2

France — which remains reluctant to move closer to NATO — to integrate its military planning and doctrine with European allies.

Second, the WEU could play an important role in solving the German question because it would ensure Germany's military integration into a broader defense community, even as NATO's role decreases. This would assuage some of the understandable fears of its neighbors. Germany will be willing to go along, however, only if such countries as France and Britain are willing to accept Germany as an equal partner. This will mean, for example, that Paris will have to take German interests into account when considering such now-sacrosanct issues as the targeting of its nuclear weapons – many of which are aimed at German territory. Ground defense would be the first NATO mission to devolve mainly to the WEU from NATO. This would happen over the next five years. Gradually, the European force could accept other missions, including eventually the development of a West European nuclear force.

Finally, the WEU could become the main organization for coordinating European military efforts in such areas as the Persian Gulf, and for promoting European solutions to European regional or national conflicts. NATO would remain the umbrella organization for deterring, and if necessary fighting, a major war in Europe.

♦♦ **Expand WEU membership, eventually to include East European states.** The WEU could form the core of an expanding European security organization. Over the next few years it could develop formal ties with the European Community, and perhaps expand its membership to include all EC members choosing to participate in Community military matters. Within the next decade or so, the WEU, perhaps under EC auspices, could expand further to include the new democracies of Eastern Europe. In this way, East European countries eventually could be integrated into European defense without having to expand NATO eastward.

♦♦ **Encourage regional alliances among East Europeans.** In the short run it may not be feasible for the WEU to spread its defense umbrella to Eastern Europe. In the meantime, regional alliances among East Europeans offer the best short-term solution to providing some military reassurance to countries now gaining their freedom from the Soviet empire. Example: a Czechoslovakian, Hungarian, Polish axis. The U.S. should encourage these groupings as an extra measure of deterrence against renewed Soviet expansionism in areas outside of

A New American Role in Europe's Balance of Power

NATO or WEU protection. The U.S. also should offer military and technical expertise to modernize East European armies once it is clear that their military establishments have cut all connections with the Soviet Union.

8) Limit the East-West security role of the CSCE but expand its role in other areas.
CSCE is Moscow's favored forum for establishing a vaguely-defined all-European "collective security" system to replace NATO and the Warsaw Pact. The purpose of NATO, however, is to balance Soviet power and prevent Moscow from using force or the threat of force to impose its political will on Western allies. Because it includes Moscow and has no military means of enforcing its collective will, CSCE is incapable of replacing NATO's security function.

In a fully democratic Europe, including a democratic Soviet Union or its successor states, CSCE would be a plausible mechanism for maintaining mutual security. A democratic Soviet Union, after all, would share the same basic security interests that now bind the other Western democracies, along with their inherent restraints on militarism and preference for negotiated outcomes. Until such a time, CSCE cannot secure Europe's peace. It can, however, help spread democracy and self-determination if used effectively by its Western members. Effective use of CSCE would include:

♦♦ **Using CSCE to ratify and reinforce the demise of the Soviet empire.** A CSCE meeting could ratify the sovereign rights of all its members to control military activities on their territory, including the stationing of foreign troops. This would give international sanction to efforts by former Soviet satellites, including what now is East Germany, to expel Soviet forces from their territory. The right of these states to withdraw from the Warsaw Pact or such other Soviet-dominated organizations as COMECON also could be ratified by CSCE. By taking such measures as inviting the Baltic States and other former Soviet republics into CSCE, once they have declared their independence from Moscow, CSCE also can be an effective forum for promoting the peaceful decolonization of the Soviet Union.

♦♦ **Expand CSCE's arms control role.** After a CFE agreement is concluded, the NATO-Warsaw Pact forum of those negotiations may no longer be viable as the Warsaw Pact dissolves. CSCE would be the logical forum for CFE II.

Chapter 2

♦ ♦ **Use CSCE to promote a European nuclear non-proliferation treaty.** As the superpowers pull back from Europe, pressures will build for European countries to deploy nuclear weapons to guarantee their security. Poland, for example, facing traditional enemies to the east and west, is a candidate for nuclear proliferation. Proliferation in Europe could be very dangerous, particularly if it were to tempt Germany to acquire nuclear weapons. Although West Germany is a signatory to the international Nuclear Non-Proliferation Treaty (NPT), this treaty will lapse in 1995 unless re-endorsed by its members. A European regional non-proliferation pact would help ensure that all European non-nuclear powers remain non-nuclear.

♦ ♦ **Use CSCE and other such organizations as the EC and WEU to address regional conflicts.** Europeans should be encouraged to take the lead in resolving regional, ethnic, and other conflicts which may arise as Soviet power in Europe recedes. America is in Europe to ensure that no single power or hostile coalition gains control of the continent. Only the Soviet Union now poses such a threat, and no other is on the immediate horizon. Europeans themselves should deal with regional conflicts that do not involve the peace and stability of the continent as a whole.

9) Find new ways to keep America involved in Europe.
While the need for a powerful U.S. military role in Europe may be declining, America still has interests to protect there. As the role of NATO moves from the center to the periphery of America's European policy, there will be a need to reinforce the American presence in Europe in other ways, including:

♦ ♦ **Establish an Atlantic Conference composed of North American and European democracies.**[58] Unlike NATO, such an organization would encompass the new democracies of Eastern Europe, and unlike the CSCE, it would exclude the Soviet Union as long as it remains communist. While it would have no direct role in European defense, it would help reaffirm America's ongoing stake in the affairs of Europe, thereby reinforcing America's security commitment to

---

58 See Chapter 1 for more on the Atlantic Conference.

A New American Role in Europe's Balance of Power

Europe, even as the U.S. moves toward the role of a mainly offshore European power.

♦ ♦ **Strengthen U.S. bilateral defense relationships in Europe.** U.S.-German bi-lateral relations will be among the most essential, and the most problematic, of U.S.-European ties in coming years. During the Cold War period, the U.S.-German relationship, managed primarily through NATO, was the cornerstone of European security. It reassured West Germany against Soviet military power, particularly its nuclear arsenal, and it helped reassure France, Britain, and other European states against Soviet power and a revival of German power. While Europeans will have to wean themselves of this dependence in coming years, U.S.-German military ties for the time being will remain critical to European security regardless of NATO's fate. A U.S.-German defense treaty assuring, for example, continued U.S. basing rights in Germany, could help solidify these ties even if NATO's influence wanes. From a U.S. perspective, a bilateral defense treaty with Germany would assure a continuing U.S. military role in central Europe, where the U.S. retains vital national interests.

Britain remains a key U.S. ally in Europe. While Britain will not have the economic or conventional military power of a united Germany, America and Britain have a historical "special relationship" in the defense field which predates the Cold War. This will remain essential for both, partly as a hedge against a shift in German policy — whether toward neutrality, demilitarization, or remilitarization — that posed a threat to Western security. If, for example, Germany were to expel American forces from its territory, London would welcome the added assurance provided by the presence of U.S. forces in Britain and a close military relationship with the U.S. For the U.S., Britain then would become the focus of the U.S. military presence in Europe. Even if Anglo-German and U.S.-German ties remain strong, the "special relationship" holds advantages. In Britain, Margaret Thatcher's Conservatives and the oposition Labour party now are commited to the purchase of U.S. *Trident* nuclear submarines and ballistic missiles in the 1990s. Moreover, a U.S.-British option in defense as well as economic and diplomatic relations, gives both countries additional leverage in dealing with a European Community dominated by France and Germany.

The U.S.-Turkish bi-lateral defense relationship, often neglected by Washington, also will remain critical regardless of NATO's fate. This

Chapter 2

was demonstrated during the recent crisis in the Persian Gulf, when Turkey stationed U.S. F-111 bombers at the NATO base at Incirlik within strking range of Iraq, and shut down the Iraqi oil pipeline through Turkey to the Mediterranean Sea.

10) Maintain a balance of power as Europe moves toward a new order.

Timing is essential in the creation of a new European security system. For the time being, NATO and the U.S. will remain central to European defense. If the Soviet withdrawal from Eastern Europe continues and a conventional arms agreement is reached between East and West, such European defense organizations as the WEU gradually can take over many of NATO's roles, beginning in the next few years with ground defense. If the Soviet Union progresses toward democracy, a development which surely would entail its breaking apart to some extent, then the 35-nation CSCE may become a viable alternative as a European security organization. If Europe jumps the gun, however, and leaves the secure chrysalis of NATO before a new order has developed sufficiently to stand on its own, peace will be in jeopardy.

CONCLUSION: AMERICA AND EUROPEAN SECURITY

Europe encompasses the single greatest aggregation of technological, economic, and military power in the world. America has an abiding interest in preventing any power or coalition from controlling Europe and turning its resources against the United States. Twice this century the U.S. has fought European wars to prevent expansionist German empires from doing so, and since World War II it has remained in Europe at great cost and risk to deter the further expansion of the Russian empire. Today, this empire is collapsing and Soviet power is in retreat.

In coming months and years, it remains for the U.S. to follow up this victory through a diplomatic offensive aimed at pushing the Red Army back behind Soviet borders and encouraging the spread of Europe's democratic revolution into the Soviet Union itself. The U.S. also faces the task of helping to establish a new European balance of power — reinforced through such alliance systems as NATO and the West European Union (WEU), international organizations including the Conference on Security and Cooperation in Europe (CSCE), and arms

A New American Role in Europe's Balance of Power

control agreements such as a Conventional Forces in Europe (CFE) treaty — capable of preventing a revival of the Soviet or any other threat to Europe.

In the best of worlds, the revolutions that have swept through Europe will reach within the borders of the Soviet Union, putting an end to Russia's internal empire. If the Soviet Union manages to hold together, however, it is likely to remain the major threat to European security for the foreseeable future by virtue of its nuclear forces and formidable mobilization capabilities. Even as the Soviet threat diminishes, therefore, the U.S. will have a role to play in balancing residual Soviet military capabilities in Europe. Nevertheless, given a reduced Soviet threat, the U.S. should be able to step into a less costly and less risky role as a mainly offshore power in a new European order.

Assuming a CFE accord and the withdrawal of most Soviet forces from Eastern Europe, U.S. ground forces in Europe could be cut from 250,000 to about 50,000, backed mainly by reserve manpower in the U.S. The U.S. Air Force also would remain in Europe, although at least two of the current eight tactical air wings will likely be cut as a result of a CFE Treaty. U.S. naval forces would retain the mission of protecting the critical North Atlantic sea lanes between Europe and the U.S. American forces in Europe still would be nuclear armed, although U.S. nuclear weapons in Europe could be limited to aircraft-launched weapons, given Soviet reciprocity. All these European deployments of U.S. forces would, of course, be contingent on the agreement of allies.

As the role of NATO in Europe declines with the reduced U.S. military presence, West Europeans will have to take on increasing responsibility for balancing residual Soviet power on the continent. This could be done through the West European Union (WEU), which should establish a standing military planning committee and initiate regular meetings of national military commanders. Within five years, Europeans should be capable of providing for their own ground defense, with mainly reserve reinforcement from the U.S.

Gorbachev and others have proposed that the CSCE serve as the foundation for a new European security order. But CSCE operates by consensus and has no military enforcement arm. It therefore is incapable of balancing Soviet power, which likely will remain the major military threat to Europe even after a CFE agreement and the withdrawal of the Red Army to within Soviet borders. Only in a fully democratic Europe, including a democratic Soviet Union or its succes-

Chapter 2

sor states, would CSCE become a plausible mechanism for maintaining mutual security. In such a Europe all states would share the same basic security interests that now bind the Western democracies, along with their inherent restraints on militarism and expansionism.

The creation of a democratic Europe is the ultimate objective of U.S. and allied policy. Until this effort succeeds, however, the immediate focus will have to remain on effectively balancing Soviet military power.

While the strategy and deployment of U.S. forces in Europe should be flexible, U.S. interests in Europe are enduring. The U.S. will have to retain a strong presence in Europe — diplomatic, economic, and if necessary, military — to protect these interests. As the British realized in the 19th Century, even an offshore power must remain engaged in European affairs during peacetime to convey the will to defend its interests should the continent be threatened by war. An America with neither the military capability nor political will to influence Europe's balance of power ultimately will leave the fate of its interests for others to decide.

Chapter 3

Beyond 1992: Promoting America's Economic Interests in Post-Cold War Europe

Ronald Utt and William D. Eggers

Until late 1989, the economic future of Western Europe could have been predicted with some confidence: the region was moving toward further economic integration. Whether this would happen on schedule by the end of 1992 was, of course, a different matter; the timetable surely could slide. And whether integration would unleash or suffocate economic energy also was a different matter. In general, however, few experts doubted that Western Europe was headed down a path that relatively soon would lead to economic integration and that this would generally be economically beneficial.

By mid-1990, predicting Western Europe's economic future had become much more problematic. This is because of two extremely important developments: 1) the East European revolutions, which have swept away command economies and are installing versions of free market economies wanting closer economic integration with the West; and 2) German unification, which could produce an economy that vastly overshadows all others in the region. How these two

Chapter 3

developments will affect the planned 1992 European Community integration — known as EC '92 — and how they will affect each other are unpredictable. Will German unification, for example, distract Germany from fulfilling its commitments to EC '92? And will the EC need to be restructured fundamentally to accommodate East Europeans as members?

These are questions that must concern Americans attempting to devise policies for how to deal with Europe in the 1990s. The economic changes in Europe are creating new challenges for American economic policy. These changes offer both opportunities and dangers.

Opportunities

- United States businesses stand to gain from the EC's removal of economic barriers, reduced paperwork, cheaper distribution costs, and new market opportunities in Western Europe and in the developing economies of Eastern Europe.
- The development of the East European states may be sufficiently rapid that they will join the EC sometime in the late 1990s and create a truly continental economy.
- Future German economic might could be the engine to drive the economic growth of the East European countries by providing managerial expertise, investment capital, and advanced technology to the region.

Dangers

- The gains of EC '92 may be offset by numerous EC bureaucratic regulations, the effect of which could lead to even greater economic stagnation in Europe.
- The powerful EC institutions emerging from EC '92 could erect protectionist measures which discriminate against U.S. and other foreign firms.
- The competitiveness of EC firms may be further weakened by the promotion of monopolistic partnerships and by government subsidization of selected industries.
- Rather than becoming the next Southeast Asia, Eastern Europe could become the next Latin America — mired in foreign debt and lacking the political will to introduce radical free market reforms.

Promoting America's Economic Interests

♦ The tremendous costs of unification and a drift toward increased government meddling in the marketplace could slow economic growth in Germany significantly over the course of the decade.

The U.S. has a tremendous amount at stake in how these developments unfold. U.S. economic policies toward the continent should focus on promoting free trade and free markets. After all, the post-World War II, liberal regime of free trade has created the world's unprecedented economic growth and wealth. As a simple rule of thumb, therefore, U.S. policy should support all proposals in Europe that decrease government involvement in the market and remove obstacles to the free flow of trade and investment across national borders. By the same token, the U.S. should oppose policies that increase government intervention in the marketplace. In coordinating this policy, the U.S. should:

♦♦ **Support the integration of free markets throughout Europe.** America consistently has supported European economic integration since the end of World War II and strongly endorsed the establishment of the EC. While this has been motivated largely by a desire to bolster European political cooperation, the reduction of trade barriers among the European states is also consistent with long-term U.S. interests of greater free trade world-wide. American support for European economic integration should be dependent on EC policies that promote freer trade and markets, not the expansion of EC bureaucratic power.

♦♦ **Oppose any efforts to discriminate against American products.** Thus far, there has been little indication that the EC plans on protecting its market from foreign competition through the use of extensive trade barriers. The Europeans, however, have a long history of protectionist policies and may, in the future, be tempted to erect trade barriers around the EC if European firms fall farther behind American and Japanese companies. Since much of the impetus behind the EC '92 project has been fear of American and Japanese competition, Washington must monitor EC policies closely to ensure that trade barriers are not erected against foreign competition. The U.S. must work through multilateral negotiations such as the General Agreement on Tariffs and Trade (GATT) and bilateral negotiations, in the form of free trade agreements, to prevent such discrimination.

Chapter 3

♦ ♦ **Press the EC to dismantle its protectionist Common Agricultural Policy (CAP).** The free market in Europe long has stopped at the farm's edge. The EC's common agriculture policy, begun in 1962, is a set of internal prices, within the Community that support EC farm incomes and external changes, intended to protect EC agricultural products from the lower prices of more efficient foreign producers. The effect is to grant absolute protection for EC farmers. The CAP not only hurts American farmers, who enjoy a tremendous comparative advantage in most agricultural goods, but also damages the fledgling democracies in Eastern Europe and the people of less developed countries around the globe, whose access to the large EC market is restricted by the CAP. Most of all, CAP should be abandoned on behalf of Europe's taxpayers and consumers who pay over $100 billion a year for this "protection."

♦ ♦ **Take the lead in removing trade barriers to Eastern Europe and press for closer economic ties between the EC and Eastern Europe.** The countries of Eastern Europe want to revive their devastated economies by increasing their economic ties to the West as quickly as possible. Most also would like greater access to the EC and its markets. Although none of the economies in the region are close to meeting the minimal standards for EC membership, they may become eligible in the late 1990s. Access to markets is the best stimulus for economic growth, rewarding entrepreneurs who devise new and improved ways to produce and market goods and services for the marketplace. America should demonstrate its continued commitment to free trade and free markets by rapidly removing trade barriers to the Eastern European countries as they liberalize their own economies and trade laws and press the EC to do the same.

♦ ♦ **Encourage and assist the East Europeans to adopt free market reforms.** Eastern Europe is replacing its failed socialist economies with the free market system. The experiences in Hungary, Poland, and Yugoslavia, where heavy borrowing from Western banks and governments failed to help the economy, demonstrate that the worse thing that the U.S. could do for these countries is provide massive amounts of foreign aid. In these countries, foreign aid was used to prop up inefficient state-owned enterprises by sheltering them from competition and providing extensive credits which allowed them to postpone needed economic and structural reforms. Over 50 percent of

Promoting America's Economic Interests

the $20 billion debt accumulated by Yugoslavia either subsidized consumer consumption or was squandered on uneconomic projects.

The lesson of this is that America should not give any government-to-government aid because it makes recipient governments depend on aid, rather than on substantial economic reforms for development. If aid is to be given, it should go directly to the private sector and should be based on what economists call the Index of Economic Freedom. The index measures how well a country is adopting free market reforms such as establishing firm private property rights, low taxes, a free price system, fiscal constraint, and easy access to business licenses.

◆ ◆ **Offer debt relief to East European countries in the form of debt-equity swaps.** A number of the East European countries have accumulated large debts to Western financial institutions and governments. The U.S. government should urge Western financial institutions to use debt-equity swaps to reduce the debts of the East European nations. In a debt-equity swap, Western investors would buy the debt of Hungary, Poland, or other countries at a significant discount from a creditor bank. The debt then would be traded for local currency, bonds, or shares in state-owned enterprises from the debtor governments.[1] Debt-equity swaps attract foreign investment and facilitate the privatization of state-owned enterprises, while reducing the debt of the debtor countries.

◆ ◆ **Support lower trade barriers between North America and Europe, and establish a North Atlantic Free Trade Area.** Washington should take the lead in lowering trade barriers between North America and Europe, with the aim of establishing a free trade area linking the two continental economies. Building on the close ties that already exist between both sides of the Atlantic, the U.S. along with Canada, and possibly Mexico, should call for a free trade area that includes North America, the EC members, other West European countries, and the newly free East European countries. A free trade area would encourage continued economic growth in the world's two largest markets,

---

1 See Melanie S. Tammen, "Energizing Third World Economies: The Role of Debt-Equity Swaps," Heritage Foundation *Backgrounder* No. 736, November 8, 1989, p.1.

Chapter 3

and provide a more attractive alternative to a potentially insular EC. It also could blunt protectionist pressures in the U.S.

COMING OF WEST EUROPEAN ECONOMIC INTEGRATION

The European Community was created by the Treaty of Rome. Signed in 1957 by Belgium, France, Italy, Luxembourg, the Netherlands, and West Germany, the treaty's chief purpose was to commit the signatories to create a common market by eliminating the many economic barriers between them. Although the six ultimately became twelve, and the institutional structures that emerged grew to form an extensive new layer of government, the chief purpose of the treaty — the formation of a true common market with minimal barriers to the flow of trade, labor, and finance between the nations — largely eluded the members. After more than three decades, barriers still impede the flow of commerce between countries. Quotas, tariffs, time consuming inspections and paperwork, and limits on the flow of labor are barriers that exist at every border. Different technical standards for products, licensing requirements, and restrictions on the flow of finance and professional services create other cross-border obstacles. And differences in taxes and monetary systems add to the cost of trade between member countries.

By the mid-1980s, the EC countries began to fall economically and technologically behind the newly-resurgent U.S. and the rapidly-growing East Asian market economies stretching from Japan to Singapore. The term "Eurosclerosis" was coined to describe this condition. The U.S. per capita gross national product (GNP) measured $18,530 in 1987 compared to just $14,400 in West Germany and $15,760 in Japan.[2] Between 1976 and 1983, the U.S. economy grew at 2.5 percent adjusted for inflation while the EC increased at the rate of 2.3 percent.[3] And, between 1984 and 1989, the Japanese economy mushroomed by 4.5 percent and the U.S. grew by 4.0 percent, while the EC countries grew

---

2 *World Development Report 1989*, Published for the World Bank by Oxford University Press, 1989, p. 165.
3 *Economic Report of the President 1990* (Washington D.C.: U.S. Government Printing Office, 1990), p. 419.

by just 2.9 percent, widening the income gap between the EC and its competitors.

Even in manufacturing, an area where America is often portrayed (incorrectly) as performing poorly in the 1980s, the EC again failed to match the Asian or American performance. Industrial production between 1980 and 1989 rose by 41.8 percent in Japan, 30.9 percent in the U.S., and a paltry 16.6 percent in the EC.

Job creation in the EC also lagged behind its competitors and, as a result, unemployment remained high in most EC countries for most of the decade. The number of workers employed in the U.S. between 1980 and 1987 rose by 13.2 percent; employment in the EC increased by only 1 percent — and this was due entirely to expanding government bureaucracy. The total number of private sector jobs in the EC actually fell over the same period. This situation could worsen as the Europeans find themselves poorly positioned in many of the technologies of the present and the future, such as in advanced manufacturing, automated machine tools, computers, mass-produced electronics products, robotics, and semiconductors. Jobs in these countries could continue to shift to Pacific Rim countries, including America.

This combination of unfulfilled goals and lagging economic performance prompted the EC in 1985, under the leadership of its President, Jacques Delors of France, to embark upon an ambitious plan to transform what was little more than a customs union into a common market. To accomplish this, Britain's Lord Cockfield, then Commissioner for the Internal Market, led a task force whose goal was to identify the remaining barriers to full economic integration and recommend how to remove them. The task force's 1985 report, "Completing the Internal Market," proposed an array of new laws to remove barriers to commerce and harmonize standards on consumer goods and regulations on a variety of issues, including telecommunications and insurance.

To facilitate and speed the enactment of these laws, the Community members agreed in 1987 to the far-reaching Single European Act. This amended the 1957 Treaty of Rome to allow majority voting on issues before the Council of Ministers, a body comprised of the Foreign Ministers of each EC member state. Before this, unanimity was required for approval of Council of Ministers decisions, thus giving each member effective veto power.

Chapter 3

The terms "EC '92" or "Europe 1992" are derived from the Community's intention to have these laws in place by December 31, 1992. As of mid-July 1990, 164 of the 282 directives had been adopted by the Council of Ministers, the remaining 118 were still before the Council. Of the 164 directives adopted by the Council, only 19 were enacted by all the member countries by mid-July 1990.

Although these directives are expected to be in place by the end of 1992, as laws in each of the member countries, additional measures are planned to advance economic integration. Important items still under review and likely to be addressed in the remaining years of this century include the development of a common labor policy, a unified anti-trust policy, and greater coordination of monetary policies, including a common currency, and a centralized European Bank.

THE INSTITUTIONAL STRUCTURE OF THE EC

The EC's governing institutions consist of the European Commission, the Council of Ministers, the European Parliament, and the Court of Justice.

The Commission has the sole power to initiate and draft legislation, which must be approved by the Council of Ministers before becoming law. The Commission is comprised of seventeen commissioners appointed by the governments of the member states for four years. They are supposed to represent the EC rather than the national interests of their member state. The Commissioners also manage the EC's extensive bureaucracy of "Eurocrats," which is divided into 23 departments called Directorates-General (DG), each headed by a commissioner.

The Council of Ministers is made up of senior representatives from member countries. Its composition may differ from one meeting to another depending upon the issue under discussion. On tax issues, for example, the representative from France may be its Minister of Finance, but a meeting on farm policy would require attendance by the Minister of Agriculture. Until the passage of the Single European Act in 1987, each minister held veto power over legislation because of the rule requiring unanimity among Council members.

The European Parliament, which is directly elected by the citizens of the member states, has little substantive power but does serve an important advisory role. The Parliament has the opportunity to review legislation at least twice. Legislation always originates with the Com-

Promoting America's Economic Interests

mission, goes to the Parliament for review and comment, and then to the Council of Ministers for a final decision. If the Parliament rejects the Council's decision, then unanimous vote from the Council of Ministers is required to pass the directive. Therefore, the Parliament's vote can carry a great deal of weight depending upon the issue. For example, parliamentary concerns, backed by public pressure, forced the EC in 1988 and 1989 to increase restrictions on automobile exhaust emissions.

Most Commission legislation takes the form of either a directive or a regulation. Directives, which account for the majority of EC '92 legislation, actually define results to be achieved, but do not become law until introduced and enacted through the existing legislative processes in each of the member nations. Regulations, by contrast, are effective immediately throughout the Community and require no action on the part of a member. An example is EC regulation No. 763/90, imposing a provisional anti-dumping duty on imports of tungsten from China.

WHAT IS EC '92?

The proposals comprising EC '92 fall into two groups: those that enhance the economic potential of the EC, and those that will have the opposite effect by limiting competition or by increasing the regulatory burden on EC economies.

The directives that enhance commerce include those aimed at creating a common market. This would be done by reducing cross border impediments to commerce, particularly in the burdensome licensing requirements and regulation of airline and truck transport, and by a harmonization of technical and product standards. The European Committee for Electro-technical Standardization, for example, would develop a common set of technical and safety standards, which when met by a product, would allow it to be sold throughout the EC. Product standards are specifications that set forth "some or all of the properties of a product in terms of quality, purity, nutritional value, performance,

Chapter 3

dimensions, or other characteristics."[4] The purpose of standards is to ensure minimum levels of controls over products. Different sets of standards in each country can distort trade. The Netherlands' Phillips Industries N.V., for example, must make seven types of television sets to meet the different standards now existing in EC countries. For this, Phillips hires 70 extra engineers and spends $20 million more each year.[5]

Harmonizing product standards among EC members is a key goal of the EC '92 process; more than 80 of the 282 directives are for this purpose. Standard harmonization will mean that manufacturers will have to meet just one standard rather than twelve separate national standards. This reduces production costs, which in turn, should mean lower prices to consumers. Standardization, moreover, can increase competition by allowing smaller companies to expand into new markets without incurring the additional costs of modifying products to meet each individual country's specifications.

While standardization and harmonization likely will result in economic efficiency, they can also be used to suppress competition and stifle innovation. This can be done in a number of ways. First, if inflexible and difficult to modify, technical standards could be used to discourage the domestic manufacture of new and better products that do not conform to the existing standards and to keep such products from entering the country from non-EC countries. Second, if complicated or unclear, standards could hurt non-EC producers more than EC-producers. Third, if the EC does not recognize U.S. product testing on how, for instance, the product affects consumer health, safety, and the environment, American companies would have to test their products twice, in the U.S. and in Europe. This would increase costs to American manufacturers and make their products less competitive.

Another EC '92 improvement will be reducing barriers to the flow of capital across national borders. An EC banking directive, termed the Second Banking Directive, permits banks to establish branches and subsidiaries throughout the EC yet remain subject to the supervision

---

[4] "Definitions: Working Paper by the Secretariat," GATT documents, MTN/NTN/W/14, June 26, 1975, 5.
[5] Bruce Stokes, "High Tech Tussling, " *National Journal,* May 13, 1989, p.1183.

Promoting America's Economic Interests

of its home country. Once a bank obtains licensing in one EC member country, it would have the right to open up branch offices in all other EC countries. This means that money and capital can flow to wherever an advantage can be gained for investment and financing. As yet, there are no plans to standardize banking regulation, although a bank authorized to provide certain commercial banking activities in one EC state may also do so in other EC states. This will force all EC states to drop their restrictions on foreign commercial banking.

An early version of the banking directives had required something called "country reciprocity," meaning that the U.S. would have had to grant privileges in the U.S. to European banks which exceed those that American banks have in the U.S. in exchange for the benefits of the Europeans opening theirs. This would have put American banks at a disadvantage in gaining EC entry because of the many limits that U.S. regulations place on foreign and domestic banks and because of the extensive and vastly differing controls on banks by the 50 American states. After strong protests from the U.S. Treasury, the reciprocity requirement was dropped and American banks will now have full access to the EC market.

Initiatives that ease licensing requirements, eliminate trucking quotas that restrict country-to-country hauling, and partially deregulate aviation, will take effect by 1992. These will improve the EC transportation system enormously. They will move toward a common transportation infrastructure which will make shipping cheaper, faster, and smoother. Now, for example, a trucker transporting cargo from one country to another has to carry up to 35 different customs forms to be checked at the borders. This requirement, which wastes time and creates inefficiencies, will be eliminated by 1992. Similarly, airline fares will be regulated less and airlines will have better access to markets across national borders. EC carriers, for example, will be able to set their own fares beginning in 1993. Further, all the EC likely will be considered one country in the eyes of the law, which means that there will be no restrictions, for example, on a German airline flying from London to Liverpool.

Intellectual property rights are another area where EC proposals should encourage innovation and boost business. According to a March 1990 study by the Chamber of Commerce of the U.S.:

> Proposed EC initiatives will create Community-wide patents, trademarks, and trade secrets that will be simpler to obtain and

Chapter 3

recognized on a uniform basis throughout the twelve member states. Substantial harmonization of divergent patent and trademark laws will consequently result. These initiatives will reduce the cumbersome and expensive procedures faced by small businesses operating in several member states. The enormous legal expenses of such operations can be a deterrent for such companies expanding operations within the community.[6]

The EC's long-term goal of creating a single, competitive, telecommunications market also should produce significant economic benefits. The telecommunications market now consists largely of national monopolies of government-owned telephone companies, such as the West German giant monopoly, *Bundespost*, which charge high fees to consumers. Directives under consideration by the Council of Ministers in mid-1990 could lead to a common market for terminal and network equipment, plus telephone services. The EC also is requiring that postal, telephone, and telegraph administrations of EC states accept bids from other telecommunications companies. By removing restrictions, these changes will introduce competition, which will improve service and reduce costs to consumers. Eventually, EC members are expected to dissolve the state-owned telecommunications monopolies.

Not all of the effects of the proposed EC '92 directives, however, will be positive. There already are regulations, directives, and initiatives that could create more regulatory burdens and limit competition. The greatest risk is that the EC bureaucracy will grow too much and too powerful. While the Community's intention is for reform, history offers few examples of dynamic and innovative bureaucracies.

Until recently, the foreign ministers (or their representatives) of EC-member states could veto initiatives proposed by the European Commission. This is because Council decisions required unanimity among all EC members. The existence of such a veto could check bad government. But with the Single European Act in 1987, which replaces consensus with a "qualified majority" (a somewhat complex construct that is a bit more than a simple majority) on many significant issues, the balance of power has shifted away from national sovereignty toward

---

6   *Europe 1992: A Practical Guide for American Business* (Washington, D.C.: U.S. Chamber of Commerce, 1989), p. 61.

Promoting America's Economic Interests

European integration. Now countries are bound to decisions they might oppose.

Adding to this are the new powers accorded to the European Parliament by the Single European Act. This body, consisting of 518 popularly-elected members, has no direct legislative powers. Yet in its consulting and advisory capacities, the Parliament wields considerable influence. What poses a danger to economic growth is that a majority of the elected representatives to the Parliament are from leftist groups, especially the socialists, and communists. Added to these are the "Greens," who advocate an aggressive program of environmental regulation and reform. With the Greens, socialists, and communists holding a majority in the Parliament, the prospect is dim for legislation favoring free markets and enhancing commercial prospects. To date, these groups have used the Parliament's "bully pulpit" to expand costly environmental regulations, such as draconian limits on auto emissions.

If the EC uses its increased regulatory authority to impose very tough environmental regulations, EC commercial competitiveness will diminish as production costs rise and as firms are forced to add costly equipment to meet more rigid air and water quality standards. Example: legislation passed by the EC requires that chlorofluorocarbons, or CFCs, be reduced to 85 percent of their present levels as soon as possible and that CFCs be eliminated by the year 2000. This means that food producers will need to install in all their trucks a new freezing technique for foods. At the same time, the EC intends to establish the European Environmental Agency to assume some of the new environmental responsibilities, such as the power to monitor enforcement of costly and extensive regulations in such areas as controlling chemical pollution, and in petrochemical industries.

If the operations of this agency are comparable to the U.S. Environmental Protection Agency, these regulations could overwhelm and offset whatever positive benefits arise from the EC initiatives for deregulation. According to a 1989 study of regulatory trends in the U.S. economy, by the Harvard University Energy and Environmental Policy Center, the expansion of environmental regulations over the past two

Chapter 3

decades has impaired the economy significantly. The study finds that environmental regulation has cut American GNP growth a total of 2.5 percentage points from 1973 to 1985. This is equal to over 10 percent of the share of total government purchases of goods and services in the national product in the same time period.[7]

In addition to environmental initiatives, the new EC bureaucracy is likely to impose regulations covering workplace safety, energy conservation, and anti-trust, and to introduce a panoply of labor initiatives. For example, the charter of basic social rights, the so-called "social charter," under consideration by the EC Commission. If adopted, the "social charter" would enable the EC Commission to act as an international social welfare state. Labor's rights under the social charter would include "fair" wages, improvement of living and working conditions, social security, free association and collective bargaining, vocational training and education, equal treatment for men and women, consultation and participation for workers, health protection and safety at the workplace, protection of children and adolescents, and welfare for the elderly and disabled. While all of these surely are desirable goals, they could be quite costly and disruptive.[8] Companies will have to impose these extra costs on consumers. Another likely result of the adoption of the social charter would be increased unemployment as businesses cut back on employees to reduce costs.

A similar threat is posed by another directive that would make worker participation in management mandatory for companies with more than 1,000 employees. Called the "Company Law" directive, this would force EC businesses to allow workers to share in company decision-making. This could reduce the competitiveness of EC businesses. The reason: workers would be less willing to pursue risky business ventures that could result in layoffs, or where the pay-off for the investment is long term. Another directive on companies could

---

7 "Environmental Regulation and U.S. Economic Growth," Harvard University Energy and Environmental Policy Center Discussion paper, November, 1989.
8 The EC regulations would be at least as costly to the EC economy as the U.S. Occupational Safety and Health Administration (OSHA) is to the American economy. See for example, Steve Hanke and Stephen J.K. Walters, "Social Regulation: A Report Card, "The National Chamber Foundation, March 1990.

Promoting America's Economic Interests

limit takeovers by requiring a company to announce a takeover bid as soon as it decides to make a bid. Companies would lose the important element of surprise that is key to most takeovers.

The EC's proposed directive on public procurement could hurt American firms. This covers government purchases of products and services from privately-owned suppliers. These proposed regulations would permit the government agencies and state-owned enterprises of EC countries to refuse to purchase products made with less than 50 percent of materials produced within the EC. It also would allow a 3 percent price preference for EC suppliers, requiring foreigners to beat the EC supplier-price by more than 3 percent to be the winning bidder. This could penalize American firms that do not have an EC subsidiary. The NEC Corporation of Japan, for instance, stopped buying American-made chips for computer circuit boards assembled in Britain. NEC did this, it appears, to ensure that the local content requirements defined the computer chips as European-made so that they could be sold to EC government entities.[9] As a consequence, two U.S. semiconductor manufacturers lost multimillion dollar exports in the first quarter of 1989.[10] To be certain to circumvent these restrictions and sell to EC government entities, U.S. firms will have to establish EC-based subsidiaries.

The EC bureaucracy intends to promote advanced technology. To do this, the EC will create transnational government-business "partnerships" which will receive large sums of funds from both government and industry to promote certain sectors judged to be important future industries. According to the U.S. Chamber of Commerce's 1989 major survey of the EC '92 process:

> EC 1992 has spawned enthusiasm for government support of cooperative research, with the emphasis on providing the technology base that will enable European industry to become more self-reliant and competitive in world markets. Although not formally a part of the 1992 program, the Community has established a strategic R&D program to keep pace. Its R&D efforts

---

9   Local content requirements define an EC product versus a foreign product.
10 Stokes, *op. cit.*, p.1182.

Chapter 3

have two components: basic scientific research, and research stressing commercial applications . . . .
These R&D programs bring a large element of public subsidization to private industry, which holds potential for future U.S.-EC trade tensions.[11]

The EC research and development program is ambitious and costly, involving major cooperative efforts along several technological fronts. One of the chief vehicles is the European Research Coordination Agency (EUREKA), created in 1985 to develop commercial applications from basic research. It has fostered nearly 300 projects supported by business and government in such areas as biotechnology, energy, information technology, robotics, telecommunications, and most recently, in high-definition television (HDTV) and semiconductors.

In addition to EUREKA, other major government-business "partnerships" include Advanced Informatics in Medicine, a Biotechnology Action Program, Basic Research in Industrial Technology for Europe, Development of European Learning through Technological Advancement, European Strategic Program for Research and Development in Information Technology, European Research in Advanced Materials, and several others in nuclear fusion for commercial energy, transportation safety technology, and telecommunications. Tens of billions of dollars, half from government and half from industry, will be devoted to these and other programs in the next decade.

In its efforts to catch up to America and Japan in new technologies, the EC will rely heavily on government guidance, coordination and funding. By combining the resources of what it identifies as its best and its brightest, Europe will attempt to pick and foster commercial winners. Experience shows, however, that this almost always is a recipe for economic disaster. There is little evidence that government committees directing capital resources can "pick winners" better than the decentralized market. The U.S. government's program in the late 1970s to invest massive amounts of money to develop synthetic fuels, solar power, and look for other energy sources, for instance, has largely been

---

11 U.S. Chamber, *op. cit.*, p. 64.

Promoting America's Economic Interests

a failure because these industries have been uneconomical.[12] And the record of Japan's famed MITI is very spotty in picking industrial and export winners.

THE FREE MARKET REVOLUTIONS IN EASTERN EUROPE

In a year of unprecedented political upheaval, most Eastern Europeans have deposed their Communist leaders, started creating democratic institutions, established civil liberties, and begun the process of shifting their economies away from communism toward the free market.

For the typical citizen of Eastern Europe, socialism's failure was not an intellectual abstraction; it was the day-to-day deprivations that transformed a once-prosperous Central and Eastern Europe into a society with a Third World standard of living. Even basic products such as food were perpetually in short supply and of extremely low quality. Technological change came slowly, and wide-scale obsolescence characterized much of the industrial base.

The new leaderships in Eastern Europe have embarked upon the task of converting their failed, centrally-planned systems into market economies. Progress could be slow, painful, and halting if the transition is not pursued aggressively. One problem is that no blueprint exists for countries shifting to market capitalism from socialism.

Under the best of circumstances this will be difficult. Unlike British Prime Minister Thatcher – who in the 1980s turned the British Treasury from a deficit to a $15 billion surplus, and privatized $38.1 billion worth of over two dozen state-owned enterprises – the leaders of Eastern Europe lack well-defined property rights, a tradition of entrepreneurship, an extensive private sector, and commercial and financial markets. Most elements of a market system were destroyed two generations ago; their re-creation is one of the most urgent priorities confronting each of these countries. It took ten years for Thatcher to privatize two dozen state industries; Poland needs to privatize some 7,000 state-owned enterprises in much less time.

---

12 Bryan Johnson, "Managed Trade: Making America Less Competitive," Heritage Foundation *Backgrounder* No. 778, July 25, 1990, p. 9.

Chapter 3

Of the structural problems facing East European reformers, the most serious is the absence of property rights. No laws protect an owner from arbitrary seizure by the state or another citizen. No contract law exists to define what is owned or determine its lawful transfer. And no courts exist to enforce ownership or settle disputes. Absent property rights, individual entrepreneurs and foreign investors understandably are reluctant to make investments. Without well defined private property, a borrower can provide no meaningful collateral for loans to protect lenders and encourage investment. As a result, financial markets cannot be created and the savings of investors cannot make their way into capital investments.

Another structural problem is the absence of commercial codes. Without a uniform commercial code governing sales and contracts throughout the country, a businessman has no certainty regarding the enforcement of contracts. Commercial codes reduce this uncertainty significantly by providing rules for breaches of contract and for what rights or liabilities a breach creates in the parties to the contract.

Yet another problem is Eastern Europe's very high tax rates. They are hostile to enterprise. Even after Poland's "shock treatment," for instance, the turnover tax (a tax companies pay on all business) is a very high 20 percent on manufacturing. Firms have to pay a social security tax of 40 percent of wages, and corporate income taxes are a high 40 percent of taxable profits. Making matters worse, even in Hungary and Poland, where economic reforms are farther along than elsewhere in Eastern Europe, tax laws remain very arbitrary. It is unclear what taxes apply to what businesses. This drives underground a tremendous amount of economic activity in areas like retailing, transport, and light manufacturing. The absence of effective accounting systems and standards makes measures of income and profits open to wide interpretation and random taxation. Functioning financial systems such as banks and stock exchanges are also largely nonexistent, making it difficult to accumulate capital.

Added to these difficulties is the continuing role of the state planning bureaucracies which have spent the last four decades fixing prices, setting production quotas and allocating resources, including labor, to uses that not only fail to meet the needs of the citizens, but lead to goods that few buy. Even in Hungary, the state still controls 85 percent of the economy. Plans to reduce this share are still in the early stages of development and discussion.

Promoting America's Economic Interests

EAST EUROPEAN VERSUS WEST EUROPEAN ECONOMIES

	GNP (billions)	Growth (%)	Inflation (%)	Debt (billions)	Per Capita* Income ($)
EASTERN EUROPE					
Albania	3	5	—	5.6	1,265
Bulgaria	68	6.2	3	6.9	5,464
Czechoslovakia	158	1.6	.2	5.5	9,216
E. Germany	207	3.0	1.2	20.9	8,558
Hungary	88	1.6	15.6	18.6	2,297
Poland	268	4.5	57.7	39.2	1,677
Romania	126	2.9	—	3.2	2,764
Yugoslavia	58	1.5	260	19.8	1,183
Averages	122	3.3%	56.3%	15	$4,054
WESTERN EUROPE					
Austria	126	4.2	1.9	15	16,776
Belgium	153	3.9	1.2	29.7	14,926
Britain	826	4.4	4.9	101	14,996
Cyprus	4	6.9	3.5	1.4	6,109
Denmark	99	.3	4.5	44	20,940
Finland	105	4.5	5.1	30.3	21,004
France	940	2.3	2.7	63.5	17,003
Greece	53	1.2	13.5	20.5	5,244
Iceland	6	−2.4	37.5	1.1	23,560
Ireland	32	2.5	2.1	29.2	8,752
Italy	828	2.5	5.0	105	14,430
Luxembourg	8	3.0	1.6	.4	17,478
Netherlands	210	2.1	.7	16.5	15,371
Norway	90	1.5	.7	50	21,474
Portugal	41	3.5	9.6	18.5	4,061
Spain	344	7.9	4.8	32.3	8,721
Sweden	179	2.0	5.8	41.7	21,077
Switzerland	184	3.0	1.9	31	27,740
Turkey	64	3.4	75	36.4	1,209
W. Germany	1206	3.5	1.1	17.4	19,665
Averages	275	3.0%	9.2%	34.3	$14,996

All figures for 1988.

* All Eastern European figures are estimates, since no economically meaningful exchange rates exist between East European currencies and the U.S. dollar.

Sources: *The Military Balance 1989-1990*, (London: International Institute for Strategic Studies, 1990).

Report On Allied Contributions To The Common Defense, (U.S. Department of Defense, April 1990).

U.S. Chamber of Commerce.

Chapter 3

Central control poses another threat. The vast majority of the existing enterprise managers and state planners attained their positions for political reasons, rather than for their business and technical expertise. These planners are the very people whose livelihood is directly jeopardized by a shift to competitive markets and decentralized decision-making. As a result, they delay the transition process by creating obstacles or simply by refusing to act. In Hungary, for example, the government set out to privatize Budapest's restaurants, all of which were state-owned. Their efforts were thwarted by the Ministry of Industry and Trade, which managed to make buying the restaurants very unattractive or impossible for investors by setting impossible terms for transferring ownership.

Despite the numerous obstacles, historical experience from Chile to the Republic of China on Taiwan demonstrates that once an appropriate framework for a free-market economy is in place — such as private property rights, rule of law, commercial codes, and low taxes — economic growth follows. Chile, for instance, has decreased the number of state-owned enterprises from 500 in 1973 to 27 today. The Chilean government has privatized the social security system, eliminated consumer subsidies, freed prices and wages, and lowered customs duties by 15 percent. The result: a fourfold increase in labor productivity between 1970 and 1979, and an average annual economic growth rate of 5.8 percent from 1985 though 1987.

Important to the success of the Chilean program was the adoption of a number of reforms simultaneously, such as debt-equity swaps, lowering the deficit and inflation, and privatizing industries. Incremental reforms that free some sectors while leaving others subject to control actually may make things worse, or at least make the transition process more painful than necessary. In Poland, for example, the government lifted price controls but did not free the enterprises to increase production of goods and services. The result is that production has been stifled by burdensome business licensing and high taxes.

It is too early to tell whether Eastern Europe will become the next Southeast Asia or fall into the debt and stagnation of South America. In most East European countries there is reason for both pessimism and optimism. The bad news is that even though Hungary has been reforming its economy cautiously and incrementally for over two decades, its new leaders still talk of the need for a "social market economy."

Promoting America's Economic Interests

The good news is that, as the only East European country to have enacted a comprehensive commercial code, Hungary now benefits from major investments and joint ventures between Hungarian enterprises and firms from Western Europe, America, and Japan. Hundreds of joint ventures have been registered since 1988. Salgotarjan Glass Wool Ltd, a Japanese-Hungarian joint venture started plant operations in November 1989. Levi Strauss and Company, the American clothing manufacturer, owns 51 percent of a joint venture with a Hungarian firm and has doubled its employees' pay while making a profit. Western financial firms have rushed to start up investment funds in Hungary, including the Austro-Hungary Fund, First Hungary Fund, and the Hungarian Investment Co. As of July 1990, over $200 million in investment funds have been raised abroad for Hungary and five more funds are planned.

Hungary's privatization plan is taking shape with 38 companies as of July 1990 listed by the State Property Agency for the first round of privatizations. Hungary has set up a Western-style banking system, has the most advanced telecommunications system in Eastern Europe, slashed the state budget deficit by 80 percent, and cut rent and consumer subsidies. As the EC '92 process accelerates, Hungary, as a gateway to the EC for American and Japanese corporations, will benefit because the influx of capital and technology will increase the competitiveness of its companies.

After a year or so of cautious fits and starts, Poland by mid-1990 was adopting sweeping reforms – with successes and failures. By devaluing the currency, the *zloty*, by 35 percent, and pegging it to 9,500 *zlotys* to the dollar, Warsaw made the currency convertible in 1990. The money supply was drastically reduced in the first quarter of 1990. Inflation was brought down from 79 percent monthly in January 1990 to 3.4 percent monthly between May and June. The budget has been slashed, subsidies have been cut, and easy credit to state-owned enterprises has been reduced significantly. The elimination of many of the constraints on production, such as price controls and bureaucratic allocation of resources, has increased the supply of consumer goods, especially food.

The chief problem with the Polish program, designed largely by Harvard economist Jeffrey Sachs, is that it has plunged the economy into severe recession. The main reason is that the program has been overly concerned with controlling consumer demand, rather than with

Chapter 3

freeing supply and creating a climate that encourages economic dynamism. Taxes on business are too high, property laws unclear, business licenses still difficult to obtain, and by compelling businesses to pay a social security tax equal to 40 percent of an employee's wages, the government is making labor costs inordinately high. Consequently, Poland's private sector and market-oriented industries have been hurt the most by tight credit and falling demand. Though the large state-owned enterprises have had to cut back production, they can merely charge higher prices because it is irrelevant to them whether consumers purchase the goods or not.[13]

The rigid austerity program of Poland, designed specifically to stamp out hyperinflation, need not serve as a model for other Eastern European countries. A more sensible economic reform would free supply and encourage entrepreneurship and the formation of small businesses by lowering or eliminating taxes on business, enacting clear laws defining private property rights, lifting wage controls on the private sector, and making business licenses easily obtainable. In addition, East European governments immediately should privatize small transport and retail industries. Successful economic growth in Poland and elsewhere in Eastern Europe depends on the extent to which East European governments adopt these economic growth policies.

The Czechoslovak government is committed to a free market economy; however, its situation is different from the Polish. The Czechoslovak external debt is very low, the economy is comparatively stable, inflation was 3.4 percent year-to-year as of June 1990 (low even by Western standards), the country has a strong history in industry, and the living standards are high compared to most other East European countries. The country is dominated by huge, state-owned enterprises, which are nearly independent of weak state planners.[14] The first aim of the government is to disband the state monopolies by cutting off subsidies, tightening credit to the state sector, cutting the fat from the

---

[13] Anne Applebaum "Only Half a Revolution in Poland," *Wall Street Journal*, July 6, 1990.
[14] "No Third Way Out," interview with Vaclev Klaus, finance minister of Czechoslovakia, *Reason* magazine, June 1990, p.30.

state budget, and contracting the money supply. Privatization will begin in fall 1990. The long-term outlook for the country's economy is good; what must be done is to speed the economic reforms and improve the unattractive joint venture laws. Prague should establish clear rules for repatriation of profits and offer tax incentives for joint ventures.[15]

In Yugoslavia, the central government's tight monetary and fiscal policy launched in December 1989 has cut inflation from over 28,000 percent per month at the end of 1989 to less than 4 percent per month in July 1990. Sharp cuts were made in the 1990 budget. The Yugoslav currency, the *dinar*, is convertible and pegged to the West German Mark. Yugoslavia has better economic ties to the West than most other countries in the region. The government, however, has failed to institute free market structural reforms. It has neither established clear, unambiguous property rights, nor reformed the banking system, nor disbanded the workers' self-management system (which encourages risk-averse, short-term business strategies and inflationary increases in workers' pay). Volatile ethnic tensions, meanwhile, make the future of any economic reforms uncertain, because the prospects of armed conflict or the state expropriation of privatized enterprises increase considerably the risk of business investment.

Bulgaria and Romania are reforming economically more slowly than the other East Europeans. Romania's continuing political instability deters significant foreign investment. Bucharest unveiled a plan on June 28, 1990 that calls for wide-scale privatization and a market economy. Nevertheless, the economic outlook in Romania remains the bleakest in Eastern Europe. The per capita income is the lowest in Eastern Europe; fuel for home heating is sufficient only for a portion of the day, and food is strictly rationed.

Bulgaria is still a question mark because many analysts doubt the new socialist government's commitment to a rapid transition to a free market economy and because the political situation is still turbulent. On August 1, 1990, however, Bulgaria's Parliament elected Zhelyu Zhelev, the UDF leader, to the national presidency. This opens up the possibility that leaders of the UDF may take posts in the government. This could speed the transition toward a market economy, because the

---

15 Major changes in foreign investment laws are expected sometime in fall 1990.

Chapter 3

government may be able to better muster broad-based support for a more radical economic reform plan. As of August 1990, some 40 percent of prices were freed, some foreign trade was liberalized, and imports of consumer goods by individuals were allowed. Bulgaria has some long-term strengths, such as its relatively strong tourist and software engineering industries, and its recent agreement with the National Chamber Foundation, a free market research organization, to develop a radical and comprehensive program to guide the transition to a free market economy.

IMPLICATIONS OF EC '92 PROCESS FOR EASTERN EUROPE

The EC '92 process is likely to be a boon for Eastern Europe. Its emerging democracies will find it easier to integrate their economies with those of Western Europe as trade barriers are reduced and technical standards are harmonized throughout the EC market. The prospect of greater access to the world's largest market will serve as a powerful inducement to the East European countries to accelerate the economic reforms that eventually could make them eligible for membership in the EC. EC '92 also will force the East Europeans to adopt free trade policies if they want to be allowed to participate in the market.

The East European countries, meanwhile, will benefit from investment by companies seeking access to the EC. General Electric Corporation's acquisition of the Hungarian lighting manufacturer, Tungsram Company Limited, will allow it to compete in the EC lighting market more cheaply than if it had built a plant in France, for example, and hired costly expensive French labor. Such investment benefits the East European countries by bringing in capital, technology, and management skills at a much faster pace than would have been the case had they not been able to sell on the EC market.

The evolution of the EC in turn will be greatly affected by the liberation of Eastern Europe. Most East European countries had extensive trade with Western Europe before World War II. These countries are eager once again to form close economic ties with the West and the EC likely will allow greater access to its markets for these countries as a way of stimulating their economic development and of demonstrating political support for their democratic reforms. By "association agreements," the EC will grant the East European countries

Promoting America's Economic Interests

free entry into the EC for joint projects, while allowing East Europeans to protect their markets during a transitional period.[16] The association agreements also hold out the possibility for future free trade with the EC. Eventually they could lead to a free trade zone and, in the long-run, prove to be more economically beneficial for the East Europeans than membership in a heavily regulated, bureaucratic EC. East European countries could receive the benefits of free trade without having to comply with some of the more onerous EC social labor regulations.

The prospect of expanding to the East is strongly resisted by most EC members because it would weaken the nature of the tightly integrated community. At a Commission meeting in early summer 1990, EC President Jacques Delors said it would take 15 to 20 years for East European countries to be eligible for EC membership. Yet, in August 1990, British Prime Minister Thatcher called on the EC to declare unequivocally that it will accept East European countries as members as soon as democracy has been cemented and their economies transformed.

The EC countries of Southern Europe – Greece, Italy, Portugal, and Spain – already feel the pinch of competition from Eastern Europe, which offers an alternative investment opportunity to the EC Southern countries. The East European governments have begun to offer very attractive tax incentives to Western firms, such as tax free zones in Bulgaria, and tax allowances of up to 100 percent for businesses in the first three years of operation in Poland and first five years in Hungary. Hungary and Czechoslovakia, in particular, are well positioned to attract American and Japanese companies. Most analysts expect that the East European countries eventually will be granted free trade into the EC. This makes them prime locations for non-European firms that seek to gain access to the EC market. Wages are lower in Eastern Europe than Southern Europe's lowest-wage state, Portugal, and the work force is better educated. If, as is likely, the EC's Southern European countries deem the competition from the East too great, these countries will lobby the EC for protectionist measures against goods from the East.

---

16 "European Community Survey," *The Economist*, July 7, 1990, p.19.

Chapter 3

There is little reason, however, for concern that Eastern Europe will retard Southern Europe's economic growth by siphoning off Western investment funds. For one thing, there seems to be sufficient investment funds to go around. European corporations have posted especially high profits the past few years, while U.S. and Japanese firms are eager to break into the EC market by setting up subsidiaries. Some firms will choose to set up subsidiaries in Eastern Europe, others will opt for the benefits of the more advanced market conditions of Southern Europe. For another thing, in the long run, the competition will help Southern Europe because it will force these countries to liberalize their economies and to resist costly social and labor regulation that would drive business investment to Eastern Europe.

GERMAN ECONOMIC POWER IN THE NEW EUROPE

One Eastern European country has joined the EC already: East Germany. It became an EC member when Germany united in fall 1990. Even without East Germany, West Germany had boasted the most powerful and dynamic economy in Western Europe. The prospect of a German economic behemoth after reunification thus is a source of concern for many of Europe's peoples and leaders.

German reunification raises three central questions for European and U.S. leaders. First, what effect will reunification have on the German economy? Second, will a unified Germany dominate Europe economically? Third, how will reunification affect the future of the European Community?

The German Economy

It may be a cliche, but this makes it no less true, that the West German economy is the engine of European growth. Less well known is that approximately 30 percent of West German manufacturing by foreign companies, one-half of this by American firms.[17] These firms will profit if East Germany grows quickly and will suffer if the German economy stagnates because of the economic strains caused by reunification.

---

17 "The Wealth of a Nation," *Newsweek*, July 9, 1990, p. 31.

Promoting America's Economic Interests

The transition process now underway is creating a remarkable degree of dependency by the East Germans upon the guidance, good will, and financial resources of West Germany. Whereas the other East European countries will have to create indigenous sources of enterprise that will power the process of economic growth, the East Germans will be dependent upon the West Germans to provide it. Most economic policy decisions will be made in the West: Western managers, companies, and investors will dominate the economic transition and Western political leaders will continue to dominate the political parties. There seems to be a widespread feeling among East Germans that West Germany will and should bring prosperity to East Germans quickly and with a minimum amount of suffering.[18]

There are two possible economic scenarios for the impact of unification on the East German economy.

The first one is rapid, wide-scale unemployment, caused by the swift closings of East German companies, resulting in considerable political unrest and the resurgence of the Left throughout Germany. In this scenario, the West German government decides to appease the East Germans by offering expanded benefits and employment assurances to prevent a massive exodus to the West. The end result: an expansion of the bureaucracy, huge amounts of public spending for unemployment relief, and massive amounts of subsidies to keep prices low and to shore up the remaining East German state-owned enterprises. Such economic policies would damage the German economy. The West German economy is already saddled with the highest tax rates on business of any Western country, a giant, intrusive bureaucracy, an inflexible labor force (the result of very powerful unions), and voluminous rules and regulations on business. An expansion of state intervention in the economy would stifle entrepreneurial activity, increase inflation, discourage the flow of capital into East Germany, and the German economy would likely suffer a prolonged period of stagnation.

In the second scenario, East Germany's economic development could be driven by West German private capital and East German entrepreneurship. Start-up, small and medium-sized firms, financed by

---

18 "Survey: The New Germany," *The Economist*, June 30, 1990, p. 21.

Chapter 3

loans from West German banks, could spring up across East Germany. The absorption of 17 million East Germans makes the German economy stronger and more dynamic. Low-wage East Germans would help keep West German wages low and therefore keep Germany very competitive. This plus a tight credit policy from the German Central Bank would lower the purchasing power of East Germans and thus dampen inflation. In effect, this optimistic scenario envisions a second "German Economic Miracle."[19]

It is too early to predict which, if either, of these scenarios ultimately will take place. It is likely that, in the short-run, the heavy costs of unification — driving up German budget deficits from 19.2 to 100 billion Marks — will slow the West German economy. Much depends in the long run on the willingness of the West German government to resist political pressures to interfere with the economy.

The Unjustified Fear of German Economic Power

The prospect of increased German economic might causes great anxiety among many Europeans. British Prime Minister Thatcher convened a secret seminar with a group of historians in April 1990 to advise her on how to deal with a unified Germany. A memo from the historians to Thatcher discusses the fear that the dramatic changes in Europe in the past year "must by all means not mean that a united Germany would

---

[19] The first German economic miracle was ignited on July 21, 1948. On this date, the allies introduced currency reform by "tenthing" the money supply. Then, in July, disregarding the objections from the Allied military government supervising occupied Germany, Ludwig Erhard, a member of the German provisional governing council, removed most of the Allied economic controls, including wage and price controls and rationing. Within weeks, goods filled the formerly empty stores, business activity was rejuvenated, and job opportunities improved. Germany has been booming, almost without interruption, ever since. There are significant differences between post-war Germany and present-day East Germany. The institutional elements of a market economy were already present in Germany. They were simply handcuffed by Nazism, war, and allied economic controls. As soon as the controls were lifted, the institutions of a free market economy soon reappeared in Germany.

Promoting America's Economic Interests

now achieve by economic means what Hitler could not create by military means." Apparently similar views are held by several members of the British cabinet. Nicholas Ridley, British Secretary for Trade and Industry, was forced to resign from the cabinet in late July after making a number of provocative statements about a unified Germany and the EC in an interview with *Spectator* magazine. He said, for example, "... I'm not against giving up sovereignty [to the EC] in principle, but not to this lot. You might as well give it to Adolf Hitler, frankly."

Ridley is not alone in his views. According to an April 1990 poll of Britons conducted by Market and Opinion Research International, 50 percent of Britons fear that a unified Germany will become a dominant power in Europe, and 53 percent worry about a return to Nazism or Fascism. French fears of Germany are more of a military nature,[20] but economic fears exist in France too. Elsewhere in Europe, business leaders worry that German business strength will muscle them out of business. They evince the specter of the menacing German economic machine turning the East European countries into nothing more than low-wage sweatboxes for German industry.

While such worries are understandable, they are unjustified. There are already ominous signs, for example, that the East German economic reconstruction is being financed primarily by wealth transfer payments from the West German taxpayers to the East German citizens and industries. If this continues, then talk of German economic dominance will be muted as the German economy slows. The East German government is using subsidies to prop up inefficient agriculture and industry. West German Chancellor Helmut Kohl is likely to continue and even extend such subsidies until, at least, after the all-German elections on December 2, 1990. The Bundesbank, meantime, has had to increase interest rates to over 9 percent to counter greater than expected inflation.

---

20 France's defense spending is rising at the same time that the defense budgets of America and Britain are being cut. French President François Mitterrand has instructed his Defense Ministry to begin constructing the *Hades* nuclear missile, which, launched from France would land in Germany.

Chapter 3

The strong West German labor unions are assuming control over the East German unions. They are lobbying to guarantee the East Germans a 37-hour work week and five weeks of vacation each year.[21] Sharp pay rises, the result of union pressure, have occurred in a number of East German industries well before any increase in productivity has taken place. These pay rises will severely hurt East German firms, whose only competitive advantage over West Germans was very low wage costs. The increases in wages, coming before an increase in productivity, will bankrupt more East German enterprises and increase unemployment.

Also proving very harmful is the 1.8 to 1 conversion of the total money stock of East Germany (the market ratio is 6 to 1). As noted by economist Warren Brookes, "arbitrarily raising the value of the E-Mark priced the already uncompetitive inputs of the East German economy still further out of the world market."[22] This increases labor costs greatly and discourages foreign investment in East Germany. This then boosts unemployment and creates disincentives for entrepreneurship. Another distressing development is that already there is talk of imposing tariffs or import controls to protect East Germany's inefficient industries from foreign competition. Instead of the decade of German economic ascendancy in Europe, the 1990s could be the decade when socialism was transplanted from East Germany to a unified Germany.

Even assuming a more optimistic scenario — that after the all-German elections, the new German government turns things around, government subsidization of East Germany's transition is scaled back and increased economic and labor regulation is avoided — fears of German economic dominance, while understandable, are still irrational. West European countries worry about losing control over their national economies and about being economically dependent on the German economy as Latin America is on the U.S. economy. But, already, national markets are tied closely together by the international flow of funds and goods. German firms can borrow from Nebraska farmers on the Eurodollar market. Global financial integration

---

21 Peter Fuhrman, "Ludwig Erhard, where are you? *Fortune*, August 6, 1990.
22 Warren Brooks, "Could the tab revive socialism?" *Washington Times*, August 22, 1990, p.G2.

Promoting America's Economic Interests

through the development of the Euromarkets, means that billions of dollars, Marks, and yen can be shifted halfway around the world in a matter of minutes. Constrained by these global markets, governments have already lost much of the ability to pursue inflationary, economically destructive domestic policies.

Increased German economic growth will benefit rather than hurt the rest of Europe, especially Eastern Europe, because it will fuel the economic growth of Europe. It is estimated that the unification of Germany will mean that an additional $25 billion of goods will be imported in East Germany. With West German industry at nearly full capacity, this gives American, Asian, and European businesses the opportunity to increase exports to this expanded consumer market.

German growth would also transfer prosperity to Eastern Europe by bringing in capital, advanced technology, managerial expertise, and by fostering international trade. West German businesses are making very substantial inroads there. West German trade already accounts for two-fifths of the West's trade with Bulgaria, Czechoslovakia, Hungary, and Poland. West German capital is responsible for 30 percent of foreign capital in Hungary and 35 percent in Poland. Siemens A.G., the West German electronics group, has embarked on joint ventures in Czechoslovakia, Poland, and the U.S.S.R. The East Europeans desperately need this private investment.

The U.S. has nothing to fear from increased German economic growth. The U.S. economy is five times larger than Germany's. American firms, which own 15 percent of German manufacturing, will prosper as the German economy grows. Increased German economic power will also mean that Germany, rather than the U.S., will be called upon to bear the brunt of the aid burden to Eastern Europe.

Germany and the European Community

The framework of the EC is being redrawn to contain Germany. Apprehension over the future role of Germany in Europe is so great that European leaders are displaying schizophrenic tendencies. Fearing a resurgent, powerful independent Germany, EC member states hope, on the one hand, to bind Germany as closely as possible to the EC by increasing the EC's bureaucratic powers over Western Europe. Yet, at the same time, they fear that an economically preeminent Germany will dominate the EC. Britain, in particular, will likely try to

Chapter 3

hold on to its national sovereignty in economic and political matters, instead of handing over powers to an EC that is deemed dominated by Germany.

Thus far, there is no evidence that German unification will slow European integration by deterring Germany from its commitment to the EC. In fact, the government of Chancellor Kohl has called for accelerating the EC process. At a European Council meeting in Dublin, on April 28, 1990, Kohl and French President Mitterrand unveiled a series of proposals to hasten monetary union. They also pledged themselves to political union by 1993.[23] The German government also said that any investment breaks or subsidies given to West German businesses to induce them to set up operations in East Germany will be available to all EC companies.[24]

PROMOTING AMERICAN ECONOMIC INTERESTS IN EUROPE

America's greatest concern about the EC '92 process has been whether it will lead to a "fortress Europe," a vast trading bloc erecting barriers against foreign firms. American pressure already has blocked some protectionist EC directives, such as attempts to limit U.S. banks' access to the EC market. Other EC proposals are clearly beneficial, such as that conferring EC status on subsidiaries of foreign firms; this would allow them to compete on an equal footing with EC companies for government contracts. On the whole, indications now are that the EC does not intend to erect a wall of trade barriers around Europe. To be sure, some problems remain which need to be worked out. For example, EC limits on doing government business with foreign firms could limit opportunities of American firms, while the EC's heavily protected agriculture market hurts U.S. farmers. But so far there has not been a protectionist onslaught against U.S. economic interests.

Perhaps more important even than the U.S. stand against European protectionism will be the need for an American economic policy to deal with a Europe that is unifying economically. The steady march toward

---

23 Carola Kaps, "A United Germany in the New Europe," *Europe*, July/August 1990, p. 20
24 "Survey: The New Germany," *The Economist*, June 30, 1990, p.19.

economic and financial interdependence means that such European developments as high inflation in Germany or a severe recession in Britain increasingly will affect the policies that traditionally have been exclusively the domestic concerns of sovereign countries, such as fiscal and monetary policy.

To ensure that the U.S. is ready for European economic developments in the 1990s, the U.S. should:

♦♦ **Support the integration of free markets throughout all of Europe.** The reduction of trade barriers among the European states serves the long-term American interests of greater free trade world wide. For these reasons, as well as the desire to promote European cooperation for political purposes, the U.S. consistently has supported European economic integration since the end of World War II and strongly supported the establishment of the EC. The U.S., however, should not automatically support an EC that evolves into a giant, bureaucratic super-state. Instead, Washington strongly should back Britain or other governments that object to the bureaucratization and centralization of the European economies. Prime Minister Thatcher foresaw dangerous trends of the EC two years ago. She was correct when she said, "We have not successfully rolled back the frontiers of the state in Britain only to see them reimposed on a European level, with a European super-state exercising a new dominance from Brussels."

Proposals to further reduce trade barriers, such as increased cooperation between the six nations of the European Free Trade Association (EFTA)[25] and the EC should also be encouraged. And U.S. influence in Western Europe should be used to eliminate protectionist policies which hurt the struggling economies of Eastern Europe. A truly continental market open to the outside world not only would open markets between East and West, but also would expand opportunities for U.S. businesses.

♦♦ **Guard against EC discrimination against U.S. products.** Even as it supports the creation of a continental European market, Washington should ensure that European economic integration con-

---

25 The six nations of EFTA are Austria, Finland, Iceland, Norway, Sweden, and Switzerland.

Chapter 3

tinues not to be used to erect market barriers against U.S. products. Through mid-1990, at least, few EC directives and regulations were protectionist. Future regulations may be. Thus Washington must remain vigilant in monitoring EC proposals. France, for instance, is pushing to require that 60 percent of EC television network programming originate from EC countries. This is naked protectionism.

The U.S. has a variety of tools to counter protectionism if it should occur. One is the threat of trade retaliation against EC protectionism. It already has worked. The threat of a destructive trade war with the U.S. and Japan has forced the EC to modify earlier protectionist directives and continues to exercise great influence over pending legislation. Threatening trade retaliation, however, is very risky. If Europe does not back down, then the retaliatory measures taken by the U.S. will hit American consumers in the form of higher prices for goods. A threat of economic warfare also raises the danger of large competing trade blocs emerging and engaging in super trade wars.

The best tool to deter the rise of EC protectionism is for Washington to press for free trade agreements, like the U.S.-Canada Free Trade Agreement signed on July 2, 1988. Free trade agreements would induce the EC to open its market in exchange for market openings in the free trade areas. They also would be an incentive for the EC to join the free trade agreements to take advantage of the removal of barriers to trade.[26] America should offer bilateral free trade agreements to individual East European countries and negotiate a free trade arrangement with the EFTA countries as well. If Britain continues to have problems with the EC, the U.S. could offer Britain complete participation in the U.S.-Canada free trade pact, which, within a few years, could extend to Mexico.

♦ ♦ **Press the EC to dismantle its protectionist Common Agriculture Policy.** The EC's Common Agriculture Policy (CAP) is a series of policies restricting farm imports to EC countries and granting export subsidies to EC farmers. Foreign imports are limited to those agricultural goods whose demand cannot be fulfilled at a given time by EC domestic producers. These heavily protectionist policies hurt farmers

---

26 Edward L. Hudgins, "Free Trade Areas: Removing Trade Obstacles and Bucking Protection," Heritage Foundation *Backgrounder*, No. 582, June 17, 1987, p.5.

Promoting America's Economic Interests

from agricultural exporting nations all over the world, including the U.S., by restricting access to the EC, the world's largest market. Export subsidies also distort the world's agricultural markets. The biggest loser is the European Community's taxpayers and consumers. It costs EC taxpayers $44 billion and EC consumers $54 billion each year. The beneficiaries are the approximately 10 million EC farmers who are only 7.5 percent of the EC's work force.

The CAP will severely hurt the fledgling free-market democracies in East Europe. Throughout history, interrupted only by the Cold War, Eastern Europe has been a prominent supplier of food for Western Europe. Now, the East Europeans are looking to resume this relationship. The best form of aid the EC could give the East Europeans would be to dismantle the CAP and remove other trade barriers to their goods.

Hurt also by the CAP have been efforts to negotiate a new global treaty liberalizing trade – the so-called Uruguay Round of GATT negotiations. At these talks, the developing nations have balked at approving the new trade agreements in services and intellectual property rights sought by the West unless the EC and other industrial countries remove trade barriers to agricultural imports and end farm export subsidies. So far, the EC has not committed to eliminate CAP's import barriers or export subsidies.

It is time, therefore, for a full U.S. assault on CAP. For one thing, the political clout of EC farmers is declining as their numbers fall. For another, CAP can be portrayed as a danger to the environment. Writes the *Economist*, the CAP "artificially raises the returns on particular crops and thus encourages their cultivation in a manner that spoils the countryside."[27] The U.S., along with Australia, Canada, the East European nations, and other countries should appeal to the EC consumers and environmentalists, urging them to oppose the CAP. The U.S. also should encourage Thatcher to continue speaking out against the CAP.

♦♦ **Remove trade barriers to Eastern Europe and press the EC to do also.** Enormous amounts of foreign assistance are pouring into Eastern Europe ostensibly to help these countries revive their

---

27 "Farm Support Under Siege," *The Economist*, July 14, 1990, p.14.

Chapter 3

economies and transform them into free markets. The best way of helping these economies, however, is to reduce obstacles to their exports. The U.S. thus should remove trade barriers to Eastern Europe as these countries liberalize their economies and foreign trade laws. This can be done by removing: all quotas on apparel, textile, and steel; oil import fees on petroleum products (almost all of it from Romania); and tariffs on East European goods.

As the largest market in the world, and one that actually borders on Eastern Europe, the EC obviously plays a key role in promoting free trade in Eastern Europe. Many of the East European countries hope someday to join the EC as full members. Although none of the economies in the region are close to meeting the minimal standards for admission, they may become eligible by the end of the century. The West Europeans could accelerate economic growth in Eastern Europe by removing barriers to East European exports. Instead of waiting for EC membership, the East European nations should form a regional association and begin negotiating an agreement with the EC similar to that being negotiated by the European Free Trade Association (EFTA) and the EC. Called the European Economic Space, this agreement will give EFTA countries full access to the EC market, and vice versa. A similar agreement would help East European countries.

◆◆ **Encourage and assist East European free market reforms.** The political revolutions that toppled the communist regimes in Eastern Europe should be followed by an economic revolution installing free market systems. To assist this, there are some things America should not do. It should not be tempted, above all, simply to give the East European governments money. The record of the past four decades proves that economic foreign assistance of this kind creates a dependency that reduces the incentive of recipient countries to institute free market reforms. The U.S. thus must not give Eastern Europe government-to-government aid. The East Europeans, after all, need to depoliticize their economies. But foreign aid increases the politicization of the economy because the money tends to go to groups or individuals who wield political power.

What America should do is tailor its assistance to encourage establishing secure property rights and an independent judiciary, an end to government monopolies, free prices and wages, minimal government regulation of the private sector, lower taxes, establishing convertible currencies, privatizing industries, and attracting foreign investment.

Promoting America's Economic Interests

American assistance should be conditioned upon the recipient countries moving quickly on these reforms.

In place of government-to-government financial aid, meanwhile, the U.S. should create "enterprise funds." The SEED Act of 1989, in which Congress approved economic and technical assistance to Hungary and Poland, created Hungarian-American and Polish-American Enterprise Funds. These are governed by a board of directors comprised of private citizens of the U.S. and the host country. The funds provide money directly to the private sector to promote entrepreneurship and joint ventures. While it is doubtful whether U.S. government subsidization is needed to encourage entrepreneurship, enterprize funds nonetheless are a better way of giving aid than through government-to-government payments.

♦ ♦ **Reduce debt burdens on East European countries through the use of debt-equity and "e-swaps."** The East European countries have accumulated an over $116 billion hard currency debt to Western banks and governments. Interest payments on this are equal to approximately 15 percent of convertible currency exports of their countries.[28] East European economic growth will be slowed by this debt burden. To lighten it, Washington should encourage Western creditors and the East European countries to engage in debt-equity swaps to help to reduce the debts of the East European countries. In debt-equity swaps, "the lender (such as a West German bank) sells its hard currency debt at a discount to a middleman. The middleman then redeems the debt from the debtor country's government for local currency or some state-owned asset, such as shares in a factory. The lender thereby recovers part of a loan that unlikely would be repaid in full; the middleman becomes an investor in the local economy; and the debtor government's external debt is reduced."[29]

E-swaps are like debt-equity swaps except that the equity in the state-owned enterprises is sold to workers — rather than corporations and investors — through employee stock ownership plans. The reduc-

---

28 *Building Free Market Economies in Central and Eastern Europe: Challenges and Realities*, The Institute of International Finance, Inc., April 1990, p. 21.
29 Douglas Seay, "How George Bush Can Help Lech Walesa Succeed," Heritage Foundation *Backgrounder*, November 9, 1989, p.11.

Chapter 3

tion of East European debt through debt-equity and e-swaps will attract foreign investment funds, speed the privatization of state-owned industries, and finance new export-oriented investments. Primarily through the use of debt-equity swaps, Chile has retired $17.6 billion in foreign debt since 1985. By 1987, Chile's debt conversion program attracted over $600 million in investment from New Zealand and $250 million in investment from both the Republic of China on Taiwan and South Korea.[30]

♦ ♦ **Support lower trade barriers between North America and Europe and establish a North Atlantic Free Trade Area.** As the two largest markets in the world, North America (including the U.S., Canada, and Mexico) and Europe have strong interests in promoting economic cooperation between themselves. At present, however, each has been concentrating on creating a continental market. In North America, the U.S. and Canada concluded their 1988 free trade agreement and negotiations are underway for a similar agreement between the U.S. and Mexico, which could be expanded to embrace Central America and the Caribbean. For its part, the EC has concentrated on its own EC '92 project and is likely to expand its cooperation with other European states presently outside of the EC.

The waning of the Cold War may result in a loosening of U.S. political ties to Europe, but America's economic interests there will increase. As such, Washington should lead in forming a North Atlantic Free Trade Area. Building on the close ties that already exist, the U.S., along with Canada and possibly Mexico, should take the initiative in creating a free trade area that includes North America, the EC members, EFTA, and the newly-freed East European countries. A major advantage of this to the U.S. is that it blunts whatever protectionist pressures may emerge in a more narrow EC. For the Europeans, such an arrangement would give them the opportunity to rethink some of the more commercially-restrictive measures which have been proposed by the EC Commission. Moreover, the European countries may find that an arrangement that includes the U.S. could balance the

---

[30] Steve H. Hanke, "The Anatomy of a Successful Debt Swap, " in Hanke, ed, *Privatization and Development* (San Francisco: ICS Press, 1987), pp. 166-167.

greater influence within Europe of a more economically powerful and politically influential united Germany.

CONCLUSION

The reunification of Germany, Eastern Europe's transition to market economies, and the removal of trade-distorting barriers between EC member countries are making an economic revolution in Europe. The transition of East European countries to free market economies should help fuel Europe's economic expansion. The East European countries offer well-educated, low-wage workers; their pent-up consumer markets should offer substantial business opportunities. There is the danger, however, that half-way economic reforms and Western largesse, in the form of massive amounts of foreign aid, could turn Eastern Europe into another Latin America weighed down by staggering debt and political turmoil.

German reunification, meanwhile, raises three central questions for European and U.S. policy makers. First, what effect will reunification have on the German economy? Second, will a unified Germany dominate Europe economically to the detriment of the rest of Europe? Third, what effect will reunification have on the German economy?

The costs of unification could top 1 trillion *Deutschemarks* (over $600 billion), in the next decade. This probably will slow the West German economy. In the long-run, however, if the West German government resists propping up uneconomical East German state-owned industries and creating a permanent welfare class out of the East Germans, then the human capital and economic dynamism from the addition of 17 million East Germans should increase the might of the German economy. This will provide a strong engine of growth to drive Europe. Germany will offer an expanded market for EC suppliers, and give needed technology, managerial expertise, and capital for Eastern Europe.

If the EC '92 project is executed in a genuine free-market manner then it could indeed spur a prolonged European economic revival. If it is not, it will exacerbate the stagnation that has afflicted Europe through much of the 1980s. Although the process of harmonization of standards and laws and the creation of a truly common market should boost economic efficiency significantly, these savings could be reduced

Chapter 3

greatly by the inefficiencies from increased bureaucracy and regulation. The principal threat to economic growth in Europe in the 1990s will not come from America or Asia. It most likely is to come from extravagant, statist policies pursued by the Eurocrats in Brussels.

Given its clear political and security interests in Europe, as well as the EC's emergence as the world's largest market, America has a major stake in the evolution of Europe's economy. U.S. policy should promote free trade and free markets in Europe. This can be accomplished by supporting the integration of free markets throughout all of Europe, opposing EC discrimination against American business, strongly pressing the EC to dismantle its protectionist Common Agriculture Policy (CAP), supporting lowering trade barriers between North America and Europe, and eventually establishing a North Atlantic Free Trade Area.

America further can encourage free markets in Europe by removing American trade barriers to Eastern Europe and encouraging the EC to do likewise, assisting the East Europeans in free market reforms, and reducing the debt burdens on East European countries through the use of debt-equity swaps.

Just as military and political changes in Europe are creating new challenges for American foreign policy, economic changes in Europe are creating challenges and opportunities for American economic policy. America should support changes that will lead to a freer market in Europe. A prosperous Europe, better able to purchase American goods and supply quality products to American consumers, is in the interests of America. A Europe overburdened with regulation and bureaucracy in the West and floundering in the face of half-way economic reforms in the East is not.

Chapter 4

Orchestrating Retreat: Moscow in the Changing Europe of the 1990s

Leon Aron

The East European revolutions of 1989 and domestic political upheavals within the Soviet Union have forced Moscow to reassess its strategy toward Europe. This reassessment comes as a result of fundamental weaknesses in the communist regime and four decades of an American and Western strategy of containing Soviet power in Europe. Today, the Soviet Union is a power in retreat.

Even in decline, however, the Soviet Union continues pursuing some longstanding strategic objectives, such as gaining access to Western capital and technology. Yet other objectives, such as achieving unchallenged military superiority, apparently are being modified substantially to accommodate changing circumstances. As Moscow's strategy in Europe attempts to adapt to changing circumstances, America's counter-strategy must adapt as well.

Today, Moscow is forced to pursue its objectives in a much different Europe than even a year ago. The 1989 democratic revolutions in Eastern Europe have put pressure on Moscow to reduce drastically its military forces stationed there. The rapid deterioration of the Soviet economy, bordering on collapse, threatens to spark mass public unrest

Chapter 4

and even unseat the regime. Powerful secessionist movements in the non-Russian republics, especially in Azerbaijan, Estonia, Georgia, Latvia, Lithuania, and Moldavia, threaten the very existence of the Soviet Union. Even the Soviet Union's largest republic, Russia, has gone its own way under the leadership of Boris Yeltsin.

These developments, along with the unification of Germany, have made Moscow's diplomatic and military position in Europe more uncertain and precarious than it has been at any time since World War II. Facing this predicament is a new, post-Stalin generation of Soviet leaders more attuned than their predecessors to the world outside Soviet borders and with a far more realistic idea of how little the West really threatens the Soviet Union.

These leaders, led by Mikhail Gorbachev, have crafted a strategy that seeks, though may not necessarily attain, an orderly retreat and the maintenance of a secure and influential role for the Soviet Union in a new Europe. Gorbachev's first priority surely is to attempt to use Western Europe's vast economic resources to alleviate consumer misery in the Soviet Union, produce exports other than raw materials, and modernize the thoroughly obsolete Soviet economy. Moscow will try to capitalize on favorable public opinion in Western Europe to collect its own "peace dividend," in the form of credits, technology, and managerial skills for the Soviet economy. Gorbachev will continue to push his "common European home" propaganda campaign as a means of harnessing the economic potential of a united Europe, while seeking to eliminate or weaken controls over Western high technology exports to the U.S.S.R.

Politically, Moscow is likely to try to mitigate the effects of a disintegrating Warsaw Pact by turning it into a political organization, dominated by Moscow, and by using it to maintain Soviet influence in Europe. He also is sure to continue a public diplomacy campaign aimed at driving a wedge between Western Europe and the United States and, finally, will seek Western Europe's tacit acquiescence to Moscow's attempts to keep rebellious Soviet republics inside the Soviet Union.

While Soviet military power in Europe is bound to decline with the disintegration of the Soviet empire, Moscow will try to remain the single strongest military power on the continent. In pursuit of this, the Soviet Union will seek to weaken NATO by "de-coupling" the U.S. and its European allies and denuclearizing Western Europe.

Orchestrating Retreat

To deal with changing Soviet policy in Europe, the U.S. needs a changed strategic plan. Where Soviet designs are detrimental to the security of U.S. allies, as in the case of weakening NATO, the U.S. should not hesitate to thwart them. Where Soviet policies could help advance U.S. interests in Europe, such as in reducing conventional forces, these opportunities should be explored. The U.S. should:

♦ ♦ **Counter Gorbachev's idea of the "Common European Home."** The U.S. should respond by announcing plans for a "Common Democratic Home," which would include all democratic European Nations west of the Soviet border plus the U.S. and Canada.

♦ ♦ **Counter Soviet propaganda and public diplomacy campaigns aimed at alienating Europe from the U.S.** As Moscow tries to persuade the Europeans that America does not belong on the continent, the U.S. should counter by providing the Europeans with truthful information about U.S. policy through such outlets as the Voice of America and Radio Free Europe.

♦ ♦ **Rebuff Soviet attempts to slow democratic change in Eastern Europe and inside the Soviet Union in the name of "stability."** In response to the professed Soviet fears of "instability" the U.S. should tell Moscow that it, too, is interested in "stability," but a genuine stability based on radical, albeit peaceful, change toward democracy and free markets.

♦ ♦ **Prevent Gorbachev from using the Conference on Security and Cooperation in Europe (CSCE) to slow democratic change inside the Soviet Union, especially in non-Russian ethnic republics.** Instead, the CSCE review conferences should be used to press for Moscow's compliance with the 1975 Helsinki Final Act, which declared every people's right to determine freely their "internal and external political status."

♦ ♦ **Preserve the Coordinating Committee for Multilateral Export Controls (COCOM).** COCOM is a Western organization that controls exports of militarily significant technology to the Soviet Union and its allies. It consists of all NATO members, except Iceland, and includes Australia and Japan.

♦ ♦ **Develop criteria to measure political and economic changes in the Soviet Union and press the allies to adopt them as a guide in their relations with Moscow.** Criteria would include Moscow's resolving peacefully its nationalities crisis and expanding such basic human rights as freedom of religion and freedom of the press, and ending

Chapter 4

support for anti-Western communist regimes in the Third World, including Afghanistan, Angola, and Ethiopia.

♦ ♦ **Be prepared to deal with the consequences of a hard-line military or KGB coup d'etat in the Soviet Union, which could lead to the establishment of an aggressive anti-Western "national salvation" regime.** The establishment of such a regime could result in a slow-down or a halt in the withdrawal of Soviet troops from Eastern Europe, or even in an attempt to re-establish Soviet political control over Eastern Europe.

THE NEW CONTEXT OF SOVIET EUROPEAN POLICY

The East European Revolution

Moscow today faces not only a different Europe, but a different Soviet Union. New political, economic, and military realities have emerged and will continue to influence both the objectives of Soviet European policy and the means of attaining them.

The breakdown of Soviet-installed communist regimes in Bulgaria, Czechoslovakia, East Germany, Hungary, Poland, and Romania has undermined Kremlin control over Eastern Europe and even called into question its ability to wield any influence there. As the East European states test the limits of their newly-gained independence, the main instruments of Moscow's domination are unravelling and could disappear altogether. These include: the Warsaw Pact a Soviet-controlled military "alliance," and the Council for Mutual Economic Assistance (COMECON), an economic body created by Moscow to promote its economic interests in Europe.

Control Over the Warsaw Pact

Since its creation in 1955, the Warsaw Pact was used to legitimize Moscow's military occupation of Eastern Europe and to ensure its military superiority in all of Europe. The Pact also advanced Moscow's political and economic agendas in Europe: the presence of over half-a-million Soviet troops in Eastern Europe made it difficult for Western Europe to ignore Soviet preferences.

The strategic role played by the Warsaw Pact in Soviet European strategy will be seriously weakened and perhaps even eliminated in the

Orchestrating Retreat

near future. Czechoslovakia and Hungary in early 1990 extracted agreements from Moscow to withdraw all Soviet troops from their territories by July 1, 1991. The leader of the Polish Solidarity movement, Lech Walesa, presented the Soviet Ambassador to Poland with an identical demand on January 18, 1990.

Perhaps more important is the rapid disappearance from the European scene of the single pro-Soviet entity called "Eastern Europe," which for over four decades has been a key factor in intra-European affairs. As Moscow began to disengage from Europe in summer 1989, it appeared willing to give up direct control over Eastern Europe, while trying to hold onto a dominant political position in the region. Yet the independent policies of Czechoslovakia, Hungary, and Poland have made it impossible for Moscow to retain control over the foreign and national security policies of Warsaw Pact members.[1] As Soviet journalist Alexandr Bovin said in January 1990, "[East] bloc discipline will weaken, diminishing the ability of the Soviet Union to influence European affairs."[2]

Changes in COMECON

The Council for Mutual Economic Assistance was imposed by Moscow on Eastern Europe in 1949 for two reasons: 1) to utilize the region's resources to rebuild the post-World War II Soviet Union; and 2) to tie East European economies and trade to Moscow. In addition to the Soviet Union, COMECON includes Bulgaria, Czechoslovakia, Cuba, East Germany, Hungary, Mongolia, Poland, Romania, and Vietnam. The organization today is under assault by virtually all its Eastern European members.

Immediately prior to COMECON's January 9, 1990, meeting in Sofia, Czechoslovak Finance Minister Vaclav Klaus proposed abolishing the Council altogether, while Polish Trade Minister Marcin

---

1 For an analysis of the reasons Moscow's withdrawal from Eastern Europe, see Leon Aron, "Gorbachev's Brest-Litovsk: The Kremlin's Grand Compromise in Eastern Europe." Heritage Foundation *Backgrounder* No. 724, August 15, 1989.
2 Alexandr Bovin, "Perestroika mezhdunarodnykh otnosheniy — puti i podkhody" ("Restructuring of international relations — ways and approaches"), *MEMO*, January 1989, p. 66.

Chapter 4

Swiecicki argued that COMECON was outdated and had to be replaced by some other structure. Hungarian Deputy Prime Minister Peter Medgyessy meanwhile proposed establishing an inner working group within COMECON consisting of the three most democratic member nations: Czechoslovakia, Hungary, and Poland. Such a group could serve as the nucleus of a future economic community of East European democracies from which the Soviet Union could be excluded.

While the disintegration of the Warsaw Pact will diminish Moscow's ability to carry out its European policies, weakening of the Soviet Union's COMECON ties and obligations may benefit the U.S.S.R. It could save, for example, some of the estimated $11 billion to $15 billion a year in Soviet economic subsidies to Eastern European economies. These subsidies normally are supplied as raw materials, especially oil and gas, at prices below those charged on the world market. Moscow exported 75 million tons of crude oil to Eastern Europe in 1988. Were the Soviets to reduce oil exports to the region, great quantities could be sold to Western Europe and elsewhere, for hard currency.[3]

As Moscow insists on hard currency payments from East Europeans for its oil, instead of the ruble, Eastern Europe will begin to run huge trade deficits with Moscow; perhaps as much $10 billion per year according to some calculations.[4] Thus, the Soviet Union is likely to acquire its own "oil weapon" which it could use to regain a measure of control over its former satellites. It could threaten, for example, to cut off oil supplies unless East European countries support Soviet policies in Europe. This, in fact, is what it did to Lithuania in spring 1990.

The Soviet Economic Crisis

The troubled Soviet economy has played a key role in determining Soviet foreign policy for four decades. During times of economic turmoil, for instance, the need for Western capital and technology

---

[3] Hard currency is money such as U.S. dollars or German marks which can be used in international transactions. The ruble, which cannot be used in such transactions, is not a "hard" currency, because it is not convertible on the international market.
[4] Dr. Jan Vanus, chief economist for PlanEcon, as quoted by *The New York Times*, January 10, 1990.

dictated a soft Soviet line toward the West. Today, more than at any time in the past, the disastrous state of the Soviet economy is dictating a relaxation of tensions with the West in hopes of gaining economic assistance.

Official Soviet reports estimate that 1989's economic growth was 1.7 percent — the lowest since the end of World War II — and Soviet economists point out that this figure does not take into account inflation, which in 1989 may have been as high as 20 percent for certain categories of products. In the meantime, during January and February 1990, the Soviet gross industrial output fell 1 percent, which means an estimated annual drop of between eight and ten percent.[5]

The Soviet annual budget deficit stands at 165 billion rubles, or nearly 15 percent of the Soviet gross national product (GNP). There is no accurate exchange rate for the ruble into dollars because Soviet prices are arbitrarily set. Still, the U.S. federal deficit, which last year was $152 billion, is only 3 percent of U.S. GNP. Meanwhile, there are too many rubles in circulation and not enough goods for them to buy. As a result, according to Deputy Chairman of the State Commission for Economic Reform Andrei Orlov, "The consumer market in the USSR has collapsed."[6] Today, 95 million Soviet citizens, or nearly one-third of the population, are below the official poverty line of 120 rubles per month, $8 by the market exchange rate.[7] The number of unemployed is estimated by Western scholars to be 5.6 million, or 4.3 percent of the total work force.[8]

The Soviet Union faces a major energy crisis as a result of the inefficiency of the socialist economy, near-exhaustion of oil reserves (in large part due to massive energy exports in the 1970s), and a dearth

---

5   *Izvestia*, March 12, 1990 and *The New York Times*, March 15.
6   *Report on the USSR*, Vol. 2 (10), March 9, 1990.
7   *Moscow News*, March 11, 1990.
8   I. Adirim, "A Note on the Current Level, Pattern and Trends of Unemployment in the USSR." *Soviet Studies*, Vol. XLI (3), July 1989, p. 449.

Chapter 4

of up-to-date equipment. Oil production declined in 1989 by 17 million tons, or almost 3 percent of the 1988 yield.[9] By 1995, the amount of oil extracted from Western Siberia, the Soviet Union's major oil producing region, is expected to fall by 25 percent.[10] Using today's technology, the Soviet Union will be able to extract no more than 35 percent of the oil sources it needs in the year 2000 for domestic consumption and exports.[11]

The Soviet economic crisis has been aggravated by the past decade's drop in world oil prices. Oil sales account for the largest share of Moscow's hard currency earnings. According to official Soviet estimates, Moscow earned $176 billion in oil revenues during the 1970s. However, since 1986, the Soviet Union lost over $60 billion because of depressed oil prices.[12] This deprives the U.S.S.R. of the hard currency to buy grain and virtually anything of quality abroad, from disposable syringes to steel pipes. Higher oil prices caused by the Iraqi invasion of Kuwait, however, should alleviate this problem somewhat and bring Moscow more hard currency. Meanwhile, Soviet dependence on imports has continued to grow. According to *Kommunist*, the main theoretical magazine of the Central Committee of the Soviet Communist Party, every third loaf of bread in the Soviet Union is now made from imported grain.[13]

Gorbachev's timid economic reforms have made a bad situation close to intolerable. Caught in the no-man's land between a fully state-controlled economy and a truly free market, the Soviet economy is collapsing. Shortages have extended beyond such Soviet "luxury"

---

9   Egor Gaidar, "Trudniy vybor" ("The hard choice"), *Kommunist*, 2 (January), 1990, p. 23.
10 Leslie Dienes, "Energy: From Bonanza to Crisis," *Report on the USSR*, Vol. 1, No. 48, 1989.
11 *Ibid*.
12 V. Katasonov, "Ne neftiu edinoy" ("Not by oil alone"), *Literaturnaya Gazeta*, March 1, 1989.
13 "Sverim tsifry" ("Let's compare the figures"), *Kommunist*, 10 (October), 1989.

items as television sets, furniture, shoes, and toilet paper to toothpaste, sugar, and potatoes. Soap now is rationed at 4.7 ounces per month per person, or less than a single bar.[14] One of the key demands of striking Soviet coal miners in summer 1989 were a towel and 30 ounces of soap per month. In a letter to the main government newspaper *Izvestia* on January 30, 1990, a reader from Siberia's largest scientific and industrial center, Novosibirsk, writes that ration coupons were introduced last year "for all family members for all products."[15] Even potatoes, long a Russian staple, are rationed.[16] Headlined *Izvestia* on page one in November 1989: "Will there be enough potatoes this winter?" One result of the shortages is food riots.[17] The first of these, bringing thousands into the streets of the Soviet military-industrial center of Sverdlovsk, occurred on December 28, 1989. Gorbachev himself seems to realize the folly of half-measure reforms; he is now negotiating with Boris Yeltsin on a plan to make a rapid transition to a free market economy.

The Unravelling of the Soviet Domestic Empire

The Soviet Union is an artificial political entity, most of whose ethnic republics are kept in the union exclusively by the Moscow-controlled secret police and the Red Army. The relaxation of police controls under Gorbachev has brought about ethnic and national unrest. As a result, the disintegration of the Soviet Union is a real possibility.[18]

To preserve the Union, Moscow has faced two options: 1) invade, occupy, and terrorize into submission the rebellious national republics if they secede, or 2) try to persuade such non-Russian nationalities as the Estonians, Latvians, Lithuanians, and Ukrainians to become part of a loose confederation with Russia by undertaking radical political and economic reform within Russia itself.

---

14 *Soviet/East European Report*, Vol. VII, No. 6, 1989.
15 "Talony na ves' god" ("Coupons for the entire year"), *Izvestia*, January 30, 1990.
16 *Kommunist*, 10 (October), 1989, p. 39.
17 *Moscow News*, January 21, 1990.
18 For a discussion of the systemic crisis in Moscow's nationalities policy see Leon Aron, "Gorbachev's Mounting Nationalities Crisis," Heritage Foundation *Backgrounder* No. 695, March 9, 1989.

Chapter 4

To be successful, reforms would have to be far-reaching. A multiparty political system would have to be introduced, all agricultural land would have to be given to farmers as private property, and the role of the state in the economy would have to be reduced dramatically. Anything short of these would keep the current system in place, and would fail to keep the non-Russian nationalities within the Union. Even with radical reform, some non-Russian republics still will wish to leave. Most likely would be Azerbaijan, Estonia, Georgia, Latvia, Lithuania, and Moldavia.

If all else fails, Gorbachev could suppress nationalist uprisings with military force. His problem is that using force on a wide scale would mean scuttling his policies of *perestroika* and *glasnost*. This would ruin the relations with the West that he carefully and skillfully has cultivated and ruin his chances of transforming the Soviet economy.

In addition, there may be serious domestic obstacles to a military crackdown in breakaway republics. As a legacy of the 1989 defeat in the Afghanistan war, in which at least 34,000 soldiers were killed, wounded, or missing, the Russian people may not tolerate massive armed suppression of nationality movements. Moscow was forced on January 21, 1990, for example, to abandon plans for mobilizing Army reserve units in response to ethnic violence in Azerbaijan, after mass protests against the mobilization erupted in several Russian cities, including Stavropol. "We don't need another Afghanistan," a protester in that city was quoted as saying.[19]

At the same time, Gorbachev either is unwilling or unable to make a thorough overhaul of the Soviet political structure. In the absence of acceptable options for ending the crisis, he is playing for time, apparently hoping for a gradual and non-violent change with minimum loss of face for Moscow rather than a sudden, bloody disintegration of the Soviet Union

But time is running out. The Supreme Soviet, or parliament, of Lithuania declared the republic's independence on March 11, 1990. Estonia declared a six-month transition to full independence on March 30. Declarations of sovereignty or independence have followed from Armenia, Azerbaijan, Byelorussia, Georgia, Latvia, Moldavia, Russia,

---

19 *The New York Times*, January 20, 1990, p.6.

Orchestrating Retreat

Tadzhikistan, Turkmania, Ukraine, and Uzbekistan. Regardless of whether they declare themselves independent soon or not, the real political power in Moldavia, Armenia, and Azerbaijan already is in the hands of nationalist opposition groups. Following March 4 elections to the Ukrainian legislature, the pro-independence movement *Rukh* acquired 30 percent of the seats and took control over the city council of Kiev, the Ukrainian capital.

Meanwhile, there is a probability of large-scale nationalist violence in Central Asia, as the 17 million-strong Uzbeks, the third largest Soviet ethnic group after the Russians and Ukrainians, challenge Moscow's control of the region. The Uzbeks for centuries have wanted to dominate all of Central Asia. Their hatred of other ethnic groups already has spawned violence: Uzbek mobs in the Fergana Valley turned against the Meskhetian Turks in June 1989, killing over 100, burning 700 homes and sending over 16,000 refugees fleeing to the relative safety of the Russian Republic.[20] The unrest in Uzbekistan is aggravated by overpopulation (the region's population grew 30 percent in the last decade), a 25 percent unemployment rate, and an income level 30 percent below the already meager Soviet average.[21]

Changing Views on the Role of the Military in Foreign Policy

The Soviet leadership under Gorbachev appears to be downgrading the central role of the military in Soviet foreign policy. This re-evaluation can be traced to several causes. The first is the Soviet 1989 defeat in Afghanistan, the longest war in Russian history after the 1805-1815 war against Napoleon. The Afghanistan defeat demoralized Soviet society and discredited the traditional view that military conquest is the most effective way of promoting Soviet interests.

The second cause is that, contrary to Soviet expectations, deployment of Soviet SS-20 medium-range nuclear missiles in Europe in the late 1970s failed to weaken Western support for NATO and to split the

---

20 *Pravda*, June 24, 1989.
21 The Soviet per capita national income in 1988 was 2,200 rubles (see *Pravda*, July 23, 1989). By the rate of exchange still used in business transaction ($1.66 per ruble), this corresponds to $3,652. By the rate of retail tourist exchange (10 rubles per dollar), this sum equals $220. For the U.S. in 1987, the figure was $13,473.

Chapter 4

U.S. from its West European allies. Instead, in 1983, NATO began deploying U.S. *Pershing* II and cruise missiles capable of striking Soviet territory. In doing so, the West shattered the longstanding Soviet conviction that military intimidation is the best way to gain cooperation from an adversary.

A third cause has been the vastly increased importance of advanced technology to weapons development. While the West in the 1980s pressed ahead developing supercomputers, imaging technologies, telecommunications, and other advanced technologies applicable to aircraft and missile defenses, the Soviet Union fell behind. While the technological gap was most spectacular in the case of the U.S. Strategic Defense Initiative (SDI), the proliferation of "smart," or self-guided, conventional weapons by NATO also alarmed Moscow and diminished its confidence in the effectiveness of its less sophisticated arms. As a result, some Soviet generals, like the former Chief of the Soviet General Staff Marshal Nikolai Ogarkov, began a campaign in the early 1980s to emphasize advanced technology for conventional weapons and de-emphasize nuclear forces.

A fourth cause of Moscow's reassessment of the role of the Soviet military is demographics. Because of the falling birthrate of the Slavic peoples of the Soviet Union (the Russians, the Ukrainians and the Byelorussians), the pool of available conscripts for the Soviet Army is becoming increasingly Asian. An official Soviet estimate puts the proportion of non-Slavic minorities now in the Army at 37 percent.[22] By the end of the decade, the army is expected to be half Asian, because of recruits coming from Kazakhstan, Kirgizia, Tadzhikistan, Turkmenia, and Uzbekistan.[23] Most of these Asians do not speak Russian well and hate their Slavic officers. Faced with this, the Soviet leaders may well have decided to live with a smaller force of more reliable Russians and perhaps other Slavs.

---

[22] Bill Keller, "Cry of 'Won't Give My Son!' and Soviets End the Call-Up," *The New York Times*, January 20, 1990.
[23] Murray Feshbach, "Meeting Report" (June 16, 1989), Institute for East-West Security Studies.

Orchestrating Retreat

A fifth cause is the pressure to reduce military spending. A leading Soviet economist Grigoriy Khanin said on July 25, 1989: "I do not see how we shall maintain even the present low standard of living over the next three or four years without a radical slashing of military expenditures by at least half."[24] A few months later, speaking at the Second Congress of People's Deputies, a top expert on the U.S., Georgiy Arbatov, described the military burden on Soviet society in terms unprecedented even in the era of *glasnost*. He said on December 16, 1989 that "no developed state" devotes as great a share of its gross national product to defense as does the Soviet Union.[25] The Soviet economy, he continued, has been "bled white" by military expenditures.[26]

Generational Change in the Soviet Leadership

It is a truly post-Stalinist generation of leaders that is making the changes ushered in by Gorbachev. This generation came of political age during Nikita Khrushchev's campaign, waged in the 1950s and early 1960s, to discredit Soviet dictator Joseph Stalin. The most prominent of these new leaders, in addition to Gorbachev, are Politburo member Alexander Yakovlev, Foreign Minister Eduard Shevardnadze, Academician Evgeniy Primakov, and head of the International Department of the Central Committee, Valentin Falin. They are not as ideologically rigid as their predecessors and are far more aware of the outside world. Yakovlev, for instance, served for ten years as ambassador to Canada, and Falin was for seven years ambassador to West Germany.

Most members of this political generation were too young to have served in the Soviet equivalent of the Chinese Communist "Long March": World War II. Gorbachev was 10 years old when Germany invaded the Soviet Union in 1941. He and his generation thus have no experience in this one event that possibly legitimized Bolshevist rule. As important, Gorbachev and his generation have few sentimental and personal ties to the Soviet military, and are therefore less likely to

---

24 Interview with *The New Times*, July 25, 1989, p. 25.
25 FBIS, December 18, 1989, p. 68.
26 *Ibid.*

Chapter 4

accord it the place of honor it enjoyed under the previous regime of Leonid Brezhnev, who came of age during the "Great Patriotic War," as the Soviets call World War II.

Gorbachev and his allies thus have a more realistic view of what the Kremlin for decades has trumpeted as the grave threat from the capitalist West. An influential columnist of Gorbachev's generation, Stanislav Kondrashev, wrote in the April 2, 1988, *Izvestia*, that "the notion of Western aggressiveness is exaggerated, if not, in fact, false."[27] Similarly, Soviet foreign policy scholars Sergei Karganov, Andrei Kortunov, and Vitaliy Zhurkin, wrote in the January 1988 *Kommunist* that "from the point of view of common sense, it is difficult to imagine in the name of what objectives Western armies would invade the territories of socialist states."[28] While it is arguable whether the Soviet leadership ever seriously believed in their routinely proclaimed Western military threat, the willingness of prominent opinion leaders in the Soviet Union to acknowledge publicly that such a threat may not exist breaks sharply with the past.

Finally, the Gorbachev generation has shown an appreciation of longstanding Western concerns about the Soviet military threat to the West and the dismal state of human rights within the Soviet Union. For example, another columnist close to Gorbachev's circle, Alexandr Bovin, published an unprecedented admission that the West had reasons to believe in the Soviet menace. On July 11, 1989, he wrote in *Izvestia*: "What we always called a 'myth', the Soviet threat, was not a 'myth' for the West. The [Soviet] invasion of Hungary in 1956 was not a 'myth', and neither was Czechoslovakia in 1968. The significant advantage of the Warsaw Pact in offensive potential was not a 'myth.' And neither were the SS-20 missiles [deployed by Moscow in Europe in the 1970s], which changed the nuclear balance in Europe."[29]

---

27 Stanislav Kondrashev, "Vzgliad iz Moskvy" ("Looking from Moscow"), *Izvestia*, May 12, 1989, and "Obychnye sily" ("Conventional forces"), *Izvestia*, April 2, 1988.
28 V. Zhurkin, S.Karganov, A. Kortunov, "Vyzovy bezopsnosti — starye i novye" ("The challenges to the security — old and new"), *Kommunist*, January 1988, p. 44.
29 Alexandr Bovin, "Evropa i Evropeitzy," *Izvestia*, July 11, 1989.

Orchestrating Retreat

SOVIET ECONOMIC STRATEGY IN EUROPE

The overriding objective of Soviet foreign policy is to shore up the perilously weakened domestic regime. As Soviet Foreign Minister Eduard Shevardnadze told a Foreign Ministry Party conference, the "main goal" of Soviet foreign policy was "the establishment of the most favorable conditions for domestic transformations in the country."[30]

While access to West European technology and credits always has been a central objective of Soviet European policy, Gorbachev now more than ever needs Western help if his rule is to survive. He surely hopes to buy favor with Soviet citizens by providing them with consumer goods, food, money for investment, and technology from the West. If he fails, so too will *glasnost* and *perestroika*.

The Soviet economic agenda has three key objectives. They are:

1) To restore the consumer market. The key to Soviet economic reform is to saturate the market with consumer goods to provide incentive to work honestly and to defuse enormous social and political tensions.

2) To modernize the Soviet economy. The bulk of the Soviet industrial plant is decades behind not just the West but many Third World nations. To remain a superpower, the Soviet Union will have to halt, or at least slow the decay of its economy. While from the 1930s and through the 1970s the Soviet GNP was second only to the U.S., the Soviet GNP is now has fallen behind Japan and will fall behind the United Europe in 1992 and perhaps China by 2000.

3) To generate hard currency exports to the West other than oil. The Soviet Union needs a sharp increase in hard currency earnings. Since Moscow faced a sharp drop in oil output in the 1980s, its major hard currency export, the Soviets concluded that they must begin selling the West more than oil. Yet in terms of its trade with the West, the Soviet Union even lags behind most of the Third World. Thus, according to Soviet economists, while oil and gas account for 80 percent of the Soviet exports to the West, industrial products account for less than a quarter of one percent. By comparison, for the Third

---

30 *RFE/RL Daily Report*, April 30, 1990.

Chapter 4

World as a whole, the average share of industrial exports to the West is 13 percent.[31]

Collecting a "Peace Dividend" from Western Europe

The primary means by which Gorbachev hopes to saturate the consumer market, modernize the economy and diversify hard currency exports is by persuading Western Europe to provide financial, technological, and managerial aid in return for the withdrawal of Soviet troops from Eastern Europe. The Kremlin's pursuit of European assistance now follows a distinct pattern: Every Soviet peaceful overture to Western Europe is followed by a massive diplomatic effort to secure as many economic benefits as possible.

Example: following Gorbachev's December 8, 1988, speech to the United Nations' General Assembly promising unilateral Soviet troop reductions in Europe, high-level Soviet emissaries descended on West European capitals to burnish economic relations with the West. Deputy Chairman of the U.S.S.R. Council of Ministers, V.M. Kamentsev arrived in London in February 1989 to meet with Prime Minister Margaret Thatcher and to propose that the Soviet Union and Britain increase their trade by 40 percent by 1990.[32] In the first week of July, five West European banks agreed to loan the Soviet Union $160 million to create an international bank in Moscow. The Western banks will hold 60 percent of the bank's new shares, while the rest will belong to Soviet side. The newly created bank will provide reservoir of hard currency for Soviet domestic needs.[33]

Agreements to create 60 joint French-Soviet enterprises were signed during and immediately after Gorbachev's July 4-7, 1989, visit to France. Among the joint Soviet-French ventures are a huge television

---

31 *Izvestia*, October 10, 1987.
32 TASS International Service, February 7, 1989.
33 The Western Banks are: Bayerische Vereinsbank (West Germany), Creditanstalt-Bankverein (Austria), Credit Lyonnais (France), Banca Commerciale Italiana (Italy), and Kansallis-Osake-Pankky (Finland).

factory to be built in the Soviet Union and a Caspian Sea mining company.[34]

Gorbachev's "Common European Home"

Another element of Gorbachev's strategy of wooing Western Europe is the concept of the "Common European Home." He freely admits that his is a nebulous concept, telling the European Parliament on July 6, 1989, "I do not pretend that I have a ready plan for this 'home' in my pocket."[35] He added that while military "security" is the foundation of the "European home", economic "cooperation" between East and West is its "pillar."[36] The Soviet dream, according to Gorbachev, is to "interconnect... the vast economic space from the Atlantic to the Urals."[37]

His objective in this "Common European Home" campaign apparently is two-fold. First and foremost, he wants to be ready to harness the enormous economic potential of the united Europe of 1992 by laying the groundwork of cooperation now. A second goal is political: by stressing the common European heritage of Europe and the Soviet Union, Gorbachev implies that America is an outsider, alien to Europe.

As Gorbachev made clear in his European Parliament speech, the aim of "interconnecting" the economics of East and West Europe is to rescue the Soviet economy. He said: "the idea is connected with our economic... restructuring, for which we need new relations, first of all, with the part of the world to which we belong." [38]

Gorbachev's Common European Home rhetoric has been followed with concrete action. Official relations between the Soviet-led Council for Mutual Economic Assistance, or COMECON, and the European

---

34 Moscow International Service in French July 10, 1989 (FBIS, July 12, 1989).
35 *Izvestia*, July 7, 1989, p. 2.
36 *Ibid.*
37 *Ibid.*
38 *Ibid.*

Chapter 4

Community were established in June 1988. The Soviet Union established a diplomatic mission at the EC headquarters in Brussels the following February.[39] And in December after that, Soviet Foreign Minister Shevardnadze signed an agreement with the EC on "trade, commercial and economic cooperation." Moscow reported in the wake of the agreement that the European Community would lift "virtually all restrictions on [the import of] Soviet goods."[40] Both sides, according to the Chairman of the Soviet Foreign Economic Commission Ivan Ivanov, viewed the talks as "a contribution to building a common European home."[41]

Attracting the Western Europeans

Because of its currency shortage, Moscow cannot pay for the extra Western European goods that it needs badly. To attract Western European capital and technology, the Soviet Union may be forced to take some extraordinary measures. One of them is to create so-called "free economic zones" inside the Soviet Union. These would be islands of free capitalist enterprise, immune from interference by the Soviet authorities. In his speech at the Cologne Chamber of Commerce and Industry on June 13 1989, Gorbachev asked West German industrialists to create such a zone in the Leningrad province.

Another Soviet tactic is to sell Soviet space technology services. In the Cologne speech, Gorbachev offered Soviet rockets to launch West German payloads into space. Yet another Soviet technique is to lure the West Europeans into trading with Moscow by evoking the specter of Japanese and American competition. At Cologne, Gorbachev warned that "more and more businessmen from... Japan and the United States" are becoming interested in the Soviet Union and that the Soviet government had "received interesting proposals" from them.[42] The moral was clear: if Western Europe would not do increased business with the Soviet Union, the U.S. and Japan were eager to.

---

39 Moscow TASS, February 17, 1989 (FBIS, February 22, 1989), p. 11.
40 TASS, December 19, 1989 (FBIS, December 22, 1989), p. 27.
41 TASS, July 25, 1989. (FBIS, July 26, 1989), p. 27.
42 Radio Moscow, June 13, 1989 (FBIS, June 14, 1989), p. 21.

Attacking COCOM

Because of the Soviet Union's hunger for Western technology, a top priority of its West European economic agenda has been to eliminate the Coordinating Committee for Multilateral Export Controls (known as COCOM), an organization established by the NATO allies in 1959 to prevent the transfer of militarily useful technology to the Soviet bloc. Gorbachev attacked COCOM in a July 6, 1989, speech to the European Parliament in Strasbourg. He said: "In our age, economic links without scientific-technological links are something abnormal."[43] Such links, he continued, are "drained of blood" by COCOM. The fact that the Soviet leader himself led the assault on COCOM in Europe's most important forum signaled escalation of the anti-COCOM campaign and underscored how important Moscow views access to Western technology.

The propaganda barrage against COCOM continued throughout 1989, with Moscow seeking to exploit differences of opinion between the U.S. and its allies over high technology trade with Moscow. In a detailed report on the October 1989 session of COCOM's Executive Committee in Paris, the main party newspaper *Pravda* contended that "15 NATO countries plus Japan opposed Washington's attempts to continue to use COCOM as an insuperable barrier in the way of exporting modern Western technology to the USSR."[44] According to *Pravda,* the anti-American "rebellion" at the session was not so much "economic" as "political". The newspaper said: "To all appearances, the United States' European allies in NATO are ready to support the transformations taking place in socialist countries more actively and constructively than their partners across the ocean." [45]

The Role of Germany in Soviet Economic Strategy

No element of Gorbachev's European economic strategy is as indispensable as enlisting West Germany's help in reviving the Soviet

---

43 *Izvestia*, July 7, 1989.
44 V. Bolshakov, "16:1 v pol'zu zdravogo smysla" ("16:1 in favor of common sense"), *Pravda*, October 30, 1989, p. 6.
45 *Ibid*.

Chapter 4

economy. The importance assigned to West Germany in Gorbachev's plans is underscored by the appointment in 1989 of Valentin Falin, a former Soviet Ambassador to Bonn and one of the Soviet Union's top German experts, to head the Communist Party Central Committee's International Department, which develops the general objectives and strategy of Soviet foreign policy.

As with other aspects of the Soviet economic agenda in Western Europe, public diplomacy has played a key role in advancing Moscow's objectives in West Germany. Shortly after Gorbachev's visit to West Germany in the summer of 1989, Moscow proposed to create a new autonomous republic within the U.S.S.R. for Soviet Germans, 48 years after the Republic of Volga Germans was abolished by Stalin in 1941 and all its inhabitants deported to Kazakhstan and Siberia. The recreated republic would be located around Kaliningrad, which before 1945 was Konigsberg and belonged to Germany.

Thus far, the Soviet strategy of forging closer economic ties with West Germany has been successful. During West German Chancellor Helmut Kohl's October 1988 visit to the Soviet Union, some 30 contracts, totalling $1.5 billion, were concluded between West German businesses and the Soviet Union. Eleven more agreements were signed during Gorbachev's June 1989 visit to West Germany, including one guaranteeing legal protection of German investments in the Soviet Union.

West Germany is the single largest Western economic partner of the Soviet Union, accounting for 15 percent of all Moscow's joint economic ventures.[46] West-German Soviet contracts span a broad spectrum of goods – from machine-building and medical equipment to production of textiles, glass, shoes, stockings, and fast-food restaurants. In the aftermath of Gorbachev's June 1989 visit, an agreement was signed between the Soviets and the West German company Roevin Deutschland GMBH to process timber, peat, oil, natural gas, and other

---

46 *Izvestia*, November 8, 1989, p. 4.

raw materials in the Tomsk region of Siberia. In return, the West Germans are expected to invest 400 million Deutsche Marks, or about $200 million, for the production of consumer goods in the region.[47] A group of West German businessmen lobbying for close economic relations with Moscow, called the "Eastern Committee," is headed by Otto Wolf von Amerongen, the chairman of the firm *Otto Wolf*. His was among the first Western enterprises to begin doing business with Soviet Russia in 1922.[48]

Perhaps the most significant development for Moscow has been the growth of West German financial assistance. The single largest Western loan to the Soviet Union was by a consortium of West German banks; granted in October 1988, it is $1.7 billion line of credit. West German banks also have been helpful in widening Soviet access to international financial institutions as well. For example, the Westdeutsche Landesbank, a regional bank headquartered in Dusseldorf, played the key role in arranging for the issuance in Switzerland in 1988 of the first international bond backed by the Soviet government.[49]

Back to the Future

The Soviet Union has a long history of Russo-German relations. Whenever Russia has sought to modernize in the past, Germany has played the central role. Peter the Great (1682-1725) not only imported technology and capital from Germany, he lured Germans to Russia to teach and perform skilled labor.[50] In June 1989, a high Soviet official pointedly told the West German weekly magazine, *Der Spiegel,* that

---

47 Moscow TASS, July 24, 1989. (FBIS, July 26, 1989).
48 V. Presniakov and E. Iordanskaya, "Delovye otnoshenia SSSR — Zapadnaya Evropa: ot Oktiabria do nashikh dnei" ("Business Relations of the USSR — Western Europe: from October to Our Days"), *MEMO*, November 1987, p. 82.
49 *Izvestia*, November 8, 1989, p. 4.
50 Peter the Great's policy of importing Germans continued under Catherine the Great (1762-1796) born a German princess. Most of the over 2 million Soviet Germans trace their origin to German farmers who settled the Volga region and Ukraine during Catherine's reign.

Chapter 4

"under Peter I the Germans taught us management.... Perestroika is at least as important as Peter's reforms."[51]

Through the centuries Russians have been fascinated with German technology. Germany was Russia's main trading partner from 1900 to 1914, accounting for 38 percent of Russia's total foreign trade volume, compared with 15 percent for the next largest partner, Britain.[52]

These links continued after the Bolsheviks seized power in 1917. An alliance with Germany, for example, was forged on April 16, 1922, with the Treaty of Rappallo; in it, both sides renounced any financial claims and extended full diplomatic recognition to each other. Lasting until Adolf Hitler came to power in 1933, cooperation with Germany was closer and more stable than with any other foreign country. As in the time of Peter the Great, Moscow used German managerial and technological expertise to modernize its economy and its armed forces. There were over 2,000 German engineers working in the Soviet Union in the early 1920s.[53] By 1928 German enterprises accounted for almost 20 percent of all foreign concessions in the Soviet Union, a share larger than that of any other nation.[54]

There is also a history of Russo-German military cooperation, dating back to the end of 18th Century when Russia was ruled by Emperor Paul I (1796-1801). A fervent admirer of German emperor Frederick the Great, Paul organized the Russian military along the lines of the Prussian army. Military ties continued under the Bolsheviks. The 1922 Treaty of Rappallo, negotiated in secret by German Foreign Minister Walther Rathenau and the Soviet Commissar for Foreign Affairs, Georgiy Chicherin, allowed Germany to circumvent the restrictions imposed on its armed forces by the 1919 Versailles Treaty, which ended World War I. For example, some units of the German army, or *Reichswehr,* trained secretly on Soviet territory. In return, the Germans

---

51   Nikolay Portugalov, "Restructuring in the Conscience of the Germans." *Der Spiegel*, June 5, 1989 (FBIS, June 8, 1989), pp. 170-172.
52   Presniakov and Iordanskaya, *op. cit.*, p. 83.
53   Patrick Glynn, "Dangers Beyond Containment," *Commentary*, August 1989, p. 19.
54   Presniakov and Iordnaskaya, *op. cit.*, p. 83. With the advent of Nazism, the United States replaced Germany as the main source of capital, technology and know-how during first two "five-year" plans of 1929-1937.

helped Moscow manufacture armaments, such as tanks and artillery shells, and build the world's first all-metal airplane.[55] The two countries also exchanged military instructors.

This historic relationship will surely continue now that Germany is unified. Although the West Germans will be preoccupied with rescuing East Germany's economy, they will continue to expand their economic and political relations with the Soviet Union, or if there is a break-up of the U.S.S.R., with the independent republics.

Enlisting Western Help To Preserve the Soviet Union

An entirely new item on Moscow's European agenda is the preservation of the Soviet domestic empire. As the national republics' struggle for independence intensifies, the Gorbachev regime will be looking for ways to win Western European assistance in keeping together the Union or, at least, in slowing disintegration.

Moscow may try achieve this through a CSCE meeting modeled on the 1975 Helsinki summit, where the so-called Final Act legitimized post-World War II European boundaries. Moscow can be expected to urge a new CSCE conference to discuss questions of stability, inviolability of borders, and the need to preserve the territorial integrity of states. The purpose of raising these issues would be to gain European consent for the preservation of the Soviet domestic empire.

Moscow also apparently hopes to discourage independence movements of non-Russian peoples by suggesting to them that the West is on Moscow's side. In a December 25, 1989, speech to an emergency meeting of the Communist Party's Central Committee, Gorbachev said:

> The existence of a whole, solid and powerful Soviet Union is an urgent necessity of our times . . . This has been quite unambiguously confirmed in contacts with the leaders of the most powerful states in the world—including those on whose support our internal separatists count.[56]

---

55 Glynn, *op.cit.*, p. 19.
56 *Pravda*, December 26, 1989, p. 2.

Chapter 4

Since that Central Committee meeting was convened to deal with the Lithuanian Communist Party's break from Moscow, Gorbachev's message to the Lithuanians and other would-be separatists was clear: do not count on Western help in your attempt to secede from the Soviet Union. In the light of Western reaction to Moscow's subsequent economic and political pressure on Lithuania, Gorbachev's analysis appears to have been borne out.

Political "Decoupling" of America and Europe

Another tool in maintaining Soviet political influence in Europe is to decouple Europe from America, though the Soviet leadership repeatedly denies any intentions of doing so. Moscow portrays the U.S.S.R. as a "European power," embodying and protecting a "common European heritage." America, by implication, is a non-European power, and thus deserves no special place on the continent. The Kremlin even publicly bemoans the "decadent" American influence on "European civilization." In his 1987 book *Perestroika*, Gorbachev wrote:

> Sometimes one has the impression that the independent policies of West European nations have been abducted, that they are being carried off across the ocean.... A serious threat is hovering over European culture, too. The threat emanates from an onslaught of 'mass culture' from across the Atlantic. Indeed, one can only wonder that a deep, profoundly intelligent and inherently humane European culture is retreating to the background before the primitive revelry of violence and pornography and the flood of cheap feelings and low thoughts.[57]

Anti-nuclear and anti-American themes are especially pronounced in the Soviet public diplomacy aimed at Germany. Before Gorbachev's June 1989 visit to West Germany, for example, Nikolay Portugalov, an advisor to the Chief of the Central Committee's International Department, accused the U.S. of "trying to cast the two German states in the

---

57 Mikhail Gorbachev, *Perestroika: New Thinking for Our Country and the World* (New York: Harper and Row, 1987), p. 208.

role of the battlefield in a 'limited nuclear war.'"[58] This is a theme that Germans themselves often have voiced. Its exploitation by Moscow shows a deep understanding of German fears of nuclear weapons, and a willingness to use these fears to alienate Germany from the West.

Moscow also will try to prevent the U.S. from maintaining a strong political position in Europe, if and when the Soviet military threat there recedes. This explains why the Soviet news agency TASS was so enthusiastic about a proposal, floated by Mitterrand in his 1990 New Year's speech, to create a "European confederation," of which the Soviet Union would be a member. Contending that Mitterrand's idea represented a response to U.S. Secretary of State James Baker's concept of a "New Atlanticism," which Baker introduced in his December 12, 1989, speech in Berlin, TASS claimed "opposition is broadening in Western Europe to Washington's proposals to turn NATO into a kind of super-organization... to step up the United States' influence in the European community."[59]

GORBACHEV'S MILITARY OBJECTIVES

Since the end of World War II, Soviet military policy in Europe has been designed to assure and perpetuate Soviet military preponderance on the continent and to weaken and eliminate NATO. In pursuit of these, the Soviet Union has worked toward:

1) **Denuclearizing Western Europe by creating nuclear-free zones;**
2) **"Decoupling" the U.S. from Western Europe by securing the withdrawal of American troops and nuclear weapons from the continent; and**
3) **Neutralizing West Germany by detaching it from NATO.**

Of the three goals, German neutrality seems increasingly to be beyond Moscow's reach. While Moscow originally may have sought to exchange its acquiescence to German reunification for the pledge of neutrality of a new German state, the pace of change in Eastern Europe and such events as the victory in the March 18, 1990, East German

---

58 Nikolay Portugalov, "Restructuring and the Consciousness of the Germans," *Der Spiegel*, June 5, 1989 (FBIS, June 8, 1989), pp.16-17.
59 TASS International Service, January 5, 1990 (FBIS, January 8, 1990), p. 33.

Chapter 4

elections of the conservative and pro-NATO Christian Democratic party appear to have eroded Moscow's confidence. Thus, at the end of his April 4-6, 1989, Washington visit, Soviet Foreign Minister Shevardnadze, reportedly "signaled" that Moscow "was prepared to for the first time to drop its demand that unified Germany be neutral."[60] Since that time, of course, Kohl and Gorbachev agreed on July 16, 1990, in Stavropol to permit a United Germany in NATO.

West European Denuclearization

Gorbachev has done more in five years to further the traditional Soviet objective of denuclearizing Europe than his predecessors did in the preceding four decades. As Gorbachev told the European Parliament in his July 1989 speech, "we are for elimination of all nuclear weapons by the beginning of next century."[61] A decisive step toward this was the 1987 Intermediate-range Nuclear Forces (INF) Treaty, in which Moscow and Washington agreed to destroy SS-20, *Pershing* II, and cruise missile forces in Europe. Altogether, 572 U.S. nuclear missiles are to be destroyed. The 1989 revolution in Eastern Europe and the reunification of Germany also have made modernization of NATO's short-range nuclear arsenal politically impossible due to strong German opposition.

New items in the Soviet Military Objectives in Europe

Following the collapse of the Soviet Eastern European empire, Moscow now appears to have added two new objectives to its military agenda. Gorbachev hopes to:

♦ ♦ **Prevent the hasty withdrawal of Soviet forces from Europe.** In negotiating the withdrawal of Soviet troops from the territories of such former "allies" as Czechoslovakia and Hungary, Moscow has been attempting to slow down the removal of the troops. The Soviets argued that the difference in the width of railway tracks between Soviet Union and the rest of Europe means that more time is needed to withdraw

---

60 *The New York Times*, April 7, 1990.
61 *Izvestia*, July 6, 1989.

Orchestrating Retreat

Soviet troops. Citing the need to transfer men, equipment, and machinery from the European to Soviet-type cars, Moscow demanded, and received, an extension of the withdrawal period, which is scheduled to be completed by July 1, 1991.

Another means of slowing Soviet withdrawal is to stall various arms control negotiations. Since January 1990, Moscow reportedly has become even less forthcoming at the Conventional Forces in Europe (CFE) talks in Vienna. Because of Soviet backsliding, these negotiations reached an impasse in April 1990.

◆ ◆ **Stop NATO from spreading into Eastern Europe.** Testing the limits of their independence, former Warsaw Pact members are exploring the possibility of extending their connection to the West beyond economic and cultural ties into political and even military areas. Thus on February 23, 1990, Hungarian Foreign Minister Gyula Horn suggested that his country would like to established links with NATO. This could become a strategic nightmare for Moscow for it would mean that anti-Soviet states, supported by the West, would be pressing against the Soviet Union's Western border. Moscow faced exactly this arrangement between the world wars, when Bulgaria, Czechoslovakia, Estonia, Finland, Hungary, Latvia, Lithuania, Poland, and Romania formed a so-called *cordon sanitaire,* or barrier to Soviet influence. Moscow surely would not want to experience this again.

To prevent resurrection of a *cordon sanitaire*, Moscow could wield the oil weapon by threatening to cut or suspend oil deliveries to Eastern European countries that attempt to form an alliance with the West. Another tactic may be to force former allies to become members of a new political organization based on the now moribund Warsaw Pact.

U.S. RESPONSE TO THE NEW SOVIET GOALS IN EUROPE

Responding to the Soviet objectives in a changing Europe requires that America and its allies demonstrate at least the strategic and tactical flexibility, clarity of purpose, and ingenuity that Gorbachev has. The purpose of U.S. policy should be to protect the U.S. interests by thwarting Soviet attempts to threaten the security of Western Europe. At the same time the U.S. should favor the expansion of free enterprise and self-determination throughout Eastern Europe and the Soviet Union. Where Soviet goals coincide with U.S. interests, as in avoiding

Chapter 4

war or reducing conventional military forces in Europe, they should be supported by the Bush Administration.

To create a U.S. counter-strategy for Soviet involvement in Europe, and to ensure that it be resolute in purpose but tactically flexible, the U.S. should:

♦ ♦ **Counter Gorbachev's idea of the "Common European Home."**

In accordance with the traditional Soviet objective of splitting America from Europe, the "Common European Home" campaign is aimed at excluding the U.S. from Europe. It should be countered with the idea of a "Common Democratic Home" from San Francisco to Warsaw and from Ottawa to Prague. United in dedication to Western civilization, democracy, and free enterprise, this "home" would include all democratic nations west of the Soviet border, the "Common Democratic Home" idea should be presented by George Bush in one of the East European capitals. In his speech, the President might recall Winston Churchill's March 1946 Fulton, Missouri, speech, in which he mourned the disappearance behind the "iron curtain" of such "capitals of the ancient states of Central and Eastern Europe" as Berlin, Budapest, Prague, and Warsaw,[62] and welcome these cities, their countries and the people back into the family of free nations. Moscow should be told that it, too, may join, once the Soviet Union becomes a truly democratic state.

♦ ♦ **Counter Soviet propaganda and public diplomacy campaigns aimed at alienating Europe from the U.S.**

Moscow tries to persuade the Europeans that America does not belong on the continent and that U.S. nuclear weapons are a threat. One way to counter this agreement has been to provide Europeans with truthful information about U.S. policy in Europe through the European Service of the Voice of America, which broadcasts to all European nations, and Radio Free Europe, which broadcasts exclusively to Eastern Europe. The Voice of America resumed daily broadcasts in English to Western Europe in 1983, after stopping them in 1960. Radio Free Europe has been in operation since 1950. Both radio stations are very popular with, and have earned the gratitude of,

---

62 As quoted in Randolph S. Churchill, ed., *The Sinews of Peace: Post-War Speeches by Winston S. Churchill* (Boston: Houghton Mifflin Co., 1969.)

Orchestrating Retreat

the Europeans. Thus, even as the Cold War appears to be receding, the Europeans want the stations to remain. Hungary, Poland, and Czechoslovakia accredited Radio Free Europe's bureaus in their capitals. Moreover, Czechoslovalva and Poland intend to allow Radio Free Europe to switch broadcasts from short-wave to medium-wave frequencies to make the reception as clear as that of local broadcasts. President of Czechoslovakia Vaclav Havel recently stated that Radio Free Europe and the Voice of America were "still urgently needed" because "they have a better opportunity than our media to inform about democracies in different countries around the globe."[63]

The Bush Administration should provide full funding for the stations. To improve U.S. public diplomacy in Europe, the United States Information Agency, which directs the Voice of America, and the Board for International Broadcasting, which governs Radio Free Europe, should add programs dealing specifically with the U.S. role in Europe in 1990s and beyond.

♦ ♦ **Rebuff Soviet attempts to slow democratic change in the name of "stability."**

Moscow has tried to slow the democratization of Eastern Europe and the Soviet Union by saying that stability in Europe is threatened by the fast pace of change. The U.S. objective in Europe is also stability but one based on radical, albeit peaceful, change toward democracy and free markets. In response to Soviet professed fears of "instability," the Bush Administration should point out to Moscow and to West Europeans that, with the notable exception of Romania, democratic change in Europe and the Soviet Union has been remarkably nonviolent. Furthermore, the U.S. can assure Moscow that the West will not take military advantage of Soviet withdrawal from Europe or of the national democratic movements of the non-Russian peoples inside the Soviet Union. The U.S. should stress it is in Soviet long-term interests that stability in Europe be based not on fear but on freedom of political and national choice. The sooner Moscow recognizes this, the greater is the chance for genuine peace and stability in Europe.

---

63 *The New York Times*, May 6, 1990.

Chapter 4

♦ ♦ **Prevent Gorbachev from using the Conference on Security and Cooperation in Europe (CSCE) to slow democratic change inside the Soviet Union.**

The U.S. should lead the Western opposition to Soviet attempts to secure Western support for repression of democratic movements inside the Soviet Union in the name of stability. The CSCE review conferences should be used to press Moscow's compliance with Article VIII of the "Declaration on Principles Guiding Relations between Participating States" of the 1975 Helsinki Final Act. This commits signatories, including the Soviet Union, to "respect the equal rights of peoples and their right to self-determination," declaring that "all peoples always have the right, in full freedom, to determine, when and as they wish, their internal and external political status...and [to] pursue as they wish their political, economic, social and cultural developments."

♦ ♦ **Preserve the Coordinating Committee for Multilateral Export Controls (COCOM).**

COCOM is a Western organization, which includes all NATO members, except Iceland, plus Japan and Australia. It controls the export of militarily significant technology to the Soviet Union and its allies. Until the Soviet Union is a fully democratic state, some COCOM regulations of Western exports to the Soviet Union will be needed. The reason: a danger remains that high technology could end up in the hands of the Soviet military and be used against the West. Transfer of advanced telecommunication equipment and extra powerful "supercomputers" would be especially dangerous, since it would greatly improve command and control capabilities of the Soviet armed forces.

To achieve their goals, the U.S. should:
- tie easing of any restrictions on high technology exports to the new democratic states in Eastern Europe to strict and enforceable rules against the transfers of this technology to the Soviet Union;
- prod the COCOM members to develop verification procedures to assure Eastern European compliance with these rules;
- link possible relaxation of high technology exports control to the Soviet Union to: a) total withdrawal of Soviet troops from Eastern Europe; b) emergence in the U.S.S.R. of a democratically elected national government and legislature that would exercise public control over the Soviet military; c) end of the

estimated $10 billion worth of Soviet military aid to such anti-Western communist dictatorships as Afghanistan, Angola, Cuba, and Ethiopia, and to such terrorist-sponsoring states as Syria and Libya.

♦ ♦ **Develop criteria to measure political and economic change in the Soviet Union and press the allies to adopt them to guide their relations with Moscow.**

American and allied policy toward the Soviet Union should change as Moscow changes. Reform inside the Soviet Union is the best guarantee against reversal of political changes in Eastern Europe. The criteria for Soviet domestic change could include in foreign policy:

- halt to the buildup of Soviet strategic nuclear forces aimed at the U.S. and its allies;
- withdrawal of about 550,000 Soviet troops from Eastern Europe;
- termination of Soviet military assistance to such anti-Western communist dictatorships as Afghanistan ($300 million a month) and Ethiopia ($800 million in 1989), and economic and military aid to the Castro dictatorship in Cuba ($6 billion annually);

In domestic policy, criteria could include:

- Moscow's beginning to negotiate in good faith with Estonia, Latvia, Lithuania and other republics desiring independence concerning the terms and timetable for their secession from the Soviet Union;
- direct multi-party elections leading to the creation of a legitimate national government;
- adoption and enforcement of laws protecting independent political activity;
- adoption and enforcement of laws protecting freedom of speech and press;
- drastic reductions in the manpower of the 600,000-strong secret police (KGB);
- repeal of the prohibition on hired labor for private enterprises, or "cooperatives";
- a land reform that would allow private farmers to sell and inherit land;
- private ownership of the "means of production," that is, machinery, tools and technology.

Chapter 4

As the Soviet Union complies with more of these criteria, the U.S. and its allies should adjust their policies accordingly, rewarding Moscow for positive change. If the U.S.S.R. becomes a fully democratic state, or a voluntary confederation of free states, Washington should accept it as a full member of the European democratic community. Should this happen, the U.S. could:
- lift restrictions on Western exports to the Soviet Union;
- accept Soviet participation in Western financial institutions, such as World Bank and International Monetary Fund;
- prepare to lead the West in extensive financial, technological, and managerial assistance to a newly created democratic European state that would replace the Soviet Union.

♦ ♦ **Prepare to deal with the consequencies of a hard-line military/KGB coup in the Soviet Union and the establishment of a neo-Stalinist "national salvation" regime.**

Should such a regime come to power in the Soviet Union, it may attempt to slow down, halt, or even reverse the changes in Eastern Europe. Although unlikely at this point, the U.S. should be prepared to respond to a Soviet crackdown and to calibrate its response accordingly.

Thus, if Moscow stalls conventional arms control talks and slows down the withdrawal of Soviet troops from Eastern Europe, the U.S. should:
- rule out the possibility of withdrawing U.S. troops from Europe,
- reverse the May 23, 1990, decision by NATO Defense Ministers to reduce the readiness of some units and scale back troops training programs,
- suspend the implementation of economic cooperation promised by Bush at the December 2-3, 1989 Malta summit and expanded upon at the May 30 - June 2 summit in Washington. The promised cooperation was to include such items as finance, agriculture, budgetary and tax policy, and a bilateral investment treaty,
- anull Bush's promise, made in Malta, to seek most-favored-nation trade status for the Soviet Union.

If Moscow halts completely troop withdrawals from Eastern Europe and walks out of conventional arms control, the U.S should:
- suspend most of economic, cultural, scientific cooperation with the Soviet Union and urge the allies to do the same;

Orchestrating Retreat

- proceeed with modernization of short-range nuclear weapons deployed in Europe;
- reverse the spending cuts for the European theater in the Pentagon budget;
- suspend the Strategic Arms Control (START) talks with Moscow;

If Moscow reintroduces the withdrawn troops back into Eastern Europe and attempts to overthrow the democratically elected governments of East Germany and Hungary and to prevent further evolution toward democracy in Bulgaria, Czechoslovakia, Poland, and Rumania, the U.S. should:

- respond with a presidential address to the nation on television in which the President explains the gravity of the situation and declares that the Soviet moves amount to the resumption of Cold War in Europe;
- reverse the military budget cuts and bringing the military spending to the 1981-1984 levels;
- suspend, across the board, all economic, cultural, and scientific cooperation with the Soviet Union;
- recall the U.S. Ambassador in the Soviet Union and urge the allies to recall their ambassadors from Moscow;
- mobilize world public opinion in an effort to isolate the Moscow regime economically and politically, including a United Nations resolution condemning the Soviet Union, as was done after the 1979 Soviet invasion of Afghanistan.

CONCLUSION

The 1989 revolutions in Eastern Europe, political upheaval within the Soviet Union, and the collapsing Soviet economy are forcing Moscow to reassess its strategy toward Europe. The loss of Eastern Europe and the downplaying of the military component of Soviet policy toward Europe have eroded seriously Moscow's previously dominant military position on the continent. Instead of relying on military intimidation and blackmail, Moscow now has to adopt new, more sophisticated strategies to preserve its political influence in Europe.

More than ever before, Soviet European policy is dominated by economic considerations and is aimed at harnessing Europe's tremendous financial, technological, and managerial potential to stave off a

Chapter 4

total collapse of the Soviet economy. To achieve this, and survive politically, Gorbachev will require major infusions of Western aid, most important, food and consumer goods.

Politically, Moscow will try to shore up its influence on the continent even as its military forces are withdrawn. It may attempt to use such organizations as the Conference on Security and Cooperation in Europe (CSCE) to legitimize its sphere of influence in Eastern Europe. The Soviet Union is assiduously courting a united Germany, which has helped Moscow out of its financial and political problems in the past. Moscow may seek at least tacit Western European backing for an attack on national liberation movements inside the Soviet Union itself. It may do so, for example, by manipulating the agenda and language of CSCE meetings to create the impression of Western acquiescence to the preservation of the Soviet domestic empire.

The Soviet Union has given no sign of relinquishing its position as the single most powerful nation on the continent. However, through its participation in the Conventional Forces in Europe conventional arms control talks in Vienna, Moscow has indicated a willingness to reduce its armed forces, and therefore to abandon a policy based almost solely on the threat of military force to advance its agenda in Europe. As it reduces its own military role in Europe, Moscow undoubtedly will continue its efforts to constrain the West militarily as well, by weakening the links between the U.S. and its West European allies and denuclearizing Eastern and Western Europe, or at least Germany. Moscow also is likely to seek an extended transition period during which it would keep forces in Germany if a conventional arms control treaty is reached.

In each of these instances, America and its allies should prepare to respond imaginatively and firmly. In some cases, as with Soviet attempts to weaken NATO by "decoupling" the U.S. and its allies, the West should counter Soviet measures outright. In others, as achieving an orderly withdrawal of Soviet troops from Eastern Europe, the U.S. and its allies should try to cooperate with Moscow when its conduct is consistent with the U.S. strategic objective of a more peaceful and democratic Europe.

With this objective in mind, the U.S. should seek to prevent Moscow from resurrecting the Warsaw Pact as an involuntary political organization and from using CSCE as a vehicle to slow change in Eastern Europe and the Soviet Union under the guise of "stability." Likewise,

Orchestrating Retreat

peace and democracy in Europe will not be served by weakening controls over militarily significant exports to the U.S.S.R. While opposing these and other Soviet steps endangering their national interests, the U.S. and its allies should encourage reform in the Soviet Union by such means as, for example, developing detailed criteria for measuring Soviet progress and structuring its relations with Moscow accordingly.

Today Western political and economic ideals march triumphantly throughout Europe, while communism retreats. Moscow, of course, will try to make the best of this situation by using rear-guard tactics to salvage as much influence as possible and strengthen itself to fight again in years ahead. The U.S. and its allies, meanwhile, should ensure that the gains of the past year are solidified and made irreversible. Moscow should not be given the chance to recoup its losses, except on terms acceptable to the West. This means pursuing strategies geared toward pressing Moscow to eliminate its military threat to Europe and ultimately to expand the benefits of the East European revolutions of 1989 – democracy, free enterprise, and national self-determination – to the Soviet Union itself.

EUROPE 1988

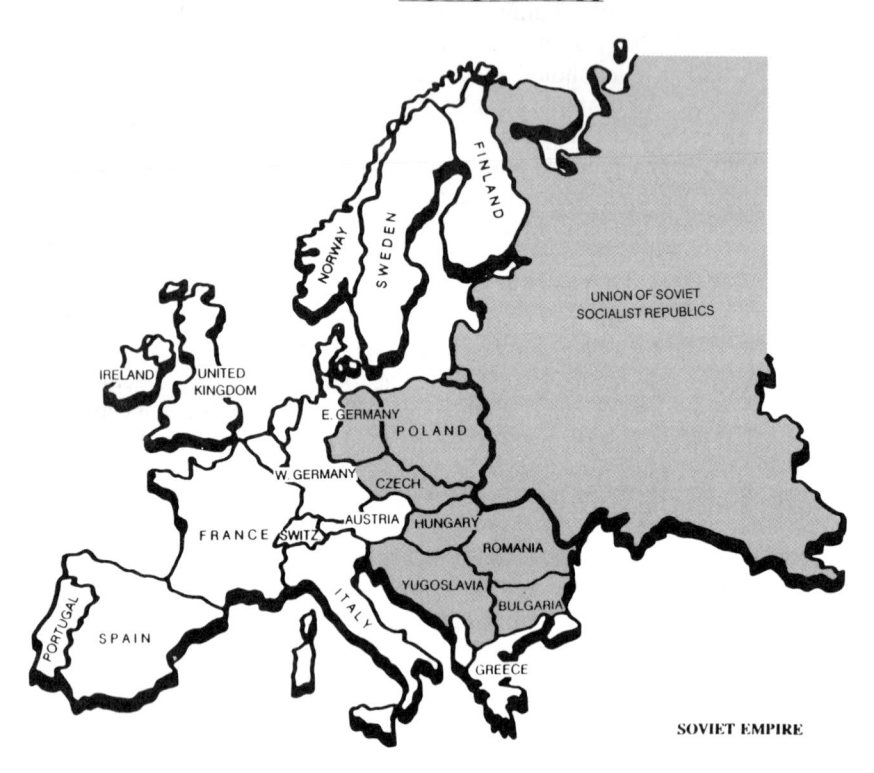

The Iron Curtain divides Germany and the rest of Europe. To the west lies free Europe, to the east the Soviet empire.

Conclusion

Jay P. Kosminsky

The East European revolutions of 1989 have undermined the Warsaw Pact and the Soviet empire in Eastern Europe, changing fundamentally the way the United States should view its involvement in European affairs. With the Soviet threat declining, the U.S. will become less directly involved in the security of Europe and more inclined to reduce its military forces there. But as America and Europe prepare to disentangle their post-war military relationship, both sides will realize that there is no *status quo ante* to which to they reasonably can return. America and Europe will have to create new political, economic, and security structures to maintain the peace as well as has the North Atlantic Treaty Organization for over forty years.

America and Europe have been transformed by their post-war relationship. America left its mark on Europe by rebuilding the continent after it was levelled by World War II. The Marshall Plan, the U.S.-led occupation of Germany, and the pervasive influence of the American economy and culture, helped the U.S. to reshape Europe, to a great extent, in its own image. America, too, has been transformed by its intimate relationship with Europe. Despite its role in World War I, America was an inward-looking power before World War II. The U.S. role in Europe during the war and afterwards changed America's image of itself. America's post-war experience in Europe turned the U.S. into a global superpower. With this role came influence, but also high costs and great risks, including that of nuclear war in defense of America's interests in Europe.

The interdependence of America and Europe during the past four decades goes well beyond their military relationship. Economic meetings among the leaders of the seven major Western powers, for example, are as eagerly anticipated and closely scrutinized by the press as any NATO summits. Dealing politically with a changing Soviet Union, strengthening the new democracies of Eastern Europe, and ensuring free trade and open markets all are non-military issues which

EUROPE 1990

Revolutions sweep through Eastern Europe, dissolving the Soviet empire. On September 9, 1989, the Berlin Wall falls, paving the way for German unification. The East European revolution jumps the border into the Soviet Union as the Baltic States of Estonia, Latvia, and Lithuania declare independence, which is not recognized by Moscow.

Americans and Europeans will face together. As Europeans and Americans begin to look out on the world they are creating, they will realize that their fates still are joined. It is on this assumption that both sides should approach their new relationship, and their response to the revolutionary forces now reshaping the continent.

PROTECTING U.S. POLITICAL INTERESTS

America has many interests in Europe. These include preventing the domination of the continent by a hostile power; avoiding major wars; expanding democracy and free markets; and keeping European markets open to American goods and ideas. To ensure that these interests are protected, America will have to participate in creating the new Europe, or risk losing Washington's ability to influence events.

Securing U.S. interests in Europe will require first and foremost that Soviet forces leave Eastern Europe and return to within their own borders. But America's vision for Europe should not stop at Soviet borders. It must include the peaceful democratization and decolonization of the Soviet Union itself. The continued existence in Europe of an authoritarian empire, the Soviet Union, is the continent's main impediment to a peaceful and prosperous future. Only when Russia is willing to divest itself of its European colonies – Armenia, the Baltic states, Byelorussia, Georgia, Moldavia, Ukraine, and others – and to reestablish formal relations with them as independent, sovereign powers, will Europe be, in George Bush's words, "whole and free." The U.S. should pursue this goal at the Conference on Security and Cooperation in Europe (CSCE), which will meet this November in Paris. Washington can do this by establishing official contacts with republics seeking independence from the U.S.S.R. The U.S. also should warn Moscow that the use of force against national movements will jeopardize political and economic ties with the U.S.

These steps should be coupled with others to make irreversible the transformations well underway in Europe. These include support for a fully sovereign reunified Germany and a foreign aid strategy that promotes free market reforms and the spread of democracy throughout Europe. They also would include targeting aid only to the private sector and offering assistance for the quick establishment of private property rights and an independent judiciary to protect them, the removal of government-imposed economic restrictions on private

EUROPE 199?

The democratic revolution begun in Eastern Europe spreads successfully throughout the Soviet Union and destroys Soviet control. In place of the U.S.S.R., its former European republics emerge as independent Armenia, Estonia, Georgia, Latvia, Lithuania, Moldavia, Russia, and Ukraine. Yugoslavia, too, splinters into its constituent states. Finally: Europe is whole and free.

enterprise, the creation of convertible currencies, and the establishment of a private banking system. The U.S. also should launch an educational assistance program for the new democracies, funded mainly by the private sector, to train business teachers and students in free market economic principles.

The U.S. should promote its vision of Europe through the creation of a standing North Atlantic Conference. This new organization would bring together all the democracies of North America and Europe in a permanent forum for advancing common interests and addressing common problems. Representing a purely political alliance dedicated to a unified, democratic Europe, this Conference could reinforce North Atlantic ties as the East-West conflict winds down. The republics of the U.S.S.R. could join if they became democratic.

Serving as a democratic parallel organization to the CSCE, the North Atlantic Conference could be used not only to coordinate aid programs for establishing market and democratic institutions in Eastern Europe, but to resolve disputes that may arise between democratic neighbors. Such an organization could do more than NATO or CSCE to define America's and free Europe's common interests. NATO is limited as a military organization; it will exclude the emerging democracies of Eastern Europe. CSCE has no common political heritage; it includes as members such non-democratic countries as the Soviet Union and Yugoslavia.

SAFEGUARDING EUROPEAN AND AMERICAN SECURITY

Revolutions can be dangerous, even for the victors. The East European revolutions of 1989 unleashed a chain of historical events with widespread, and still uncertain, consequences. Even as the borders of the Soviet empire in Europe are rolled back, new security problems are arising in Europe. These include understandable concerns, within Germany and among its neighbors, over the ramifications of German unification and the increased likelihood of regional and ethnic conflict as the Soviet empire disintegrates. The future of the Soviet Union remains Europe's biggest question mark. If it holds together, it will remain a dangerous potential enemy in possession of a superpower nuclear arsenal, deep stocks of war reserves, and an army of nearly five million. If it breaks apart violently, new dangers could arise, including loss of control over Soviet nuclear weapons. If Soviet power dissolves peacefully, however, through genuine democratization and decolonization, the greatest threat to European security will dissolve with it.

America's first objective in negotiations over the future of Europe should be to ensure the withdrawal of all Soviet forces in Europe to within Soviet borders and strictly to limit Soviet armaments. It also should include a Conventional Forces in Europe (CFE) agreement that requires the destruction of Soviet equipment not permitted under the Treaty. Otherwise Soviet weaponry equipment might be assigned to forces deployed outside the Treaty area.

In the meantime, the U.S. and its allies best can safeguard their interests and encourage peaceful change by maintaining a stable European balance of power. For now, this means continued reliance on NATO as the backbone of Europe's security system, including the integration of a united Germany in NATO as an equal partner. At the same time, the U.S. and its allies face the task of adapting Europe's security system to accomodate rapid change within the Soviet Union and the rest of Europe.

The first among these requirements should be to adjust U.S. force levels to a reduced Soviet military threat. The Soviet retreat from Eastern Europe allows the U.S. to transform and reduce its role in Europe over the next few years. If the Soviet retreat in Europe continues, and Soviet forces are withdrawn to within their own borders and limited through a CFE agreement, the U.S. will be able to become mainly an offshore European power, reducing its ground forces in Europe to about 50,000 from the current 250,000. The U.S. role in European defense would emphasize those areas in which the U.S. has a comparative military advantage because of its geography or traditional military and technological strengths. These would include nuclear deterrent forces, air power, sea power and reserve manpower.

Europeans, meanwhile, would take over primary responsibility for their own ground defense. To facilitate this, the U.S. should encourage stepped-up European military planning and coordination through the West European Union (WEU), a little-used West European defense organization which includes Britain, France, and West Germany. Immediate steps to strengthen European defense should be to create a standing WEU military planning committee of high-level officers and to initiate regular meetings of WEU national military commanders. An advantage of these steps would be to integrate France, which remains reluctant to participate in NATO's military command, more closely into European defense efforts.

In coming years, the European role in the collective defense of continent should expand. As U.S. ground troops in Europe are drawn down, a European could be appointed to the post of Supreme Allied Commander Europe (SACEUR), which has been held by an American since NATO's inception. Over time, the WEU, perhaps under the auspices of the European Community (EC), could expand to include East European democracies, thus integrating them into European defense without having to expand NATO or U.S. defense commitments eastward.

The pace of change in Europe's security system should be pegged to the Soviet threat. Reimposition of a militarist regime in Moscow, or civil war within the Soviet Union, would delay by years the timetable for America's military withdrawals from Europe and extend NATO's central role in European defense. Continued moderation in Moscow, however, will allow the Europeanization of Western defense by turning over such missions as ground defense to European forces and increasing the defense role of the WEU and other European organizations. If reform in Moscow leads to the democratization and decolonization of the Soviet Union, Europe will be positioned to move beyond military rivalries and establish a system – perhaps centered on CSCE and a newly established North Atlantic Conference – based on mutual self interest in the preservation of peace, democracy and free markets. In the meantime, the CSCE can help mediate regional conflicts, verify arms control agreements, and promote human rights inside the Soviet Union.

Even if Moscow moves peacefully toward democracy and decolonization, and the U.S. withdraws its forces from Europe altogether, the U.S. cannot afford to forget that American interests in Europe are enduring. Much like Britain in the 19th century, the U.S. will have to learn how to protect these interests as a largely offshore power, through continued diplomatic involvement and the maintenance of military strength. If it fails to do so, it will leave the fate of its most basic security interests for others to decide.

PROMOTING ECONOMIC FREEDOM

Transformations in the map of Europe ease military tensions, but increase economic tensions. So far, change in the East has accelerated the integration of Europe's economies. The goal of the EC is to form a single integrated market without internal barriers by 1992. Less than one year after the fall of the Berlin wall on November 9, 1989, the two Germanies have unified their economies, presaging the creation of a new economic colossus in Europe. And Eastern European nations, newly freed from Soviet domination, desperately are seeking the means to transform their moribund command economies as quickly and painlessly as possible along the lines of the Western free market model.

America's major interest in Europe's economic revolution is to ensure that a European market free of internal barriers is not accompanied by measures to exclude the goods of U.S. and other trading partners from European markets. This could be achieved best by creating a North American-Europe Free Trade Zone, which would eliminate barriers to trade across the North Atlantic. Short of this, the U.S. should seek free trade agreements bilaterally with Britain, the new democracies of Eastern Europe, and other European states. In addition, the U.S. should press the EC to dismantle its protectionist common agricultural policy (CAP), which restricts farm imports and subsidizes EC farmers. The U.S. should be supportive of EC efforts to create a truly "common market" without internal trade barriers, by 1992. Other aspects of "EC 92," however, such as a planned bureaucracy in Brussels, will lead to a heavy tax and regulatory burden which is apt to slow the growth rates of European economies, notwithstanding the advantages of a single European market.

The U.S. also should encourage the EC to eliminate economic barriers with Eastern Europe, to enable free markets there to emerge rapidly. The U.S., meanwhile, should encourage and assist East European governments in free market\ reforms, but should not provide large amounts of foreign aid, except through enterprise funds that send capital and expertise directly to the emerging private sector, and not to governments. The U.S. should reduce the foreign debt of emerging East European democracies like Poland by promoting so-called debt-equity swaps, which entail forgiving debts in exchange for equity in local currency, state-owned enterprises, and private companies.

COUNTERING SOVIET EUROPEAN STRATEGIES

The U.S. is not a lone player in Europe. There remains an adversary, albeit wounded, presumably still committed to expanding its own interests in Europe at America's expense. Moscow is bargaining hard at the CFE negotiations, extracting concessions from NATO. Already the Soviet Union has induced NATO to revise its nuclear strategy and to limit the size of a united Germany's armed forces. U.S. diplomatic strategies toward Europe thus must take Soviet strategies into account. Moscow understandably is trying to shore up its influence in Europe, even as its main means of exercising influence — its military power — recedes.

Moscow almost certainly will try to use such organizations as the CSCE to legitimize Eastern Europe as a Soviet sphere of influence and to strengthen its slipping grip on its own internal empire. Gorbachev already is courting a united Germany, which historically has come to Moscow's financial rescue, by offering German businessmen privileged investment opportunities and access to markets in return for Soviet acquiescence to unification. And the Soviet Union is still trying to split Western Europe from the U.S., by pressing for the elimination of U.S. nuclear weapons in Europe and the withdrawal of U.S. forces in exchange for the removal of Soviet troops from Europe.

As long as the West responds creatively to these efforts with its own agenda for a free Europe, it has little to fear from Moscow. The U.S. should promote a vision of Europe as a "Common Democratic Home" of democratic nations from Poland to the U.S.; this is in contrast to Gorbachev's "Common European Home," which often implies that there is no place for the U.S. in Europe. The U.S. should use CSCE as a forum for discussing the implications of Soviet decolonization, or the break away of non-Russian republics from Moscow's central authority. The U.S. should oppose Moscow's attempts to enlist Western support for legitimizing the dying Warsaw Pact. The U.S. should preserve multilateral export controls on the transfer of militarily-significant technology to the U.S.S.R. And the U.S. should develop clear criteria by which to measure political and economic changes in the Soviet Union.

A FREE EUROPE FROM THE ATLANTIC TO THE URALS

For most Americans, "Europe" for the past four decades ended at the Iron Curtain. Behind that spiritual and physical barrier lay a virtually ignored land, locked away and inaccessible in its own political twilight zone. Suddenly, this curtain is lifting, and a new vision of Europe is emerging. This is Europe as it should be — a free Europe.

As the revolutions of 1989 spread ever eastward into the Soviet Union itself, the true map of Europe may finally appear. It would be a Europe of great capitals from London, through Paris, Berlin, Warsaw, Riga, and Kiev to Moscow. In this Europe, military security would be assured collectively, prosperity guaranteed by borders open to the free movement of goods and ideas, and the rights of individuals protected by governments committed to human rights and human dignity. This Europe would be tied to America not because of military necessity, but by the deep political, economic, and moral bonds that underlie their common civilization.

This is the vision that should guide Americans and Europeans as they set out to reshape Europe and reforge their relationship. Already some key elements of this new Europe have fallen into place; Germany will be united, and Moscow — if current agreements are kept — will withdraw the Red Army from Eastern Europe. These developments will enable the U.S. to scale back dramatically its military presence in Europe over the next few years. During this time, America can begin building a new relationship with Europe based on open markets and partnership among democracies. If all goes well, a genuinely democratic Soviet Union, or its successor states, will be added to this partnership in coming months and years.

While this will signal the West's final victory in the Cold War, it will not bring politics to a halt. The tasks of managing the new American-European partnership will be as challenging, if not more so, than the Cold War, with its clear cut lines of ally and adversary. Creative American diplomacy will be required to deal with a Europe freed from its military dependence on the U.S., and destined perhaps to become its rival, or its partner, in the global contest for economic and political influence. But this, after all, is the Europe that America struggled long and hard to create through the Cold War and through two World Wars this century. Victory over tyranny surely will have its cost; but it pales before what would have been the price of defeat.

Men Who Have Reshaped Europe

Charlemagne - Crowned Holy Roman Emperor in Rome by Pope Leo III on December 25, 800. Charlemagne unified a large portion of Europe into a loose confederation in an attempt to restore the lost order of the Western Roman empire. As the king of the Franks, however, he moved the political focus of Europe away from Rome and made northern Europe a vital center of power in its own right.

Armand de Richelieu - With the support of King Louis XIII, Cardinal Richelieu oversees the later stages of the Thirty Years War, permanently weakening the Hapsburg Empire and establishing France as the preeminent continental power. The final terms of the war, decided in the 1648 Peace of Westphalia, after Richelieu's death, alter the European landscape for generations by splitting Germany into small sovereign states and eliminating the Holy Roman Empire as a political entity.

Louis XIV - Crowned king of France in 1643 at the age of five and reigned for 72 years as the most powerful ruler in Europe. Under his leadership, France developed influence in every country from Britain to Turkey and French culture became the model for the entire continent. Louis strove for a "universal monarchy" for Europe with himself at the head. He was countered by other states, such as England, Holland, and Spain, and a new term, "balance of power," was used to describe their actions as they combined against him.

Napoleon Bonaparte - Crowned himself Emperor of the French in 1804. Napoleon came closer than any European leader before or since to unifying Europe under his sole control. At the height of his power he controlled mainland Europe from the Atlantic Coast to Moscow. He established the Continental System which linked

European trade, gave his conquered states "constitutions," and instituted internal reforms similar to France's Civil Code. Napoleon overextended himself, was deposed and exiled, returned, and finally was defeated by combined British and continental forces under the Duke of Wellington at Waterloo, Belgium, in 1815.

Otto von Bismark - Bismark became chief minister of Prussia in 1862. After defeating Denmark in 1864, onetime ally Austria in 1866, and France in 1870, he was able to unify the formerly independent German states under Prussian leadership. In 1871, at Versailles, he proclaimed the German Empire with the King of Prussia at its head. Through a complex series of alliances, he kept Europe at peace after his initial conquests, until his death in 1898.

Adolph Hitler - As the head of the National Socialist Party, he became German Chancellor in 1933, and seized total control of the country later that year. After annexing Austria and much of Czechoslovakia, he began World War II by marching his armies into Poland in September 1939. At his acme he occupied or controlled Europe from France to Ukraine and from Scandinavia into Africa and the Middle East. Hitler's downfall began with his repulse by Russian armies at Stalingrad in 1942 and was assured after the U.S.-led allied invasion of Normandy in 1944. Before his defeat, Hitler committed genocide against European Jews, killing six million. His Third Reich ended only twelve years after it began with his defeat and suicide in Berlin in 1945.

Joseph Stalin - Rose to power in the Soviet Union in 1927 after Lenin's death and maintained control by bloody purges and the mass murder of millions throughout his 26-year rule. His relentless pursuit of increased power in Europe was marked by his 1939 pact with Hitler, which gave him temporary control over the Baltics and half of Poland. After chasing Hitler's armies out of the Soviet Union and Eastern Europe, he gradually established his own Eastern European empire, setting the stage for the Cold War before his death in 1953.

Franklin Roosevelt - President of the United States from 1933-1945. Despite American isolationism, Roosevelt tried to rally U.S. support for Britain's war effort in 1940 and 1941, and succeeded in securing the passage of the Lend-Lease Act which provided arms and materiel to nations at war with the German-led Axis. After the bombing of Pearl Harbor by Japan on December 7, 1941, Roosevelt committed the full strength of the U.S. to the war effort. After the war, however, in an effort to placate Stalin, he abandoned at Yalta his own idealistic goals for creating a whole and free Europe and set the stage for Stalin to solidify communist rule in Eastern Europe.

Winston Churchill - As Prime Minister of Britain from 1940 to 1945, Churchill led the British struggle against Hitler. As the war progressed, he began to see Stalin as a future threat to Europe, but his calls for Western drives into Central and Eastern Europe to counter Soviet armies were not accepted by the United States. At a speech in Fulton, Missouri, in 1946, Churchill coined the phrase "iron curtain" to describe the consolidation of the Soviet empire and the division of Europe.

Harry Truman - U.S. President from 1945 to 1952. Under his leadership came the 1947 "Truman Doctrine," promising aid to any nation resisting communism, the 1947 Marshall Plan for reconstructing Europe, and the 1949 creation of the North Atlantic Treaty Organization (NATO), which commited the U.S. to the defense of Western Europe.

Ronald Reagan - During his White House years, from 1981 to 1989, he oversaw the largest peacetime military build-up in U.S. history. Reagan's 1983 deployment of U.S. *Pershing II* and cruise missiles in Europe and his 1983 Strategic Defense Initiative probably more than anything else helped convince Moscow that it could not compete militarily with the West, and broke the back of the Soviet empire in Eastern Europe.

Mikhail Gorbachev - Facing the collapse of the Soviet economy and the continued strength of the West, Gorbachev, in 1989, renounced the use of military force in Eastern Europe, inciting revolutions and bringing an end to Moscow's post-war empire in Eastern Europe.

NATO Chronology

1949 — **U.S. and Western powers sign the NATO Treaty.** Citing their right to collective self defense under Article 51 of the United Nations Charter, ten West European nations plus the United States and Canada sign the North Atlantic Treaty in Washington, on April 4, 1949. The treaty commits them to "Unite their efforts for self defense and for the preservation of peace and security."

1951 — **U.S. commits forces to Europe.** President Harry Truman announces plans to send six divisions of American troops to Europe, to be placed under NATO command, in September 1950. After much debate, Congress approves the measure on April 4, 1951.

1954 — **NATO adopts nuclear strategy.** At Paris in December, NATO Ministers approve a document known as "MC-48." Adopted with little fanfare or debate, it calls for a massive nuclear response to Soviet aggression in Europe, and presages the deployment of large numbers of U.S. nuclear weapons in Europe.

1955 — **West Germany joins NATO.** After years of dispute within the alliance, the U.S., Britain, and France decide to end their formal occupation of West Germany and admit the soon to be armed nation into NATO. Nine days after the Federal Republic of Germany is admitted into NATO on May 5, 1955, the Soviet Union consolidates its Eastern European empire into a military bloc known as the Warsaw Pact.

1961 **Khrushchev erects Berlin Wall.** After Soviet leader Nikita Khrushchev proclaims that the Soviet Union will conclude a separate peace treaty with East Germany and deny Western access to Berlin, NATO leaders send word to Khrushchev that they will not be pushed out. Rather than provoke an open conflict, the Soviets begin constructing the Berlin Wall in August to divide their sector of the city from the Western zone.

1966 **France leaves NATO.** Seeking a more influential and independent role for France, President Charles de Gaulle withdraws Paris from NATO's command in March 1966, and asks the organization to move its headquarters and forces out of France. The alliance moves to Belgium in 1967.

1967 **NATO adopts flexible response.** At Brussels, in December, NATO's ministers complete the first major review of strategy since MC-48. They devise a doctrine of "flexible response" so that the alliance will have available structured options ranging from conventional forces to a limited or massive nuclear strike when responding to different levels of potential Soviet attack.

1967 **Harmel Report charts NATO's future.** Presented at the same Brussels meeting as the flexible response doctrine, a report by a group of NATO senior statesmen chaired by Pierre Harmel of Belgium, emphasizes the importance of force reductions and the defense of exposed areas adjacent to the alliance, namely the Mediterranean and the Middle East. The report is implemented in 1968, as a strategy to obtain NATO's long term goals of militarily, "creating a climate of stability," and politically moving "towards a more stable relationship" for Europe.

1972 to 1975 **Years of treaties.** Talks between the United States and the Soviet Union during a period of detente lead to the Strategic Arms Limitation (SALT) Treaty, an Anti-Ballistic Missile (ABM) Treaty, and a Four Power Declaration settling the nagging Berlin dispute in 1972. In 1975, at Helsinki, European countries, the U.S., and the Soviet Union, complete the largely symbolic Conference on Security and Cooperation in Europe (CSCE), which establishes broad guidelines for peaceful conflict resolution and respect for human rights.

1977 **NATO adopts the 3 percent solution.** In response to growing Soviet military capabilities in Europe, allied leaders agree at a summit in London, to request 3 percent annual defense spending increases from their respective parliaments.

1979 **NATO agrees to deploy U.S.** *Pershing II* **and cruise missiles in Europe.** In December, 1979, NATO Foreign and Defense Ministers agree to deploy 108 *Pershing* II launchers and 464 Ground Launched Cruise Missiles (GLCMs) in Western Europe. In line with the 1967 Harmel Report, they also sought negotiations with Moscow to limit these missiles in return for limits on Soviet SS-20 missiles deployed in Europe.

1983 **First *Pershings* deployed.** Despite Soviet threats and mass demonstrations in Germany and elsewhere in Western Europe, NATO deploys the first of its *Pershing II* and cruise missiles.

1984 **NATO bolsters flexible response.** NATO's Defense Policy Planning Committee issues the "Follow-on Forces Attack" (FOFA) guidelines in November, to bolster Western defense. The new guidelines, designed to enhance flexible response, envision strikes with long-range "smart" weapons against targets deep behind Warsaw Pact lines.

1987 **U.S., Soviets sign INF Treaty.** The INF treaty, signed in December 1987, eliminates all land-based missiles in the 300 to 3,400 mile range. Negotiating progress is also made in the areas of chemical weapons, nuclear testing, conventional forces, and confidence and security building measures.

1989 **Soviet empire collapses.** During the course of 1989, Soviet General Secretary Mikhail Gorbachev renounces the use of force in Eastern Europe, opening the way for an outpouring of nationalism and democracy in a series of uprisings across Eastern Europe. The revolutions effectively put an end to the Warsaw Pact as a military organization, and signal the beginning of the ongoing Soviet retreat from Europe.

1990 **NATO endures in a changing Europe.** With agreements expected to reduce conventional forces in Europe and reunite Germany, NATO leaders meet July 5-7 to reaffirm the role of the alliance and modify NATO strategy to meet the requirements of a changing Europe. The meeting results in an invitation to Gorbachev to address a future NATO summit, and a revision of NATO's "flexible response" doctrine that designates nuclear weapons as "weapons of last resort" for the alliance.

What U.S. Presidents Said About NATO

Harry Truman

The security of the United States is squarely based on the unity of the Western world and the continued strengthening of its joint institutions, particularly the North Atlantic Treaty Organization. It is a primary political and propaganda objective of the communist bloc to weaken those institutions and to drive a wedge between the democratic allies.

Letter to Congress, July 25, 1952.

Dwight Eisenhower

Properly speaking the stationing of U.S. divisions in Europe had been at the outset an emergency measure not intended to last indefinitely. Unhappily, however, the European nations have been slow in building up their military forces and have now come to expect our forces to remain in Europe indefinitely.

Remarks to National Security Council, November 1953.

John Kennedy

We need the capability of placing in any critical area at the appropriate time a force which, combined with those of our [NATO] allies, is large enough to make clear our determination and our ability to defend our rights at all costs – and to meet all levels of aggression pressure with whatever levels of force are required. We intend to have a wider choice than humiliation or all-out nuclear action.

Radio and Television Report to the American People on the Berlin Crisis, July 25, 1961.

Lyndon Johnson
We see it not as an alliance to make war, but as an alliance to keep peace.
U.S. Foreign Service Institute, March 23, 1966.

Richard Nixon
The original aims of the western alliance are still our basic purpose: the defense of Western Europe against common challenges, and ultimately the creation of a viable and secure European order.
Report to Congress, Febuary 18, 1970.

Gerald Ford
NATO is the cornerstone of United States foreign policy and has the unwavering support of the American public and our Congress...our commitment to this Alliance will not falter.
Brussels, Belgium, May 28, 1975.

Jimmy Carter
NATO since its inception has helped tie our nations together in political and economic and social ways.
News Conference, May 10, 1977.

Ronald Reagan
The United States would consider an attack on its NATO allies as an attack on itself. This is a commitment which is enshrined in the North Atlantic Treaty .... We share common values, common heritage, and parallel dreams. Europe's security is indivisible from our own. I can hardly think of another aspect of United States foreign policy on which there is a broader consensus.
Interview with *Le Figaro*, December 23, 1983.

George Bush
The Eastern European contries are throwing off the yoke of communism. The policy of NATO has prevailed.
News Conference, Febuary 25, 1990.

Milestones in German-Soviet Relations

April 16, 1917 — **Lenin transits Germany.** As German and Russian troops battle each other in World War I, German leaders grant safe passage through Germany to Vladimir Lenin and other revolutionaries *en route* to Russia from Switzerland. As the Germans had hoped, Lenin and his followers seize power in war-weary St. Petersburg (now Leningrad) and take Russia out of the war.

March 3, 1918 — **Treaty of Brest-Litovsk.** Representatives of the Imperial German government and the new Bolshevik regime in Moscow sign the Treaty of Brest-Litovsk, ending Russian involvement in World War I. In exchange for peace, the Bolsheviks surrender Poland, the Baltic states, Ukraine, much of Byelorussia, and a strip of land along the Turkish border. Moscow regains control over most of the territory following Germany's defeat by the Western powers and three years of civil war in the Soviet Union.

April 16, 1922 — **Treaty of Rapallo.** German and Soviet governments agree to cancel their debts to each other and renounce all war claims. Pursuant to hidden clauses in the agreement, the German military starts secretly to test weapons and military tactics on Soviet territory. These exercises are in violation of the provisions of the Versailles Treaty ending World War I, which set strict limits on German military activity. In return, Germany begins producing military equipment for the Soviets.

August 23, 1939   **Hitler-Stalin Pact.** In the secret protocols of this "non-aggression pact" between Germany and the Soviet Union, the two sides agree to: 1) divide Poland into Soviet and German "spheres of interest," 2) recognize Soviet "influence" over Estonia, Latvia, Finland, and Bessarabia, and 3) recognize German control over Lithuania and most of Poland (a later adjustment hands Lithuania to the Soviets).

September, 1939   **Joint attack on Poland.** On September 1, 1939, German troops invade Poland, igniting World War II. As agreed in the Hitler-Stalin pact, the Germans are joined on September 17 by Russian troops marching into Poland from the east. Germany and the Soviet Union divide Poland between them.

June 22, 1941   **Germany attacks the Soviet Union.** On Hitler's order the German army undertakes "Operation Barbarossa," the invasion of the Soviet Union. The German lines push eastward and take the Soviets by surprise. Hundreds of thousands of Red Army soldiers are captured.

	By the fall, Nazi troops come to within 20 miles of Moscow but fail to take the Soviet capital.
January 31, 1943	**Victory at Stalingrad.** German Field Marshall von Paulus surrenders his 300,000 man army to Soviet forces after the crucial battle of Stalingrad, in Ukraine. In the summer of the same year, the Germans launch their last major offensive at Kursk, where most of their armor is destroyed in the largest tank battle in history.
May 7, 1945	**Allied victory in Europe.** The German government surrenders to the Allies and Germany is divided into four zones of occupation, with the Soviets in the east and the other allied troops to the west.
June 24, 1948	**Stalin blockades Berlin.** Stalin cuts off all land access to the American, British, and French zones of West Berlin. The Berlin airlift commences, and Stalin backs down the following May.
May 23, 1949	**Germany formally divided.** Between 1946 and 1948, America, France, and Britain combine their German zones of occupation. On May 23, 1949, the West German state is established when a constitutional convention publishes the "basic law," or West German Constitution. In October 1949, the Soviets turn their zone of military occupation in Germany into a client East German state.

June 17, 1953 — **Red Army subdues East Germany.** Soviet troops intervene to put down anti-Soviet uprisings in East Germany.

August 1961 — **Khrushchev builds Berlin Wall.** Under Soviet direction, the construction of the Berlin Wall commences after Moscow backs down on its renewed threat to cut off Western access to Berlin in the face of NATO opposition.

August 12, 1970 — **West German-Soviet Treaty.** The leftist Social Democratic Party wins power in West Germany and, wishing to reduce tensions with the East, signs a treaty with the Soviet Union recognizing the two nations' post-war borders.

September 3, 1971 — **Four power agreement on Berlin.** Negotiations result in the Quadripartite Agreement, the first on Berlin between the four wartime allies since 1949. The agreement reaffirms four power responsibility for the city and establishes free access between its western and eastern sectors.

November 22, 1983 — **U.S. *Pershing II* missiles deployed in West Germany.** Despite tremendous political pressure from Moscow, West Germany allows the United States to begin stationing intermediate-range cruise missiles and *Pershing II* ballistic missiles on its soil.

November 9, 1989 — **The Berlin Wall comes down.** Following a peaceful revolution which deposes the Soviet-imposed Eastern German dictator Erich Honnecker, the East German government begins dismantling the Berlin Wall.

March 22, 1990   **Two Plus Four talks convene.** The four powers supervising Germany since the end of World War II and the two German states begin talks on German unification. In the meantime, progress towards one Germany accelerates as East and West Germany complete economic unification on June 30 and plan for all-German elections late in the year.

July 16, 1990   **Soviet President Mikhail Gorbachev and West German Chancellor Helmut Kohl agree on German Unity.** Meeting in Zheleznovodsk, U.S.S.R., Kohl and Gorbachev agree that a united Germany will be free to remain in NATO, and that Soviet forces will be withdrawn from Germany by the end of 1994.

Profiles of Soviet Leaders

Vladimir Ilyich Lenin (1870-1924) - The leader of the Bolsheviks, later the Communist Party, and the first ruler of the Union of Soviet Socialist Republics, formed in 1922. Lenin leads the Bolshevik Party to victory in the 1917 revolution and the civil war that follows. He establishes the secret police, or Cheka, and the Soviet Union's first political prison camps. In the last three years of his life, Lenin seems to move away from the communist orthodoxy by allowing limited private enterprise. Shortly before his death, Lenin urges his comrades to remove Stalin from the post of General Secretary.

Joseph Stalin (1879-1953) - The creator of today's Soviet Union, he rules it singlehandedly from the end of the 1920s until his death. A determined Marxist, he nationalizes all private property, including land. With the help of the West and at enormous human and material cost, he makes the Soviet Union the world's second-most industrial nation. Stalin's pact with Hitler leads to World War II. The quarter century of Stalin's terror costs the Soviet Union at least 40 million lives. After Stalin's death, Georgi Malenkov briefly gains control of the Soviet State, but quickly is overshadowed by Party boss Nikita Khrushchev.

Nikita Khrushchev (1894-1971) - As leader of the Soviet Communist Party from 1953 to 1964, he delivers a 1956 "secret" speech denouncing Stalinist terror and releases millions from concentration camps. Internationally, he builds the Berlin Wall and brings the world to the brink of nuclear war in 1962 by placing Soviet nuclear missiles on Cuba. In 1964, Khrushchev is overthrown by a Communist Party coup.

Leonid Brezhnev (1906-1982) - Leader of the Soviet Union from 1964-1982. At first, Brezhnev rules in triumvirate with Aleksei Kosygin and Nicholai Podgorny, but gradually gains sole control over the Communist Party and Soviet state. During his reign, the

Soviet Union becomes a global military superpower. Russian soldiers and military aid span the globe from Cuba and Nicaragua to Ethiopia and Afghanistan. At home, economic stagnation sets in and Party corruption becomes endemic. Brezhnev is followed by ill, older leaders, Yuri Andropov and then Konstantin Chernenko, who rule only briefly.

Mikhail Gorbachev (1931-) - Assumes power in March 1985 as the youngest Soviet leader since Lenin. He moves swiftly to relax police terror, allows greater freedom of expression ("glasnost"), withdraws Soviet troops from Afghanistan, and shows new flexibility in foreign policy. During his rule, all the East European puppet regimes are dislodged by popular uprisings. As of 1990, he fails to reform radically either the Soviet economy or the Communist Party. He presides over the political and economic disintegration of the Soviet system.